Feminisms and the Self

'Identity of our fragmented selves is woven from emotions of love, acceptance and rejection, both by particular others and politically and socially salient groups. This is an optimistic book, we can make ourselves, though not in circumstances of our own choosing! The position of the emotions at the centre of the account of the self is most welcome, and the book is written with the anchorage in experience and sensitivity to differences we hope for from the best feminist theorists.'

Kathleen Lennon, University of Hull

'The self I am, the identity I have, is affected by the politics of gender, race, class, sexuality, disability and world justice. In other words, the feelings I have, the reasons I recognise, the wants I act upon – they are all deeply political. Feminist theory and feminist politics have all been responsible for my coming to understand that my individuality is shaped by political forces, and what I feel as deeply personal is affected by public systems of control.'

Morwenna Griffiths in the Introduction

In Part I of *Feminisms and the Self*, Morwenna Griffiths grounds the methodology of the book by looking at her own autobiographical accounts and those of others. Part II looks at the construction of self-identity as a process of belonging and exclusion. The final part of the book considers authenticity and change: what does a politics of the self mean for a politics of liberation?

Coming from an Anglo-analytic tradition which is not generally as hospitable as European theory to overt political perspectives, Morwenna Griffiths' work has a controversial seam running through it. *Feminisms and the Self* vigorously counters the challenge made by postmodernism and post-structuralism which have threatened to overturn even the possibility of a feminist politics.

Morwenna Griffiths is Lecturer in Education at the University of Nottingham. With Margaret Whitford, she co-edited *Feminist Perspectives in Philosophy*. She was a founding member of the Society for Women in Philosophy and co-editor of its newsletter, *Women's Philosophical Review*.

Feminisms and the Self

The Web of Identity

Morwenna Griffiths

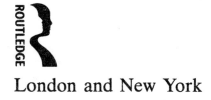

London and New York

First published 1995
by Routledge
11 New Fetter Lane, London EC4P 4EE

Simultaneously published in the USA and Canada
by Routledge
29 West 35th Street, New York, NY 10001

Phototypeset in Times by Intype, London
Printed and bound in Great Britain by
Mackays of Chatham PLC, Chatham, Kent.

British Library Cataloguing in Publication Data
A catalogue record for this book is available from the British Library

Library of Congress Cataloging in Publication Data
A catalogue record for this book has been requested.

ISBN 0–415–09820–3 (hbk)
ISBN 0–415–09821–1 (pbk)

Given our historical position we have to learn to negotiate with structures of violence, rather than taking the impossible elitist position of turning our backs on everything.

Gayatri Spivak

Je suis donc une militante politique de l'impossible.
[I am militating politically for the impossible.]

Luce Irigaray

If given a choice, I would have certainly selected to be what I am: one of the oppressed instead of one of the oppressors. But, in truth, I had no choice. And in a sad world where so many are victims, I can take pride that I am also a fighter.

Miriam Makeba

Contents

Acknowledgements

This book which has been a long time in the making, would not have been conceived, let alone written, without the help of a very large number of other people who I cannot hope to name and thank personally.

Colleagues and students from Christ Church College, Canterbury and Oxford Brookes University helped me think through some of the ideas and influenced their direction, sometimes radically – as have my colleagues and students at Nottingham University where I now work. I have also been helped in sorting out my ideas by the helpful criticism, combined with support and encouragement that I have found in more informal networks of colleagues – especially women – in educational research, philosophy of education, philosophy and other intellectual networks harder to pin down under an institutional name, such as those involved in the Girls and Science and Technology conferences in the 1980s.

Far and away the most important source of intellectual stimulation and personal encouragement has been the Society for Women in Philosophy. I could not have written this book without the continuing support of the women of this society, who, collectively and individually, have provided a space for thinking these ideas at all. This society has given us a space to learn from each other, through discussions of work in progress, an opportunity that could not have been found elsewhere. Members have also challenged and changed how I think by criticising my work, in ways that encouraged development and progress rather than retreat. They have also given support, encouragement and friendship which has allowed me to weather the isolation that I would otherwise have found given the lack of institutional support in Britain for this kind – any kind – of feminist philosophy.

Among these many, I can only pick out a few names, conscious of how many I am leaving out. I am especially grateful to some of the founder members of the Society – Alison Assiter, Judy Hughes, Kathleen Lennon, Mary Midgley, Joanna Hodge, Anne Seller and Margaret Whitford – for their continued intellectual support and friendship over many years.

I am also grateful to members of a seminar of the society – to Alison Assiter, Christine Battersby, Susan Khin Zaw, Kathleen Lennon, Anne

Seller, and Margaret Whitford for their criticisms of an earlier draft of Part I – which led to serious re-writing!

I have particular thanks to give to Alison Assiter, Kathleen Lennon, Anne Seller, Patricia White and Margaret Whitford, who commented on the final draft in spite of the shortness of time available. I also have to thank my family and friends whose patience and encouragement has continued in spite of everything. Finally, I thank my father who thought of the title and who did not live to see the book finished.

The poems reprinted on pages 48, 49 and 53 are from *In The Pink* by The Raving Beauties, first published by The Women's Pess Ltd, 1983, 34 Great Sutton Street, London EC1V 0DX. 'In the Men's Rooms' by Marge Piercy was originally published in *Eight Chambers of the Heart* (Penguin, UK) by Marge Piercy. Copyright © 1972 by Marge Piercy and Middlemarsh, Inc. Reprinted by kind permission of the Wallace Literary Agency. 'Woman Enough' by Erica Jong is reprinted by permission of Sterling Lord. Permission for the use of the poems 'Holding My Beads' and 'Epilogue' by Grace Nichols from the collection, *i is a long memoried woman*, was granted by the publishers Karnak House © 1983, 1995. 'In Spite of Me' by Grace Nichols, from the collection, *Lazy Thoughts of a Lazy Woman* is reprinted by kind permission of the publisher, Virago Press. While the publisher has made every effort to contact all copyright holders, if any have been inadvertently omitted the publisher will be pleased to make the necessary arrangements at the first opportunity.

1 Questions of the self

Questions of selves

1 INTRODUCTION: WEBS OF IDENTITY

The self I am – the identity I have – is affected by the politics of gender, race, class, sexuality, disability and world justice. In other words, the feelings I have, the reasons I recognise, the wants I act upon – they are all deeply political. Feminist theory and feminist politics have been responsible for my coming to understand that my individuality is shaped by political forces and that what I feel as deeply personal is affected by public systems of control. Equally, I know that such shaping and control are not absolute, fixed or deterministic. The individual I am and the identity I have is mine, and I shape and control it in so far as I am capable of doing so.

So how did I come to be myself? And is what I take to be myself my *real* self? These questions matter, because the answers affect what I do, and how I react to the circumstances in which I find myself. The answers also affect how I think I should associate justly with others in cooperative actions with political consequences. This book is a re-assessment of identity and the politics of identity through exploring the self.

Recently there has been an explosion of interest in self, identity, narratives of self, autobiography, and the politics related to all of these. As a result the politics of identity has come of age. There was a time when identity politics was based on the simple-minded assumption that personal identity could just be read off from the fact of being a woman, or a black person, or a black woman, or a white, working-class man: the divisions soon became unmanageable. Such politics are regularly the butt of jokes in newspapers, fiction and party politics. However, identity politics served a very useful function. It is now comparatively rare to meet people who think that gender, race, class, or sexuality are irrelevant to an individual's beliefs and attitudes.

The issues of identity politics remain unresolved. Still in question is exactly how politics and self-identity are linked. But it is clear that a discussion of self and identity must be both highly political and highly personal. This book is both. It draws on personal experience – both mine and that of others – to investigate what might be the consequences of 'being ourselves'. I argue that the consequences would be far-reaching, affecting our private feelings and our public spaces. Thus the argument is political and personal in the way that the questions are investigated, and in the conclusions it draws.

A central metaphor is the web. Spiders make webs which are nearly invisible until the dew falls on them. They are made with threads stronger than steel and take their shape from the surrounding circumstances and from the spider herself. Second, women have traditionally made webs: knitting, tapestry, crochet and lace. Their creations are constrained by the circumstances of their making but they bear the mark of the maker. They can, like Penelope in the Odyssey, untangle the webs they have made for their own reasons and to suit their own purposes. Many webs can be seen as wholes or as a conglomeration of parts. Which perspective is used depends on the purpose of the looking. Think of the Bayeaux tapestry, for instance. It is a series of pictures and symbols, or it is a whole, though *which* whole, a historical document or a political argument, for instance, is itself at issue.[1] Third, and last, the abstract noun, 'web' refers to something which is complex. It is intricate, involved, interlaced, with each part entangled with the rest and dependent on it.

The metaphor of a web can throw light on the idea of the self and its politics. It, too, is made of nearly invisible, very strong threads attached to the circumstances of its making and under the control of its maker. It, too, is made to suit the purposes of its maker, but the circumstances of the making are not under her control. It, too, can be thought of as fragments in a conglomeration, or as a unitary whole; though whether it is a whole, or which whole it is, depends on the viewer as much as on its own constitution. It, too, is intricate, entangled and interlaced, with each part connected to other parts. A value of this metaphor is its flexibility. Looked at in some ways, the self is like the whole web. Looked at in others, it is more like the nodes where the lines cross, or where the individual stitches resolve themselves into patterns and pictures as a result of the other individual stitches.

The metaphor is only a metaphor. It is not a picture. A spider and a woman are not the same as the webs they create. Selves are not so easily distinguished into their constituent parts of maker and made. Moreover, each web affects the next one. It is not just that 'No man is an Island, entire of it self'.[2] Also very important for this book is the fact that each of us is affected by the relations of power which hold between groups of people on the basis of sex, and, depending on the part of the world, on the basis of other factors such as race, class and sexuality.

In this book I try to explain the intricate entanglement which is our own self-identity. To do so I look at how selves are constructed and then in more detail at emotions and rationality, self-esteem and self-creation and, finally, at the idea of 'real self' and authenticity. As I do so, I draw implications for political change. This is the weft of the book. The warp on which the weft is woven, is made up of: the threads of an epistemology based on autobiographical experience; an argument about the constraints and opportunities of language; and, most importantly, since the analysis is a feminist one, an attention to politics.

In the rest of this chapter I set the scene by explaining the background to the way I have constructed the book: the purposes and intentions I had in writing it, the theoretical context I am working in, the politics of methodology and the audience I imagine. I go on to outline the content, first summarising the overall aims and the logic of the structure, and then giving a synopsis of each chapter.

2 PURPOSES AND INTENTIONS

The book is intended as a contribution to the understanding and politics of self-identity from a feminist and philosophical perspective. It examines belonging (and violent exclusions), emotion, rationality, autonomy and authenticity. It draws on mainstream philosophy, which is brought into question by the use of perspectives which are usually excluded from academic debate, particularly those of women and of people who are black and poor (many of whom are also women). The book begins with critical autobiography and finishes by advocating a politics of reflection and action, achieved through an acknowledgement of fluidity and frag-mentation, framed by the attitudes of vigilance, subversion, and the will-ingness to dream impossible dreams.

The book as a whole should be seen as contributing to the project of discovering and inventing feminist philosophy. The book is, therefore, both critique and construct.[3] Mainstream philosophy in the West suffers from an inappropriate purity of focus and method. This is particularly true of the Anglo-Saxon tradition, dominant in English-speaking coun-tries. The result has been to render it incapable of satisfactorily pursuing its own aim of understanding human experience, especially in the fields of epistemology, ethics, mind and politics. The book aims to question unhelpful disciplinary boundaries, as a contribution to the project of re-defining and re-aligning them.[4] I have not written in the style, or used the kinds of content, that are normal in standard, mainstream philosophy. However I claim that the book is a contribution to feminist philosophy. Thus, in itself, it constitutes a challenge to mainstream views of what counts as philosophy. The construct is, in itself, a critique.

In writing this book I have drawn on theories within feminism. Many of these feminist theorists themselves draw on philosophy, but usually not on the Anglo-Saxon mainstream, but rather on the mainstream of French and German theory. I, myself, draw more on the theories of Anglo-Saxon mainstream philosophy. I also draw, to a lesser extent, on theories from social sciences, especially education, a field traditionally of more interest to women, although dominated, academically, by men.

In more detail, the project is one of re-thinking the particular area of self-identity, that is, of re-defining and re-thinking what counts as philosophy of self-identity, what the questions are, and what would count as answers to those questions.

Personal identity and mind are questions which have been central to philosophy. In the philosophy of mind in the Western Anglo-Saxon tradition, questions of self and personal identity have tended to appear as questions about the unitary 'I' rather than about 'Who or what am I?' It has been dominated by the considerations that prompted Hume's remark in the *Treatise of Human Nature* (I.iv.2):

> It is certain that there is no question in philosophy more abstruse than that concerning identity, and the nature of the uniting principle, which constitutes a person. So far from being able by our senses merely to determine this question, we must have recourse to the most profound metaphysics to give a satisfactory answer to it; and in common life it is evident these ideas of self and person are never very fixed nor determinate.
>
> (Hume, 1962: 240)

Hume begins by thinking 'Is this still the same pen and paper?' and then moves on to consider himself. Kant is concerned with the same question. His answer is in terms of a transcendental apperception, an argument that 'I' as a category has to come before it is possible to raise questions about the identity of pens and paper. He argues that a transcendental synthesis of imagination is a precondition for all experience. This question remains alive and well. B. Williams (1973), Dennett (1978), Nagel (1979) and Parfit (1984), have been widely read and remain influential; more recently, Dennett (1991) and Thornton (1991) discuss this issue. Dennett discusses the creation of a self in terms of spinning and being spun by stories (1991: 418). His preoccupation is with questions like 'How many selves to a customer?' and whether a self of the kind he argues for could be real. Fundamentally, these are questions about the unitary I.

Self-identity and questions of the self have been central to the Women's Movement from the first.[5] However the questions of the women are not those of the philosophers, and vice versa. It has been rare for theorists to point out where the two sets of questions overlap. Feminist philosophers notice the overlap. For instance, Grimshaw (1986, 1988) draws attention to the difficulty of accounting for fragmented selves using traditional discussions of personal identity and autonomy. Benhabib (1992) and Thompson (1994) explicitly make connections between notions of the self underpinning social contract theories in political philosophy and feminists' concerns with situated perspectives forming identities. I say more about this at the beginning of Chapter 5.

Thus there is a two-fold intention to the argument of the book. In the first place, it is to investigate self-identity, including emotion, rationality, autonomy and authenticity, because these issues are important to women – and to other groups seeking liberation and acknowledgement. For instance, Gilroy writes (1993: 70):

> The vernacular components of black expressive culture are thus tied to the more explicitly philosophical writings of black modernist writers like Wright and Du Bois. They develop this line of enquiry by seeking to answer the metaphysical questions 'Who am I?' and 'When am I most myself?'

Second, the intention is to redraw the boundaries of mainstream philosophical discussion of these subjects which tend to exclude such questions as peripheral.

3 CONTEXTS

Philosophy, even 'mainstream philosophy' is a huge area, with ill-defined boundaries. As I said earlier, I draw more on Western analytical philosophy than on the modern French and German theorists, though the two traditions overlap, and are coming together. I draw particularly on the work of philosophers with interests in both camps, such as Charles Taylor and Richard Rorty. Their ideas appear interwoven with my arguments especially in Part II, where I read them 'against the grain' from the political perspective of feminism.

Feminism and feminist theory is also a large area. There is no such thing as 'the feminist perspective' or a univocal 'feminist theory'. My argument has been most influenced by the feminist movement in Britain, but also draws on work from elsewhere. I draw particularly on the work and discussions of the Society for Women and Philosophy, some of which appears in published form (Griffiths and Whitford, 1988; Lennon and Whitford, 1994; *Women's Philosophy Review*). I also draw on the work of a number of others, especially philosophers, but also those in social sciences and cultural studies. I have looked particularly for theorists who cross the boundaries of such frozen identities as gender, race, class, in order to examine and discuss the fluid, plural world in which all of these overlap. It is crucial to my argument in the book as a whole that feminist movements cannot and should not be divorced from other movements seeking justice and acknowledgement.

4 METHODOLOGY AND ITS POLITICS

The methodology of the book is one which questions the abstractions assumed by most Western philosophers, drawn as they are from the experience and preoccupations of white Western males. The questioning is begun in the first section, by returning to experience through a critical use of autobiographical material. Some of the material is drawn from my own life, but a sustained effort is also made to discover and understand the perspectives of others from excluded minorities, especially women but also including a number of men.

I have argued before that the use of personal experience is crucial to the development of a feminist perspective (Griffiths and Whitford, 1988; Griffiths, 1989). Others have questioned philosophical conclusions by questioning the experience of philosophers[6] or, to use the terminology of the French intellectual tradition, have discussed the masculine 'imaginary' as constitutive of Western rationality (Whitford, 1991).

I consider the use of personal experience in more depth in Part I, especially in the most theoretical chapter of that section, Chapter 4. I argue that experience provides a sound epistemological base, if it is treated critically using a process of reflection and re-thinking, including attention to politically situated perspectives. Such a process requires attention to language; the relation between experience and language is a theme which reappears throughout the book and which is considered directly in Chapter 9. Part I also contains autobiographical material from my own life and an annotated bibliography of autobiograpical writings of others which have particularly influenced me while writing the book. (Where these are poems, I have quoted them in full.) In Part II, this material is used as a basis from which to re-conceptualise and re-theorise self and selves. In Part III, change becomes central. Political conclusions are drawn about both personal and collective changes which can and should be made.

The methodology is explicitly political, in the sense that it begins from a political perspective and moves towards political conclusions.

5 AUDIENCE

Readers of the book will have a range of expectations – about content, perspectives and purposes. They should be able to draw from it what is interesting to them, whether they are feminists interested in politics of identity and subjectivity, philosophers interested in traditional questions of mind, or social scientists interested in social justice – and various combinations of these categories. I do not wish to be speaking only to people like myself. My intention is that readers coming from other backgrounds, with their associated preoccupations and interests should also be able to draw from this book what is interesting to them. In particular, those who would not describe themselves as 'academics' should feel included in my imagined audience. I say more about this is in Chapters 2 and 3.

Since my imagined audience is varied, the use of the pronoun 'we' is problematic. For the purposes of this book it should be taken as meaning 'we human beings'. There are times when the meaning is more restricted than that, and in those cases I have tried to make its meaning clear by the context: for instance, it might mean 'we in the West', or 'we women'.

The pronouns 'he' and 'she' are more difficult. In general I have followed Deborah Cameron's suggestion (1992: 125–6):

> In my opinion we should be tampering with language not to tell the truth, but quite openly to shame the devil. It is disingenuous to claim that the conventions we propose are simply 'better' than the traditional ones (more accurate, more precise), because really it is a question of political and ideological preferences – the traditional usage embodies one view of the world and the feminist alternative a different one, and we need to make clear that both these views are politically non-neutral.... I have made a decision to use ... 'positive language', in which all generics are feminine: *she, her*. ... I do not want my pronouns to slip by unnoticed: I want readers to think about it, and to act on their conclusions.

There are occasions when I use 'he' for the generic when I think the so-called 'universal human being' indicated is, in fact, covertly male. I say more about political change in language in Chapter 9.

6 CONTENT OF CHAPTERS: A SUMMARY[7]

Chapters 2–4 make up Part I of the book, which is titled 'Learning from experience'. In this part of the book, I establish a methodology for finding and resolving the questions with which I began this chapter, using current arguments in feminist epistemology as the basis for doing so. The methodology is one which requires attention being paid to the accounts women (including myself) give of their experience. Part II, 'Constructing ourselves', builds on Part I and uses it to theorise self-identity and its construction. In Part III, 'Changing', I focus on changing self-identities and draw out some political implications.

In Chapter 2 I discuss the reasons for using autobiographical material in the book and I also discuss some of the pitfalls of doing so. The discussion revolves round the variety of people who might read the book and also on the possibility of understanding or being understood by others who are not the same as myself. This discussion is taken up in Chapter 3 where I focus on the use of other people's autobiographies, and the dilemmas of hearing voices from the margins, without cultural tourism, and in spite of the difficulties of translation. Chapters 2 and 3 contain autobiographical material – from myself in Chapter 2 and from other people in Chapter 3; people from a variety of backgrounds and of both sexes. I draw on these autobiographies in the rest of the book. In Chapter 4 I look more systematically at epistemological questions underlying the use of autobiographical material and, indeed, underlying the use of personal experience in building feminist theory. Chapter 4 concludes the first part of the book.

Chapter 5 sets out the framework for the central thesis of the book about self-identity. Two main questions of self-identity for feminists are identified as being concerned with 'real selves' and 'fragmented selves'. In order to answer them, a theory of construction of the self is explained which takes account of material as well as of social circumstances. It focuses most closely on connections of love, resistance, and rejection. It explores the effects of these found in small groups and in large-scale structures of power like gender, class and race.

The theory of self-identity is used in Chapter 6 as the basis for a discussion of emotion and rationality as constructive or productive of the self. The chapter is framed by a dilemma for feminists about how far to trust their feelings and their reason, since they have themselves been constructed within a society dominated by masculinities. An analysis of the construction of both emotion and rationality is used as a basis for defining and discussing the politics of emotion and the politics of rationality.

In Chapter 7 the focus is on the politics of particular emotions of the self: self-esteem and the emotions surrounding self-creation. First, the politics of self-esteem are investigated: why it is that excluded and marginal groups have more problems with it and what action should be taken about this. Political conclusions are drawn about sexual and racial harassment, about violence against women and visible minorities. Second, the politics of self-creation are discussed. The valorisation of cruelty and domination which marks mainstream accounts by Rorty and Hegel is investigated and shown to be political in origin. Conclusions are drawn about the dualisms of private/public and dominant/dominated.

In Chapter 8, the theme of self-creation is further examined by looking at ideas of autonomy and independence. By attending to the experience and aspirations of women, with all their differences such as those of class or race, I draw out ideas of autonomy, showing they are different from the ones usually presented in mainstream philosophising. The analysis is used as a basis for discussion of the conditions of personal and collective freedom, particularly in relation to fear, to the fluidity and fragmentation of self-identity, and to the possibilities of finding space in which to influence public decisions.

Chapters 9 and 10 make up Part III. They focus on change and the politics of change. Chapter 9 takes up the theme of language. Assumptions and arguments concerning language are interwoven into the argument of the book as a whole. It is necessary to look at them more systematically before the main questions of the book can be adequately answered. Issues of communication and expression are raised and explored. Attention is given to themes found in the rest of the book related to: material and social; fragmentation and fluidity; and, change, power and differences.

Chapter 10 draws together the themes of the book in a discussion of authenticity: how it is possible to retain an authentic identity without looking for an essential core self, and how it is possible to organise collectively for change in a way that maintains self-identities even while altering them. I end by arguing for a fragmented politics which maintains a cohesion through a shared commitment to vigilance about oppression; to promoting subversion, ambiguity and compromise; and to dreaming impossible dreams.

Part I
Learning from experience

2 Using autobiographical accounts

1 INTRODUCTION: CAVEATS AND ASSUMPTIONS

In Chapter 1, I said that the methodology of the book as a whole is one which questions the abstractions assumed by most philosophy, drawn as they are from the experiences and preoccupations of white, Western males. This questioning will be helped by using critical autobiographical material to discover and understand alternative perspectives of those who are not white, Western males. Throughout the book I call on experience (my own and that of others) in order to critique or construct theories and abstractions. Thus, in the course of developing my arguments I find I need to tell stories which are crucial to the critique and creation of theory.

Using autobiographical material is not straightforward, whether the material is supplied by my own memory or by the accounts of other people. There are epistemological problems. Can knowledge be got this way? If so, what kind of knowledge would it be? Is it reliable at all? All kinds of questions and objections can be raised. I tackle such questions in Chapter 4, where I argue that autobiographical material is a good source of knowledge. I also argue that it is important that personal material is brought to bear on theoretical concerns.

The thought of 'calling on experience' will cause alarm bells to ring in the minds of some readers. They might think that I believe that experience is something we know directly, independently of any language, and that language can mirror it. I do not believe this at all.

I will discuss my position more thoroughly as the book proceeds, especially in Chapter 4, but also in the discussion of language which is a theme of the book as a whole, and which is discussed in most detail in Chapter 9. For the time being, I will simply explain what assumptions I make, knowing that I will be arguing for them later. They are assumptions about both language and experience.

1 My assumption is that language creates us but is also created by us. So I deny linguistic determinism.[1] But, equally, I deny that meaning can be transparently rendered (or translated). By using language we create

the world as well as discover it. My view is that language is developed in a community of participants. Understanding is constrained by that community and by the language it has developed. The language constrains what understandings members of the community are able to have and vice versa, the understandings of members of the community constrain the language they have developed.

2 Descriptions of experience are always revisable. I am assuming that I can recount my own experience without claiming that I am simply describing something independent of the description. This follows from my first assumption that there is no transparent language. I start from *this* situation and *this* situated self. I can recount my experience as it feels to me now, with my present level of understanding. It is quite possible that as I continue to think and theorise and observe, that I will understand more and my situated-self-understanding will change accordingly.

To put it another way, my direct descriptions of any piece of experience will change. Thus what I say is *not* a transparent description of direct experience. Similarly, what others say is not a transparent description of their direct experience either. Examples of my own changing understanding of my own experience appear later in this chapter. Another example is found in Maya Angelou's autobiography. She gives a number of examples of how her understanding of her experience has changed, thus changing the nature of the experience as she now tells it. For instance, she tells the story of being raped as a child. The child, who was herself, reacted to the experience by becoming mute for seven years. The adult, reacting to the same experience but with more maturity, puts it into words, including in the telling the experience of keeping silence. It is important to note that her adult self is not using a memory, as one might report a story told by someone else. She is telling her own experience. The book is autobiography and it tells her own experience as the silenced child was unable to do.

3 I am following ordinary usage in allowing for the view (a) that language needs to be understood both as a system of words and syntax, and also for the view (b) that language is primarily a means of expression and of communication between groups sharing a common interest in the world. Thus I am not identifying it, narrowly, with tongues such as 'French' or 'Swahili' nor, on the other hand, am I assuming that questions of language are located *within* one such human tongue. Thus 'language' could be a tongue spoken across religion and culture, like 'Panjabi' (whether spoken in England, Pakistan or India). It could be a particular use of a single tongue by a set of its speakers, like London-Jamaican, or it could be a way of communicating that transcends both tongue and culture. An example might be 'talking like a woman', which could stretch across an area having a multiplicity of tongues and

cultures, but in which gender is similarly constructed. Examples of such areas might be Europe or West Africa.

2 SPEAKING FOR MYSELF

I begin by considering the use of my own experiences and then go on, in the next chapter, to consider the use of autobiographical material from others, where even more problems arise. In this section, I am reporting on the considerations which led to my structuring this book in the particular way that I have. The collections of autobiographical material in this chapter and the next appear as a direct consequence of the difficulties I faced in developing a feminist philosophy of the self.

My first difficulty came from the length of time it takes to tell a story or to explain a piece of experience well enough for an audience to understand it. The scene needs to be set, the reasons given, the feelings described. The more diverse the audience, the longer the story, because the description needs to become more detailed. This length of description gets in the way of the argument – the very argument which relies on the description and which needs it. The question here is how much I have to include so that my readers will understand me.[2]

I was helped here by turning the tables for a moment, and noticing how much others have to include for me to understand them. As examples I will take the black Americans, bell hooks and Patricia Williams, and the Bengali, Gayatri Spivak, all of whom write in English. I want to understand the arguments that these women are making in their books, but to do so I need to know more of them. I am grateful that they give us snippets of their lives. As a white British woman, I need them to explain their experience, knowledge and culture. When they assume too much, communication breaks down. For instance, of the three, I find the work of Gayatri Spivak the hardest to understand and engage with. I think this is because she assumes too much, without explanation of who she is and what her cultural and personal background is. I find her interviews much easier to understand than her papers: a reversal of my usual reactions to arguments contained in published interviews.

Bell hooks is explicit that her primary audience is black Americans. This is a diverse audience, ranging from Cornell West, the Ivy League philosopher, to people who are not college educated (hooks, 1989: 81). However, there are still enough shared assumptions for her to tell shorter rather than longer stories. Patricia Williams is addressing white middle-class America in the shape of her colleagues and students (as she makes clear by explaining how the various chapters came to be written), although she would also like her book to be interesting to her own sister. Thus her stories are much longer, and she is satirical about the possibility of being understood without such stories. I find Williams is easier to engage with than Spivak, just because of these long stories. On the other hand, her full accounts of her experiences often make it hard to follow the structure of her argument, precisely because of the time she takes in telling the necessary stories.

The conclusion for me was that the answer to the question about how long my stories should be depends on who the audience is, and how likely they are to recognise allusions to shared knowledge.

3 THE PARTICIPANTS IN A DISCUSSION

If the length of the story depends on the audience, then I need to define the audience. This is not straightforward. It includes any of those who are interested in the self in relation to women, feminism or philosophy. The audience comes from different life-experiences (gender, ethnicity, class, nationality, sexuality, education, career) and from different academic backgrounds (at least, from women's studies, feminist studies, cultural studies, philosophy, social studies or my own present academic home, education): in short, they come with different sets of experience, knowledge and culture. They are something like me, but not just like me. It is still quite a narrow group – though already wider than the audience of a philosopher doing philosophy-as-usual.

Many of the audience are, like me, on the margins rather than at the centre. However, the debates about differences have made us all aware that the margin is not a shared place. My purpose is to address an audience which is often at other places on the margin, but who may have the same interests as me in the theoretical problems I am addressing.

The audience includes those white males who are closer to the centre. They are important because they have an influence over all our views. We on the margin have found that we cannot do without them. Our theory borrows from theirs and is highly influenced by them. Given the fact that they are the dominant voices in our education and in our philosophical and theoretical apprenticeships, how could it be otherwise? I do not expect them to be the primary audience, but they should be able to read this and understand it.

Faced with this disparity, although I need to start with 'I', and, although I know that the 'I' is a fragment rather than an atom (I am always part of a 'we'), I cannot assume that I know who 'we' is. I am sure that there is an implicit 'we'. In my first assumption I said that language is developed in a community of participants and that their understanding is constrained by that community and the language it has developed. Therefore, however individual an experience is, it is understood through an understanding developed in a community: a 'we'. 'We' is indeed a slippery word. Feminists have long noted how the 'we' of male academic discourse slips from inclusion to exclusion and back again, with respect to women. Women are better placed to notice this than men. Black women have further noted how the 'we' of white feminist discourse is just as dangerously ambiguous. I need others to work out with me when I am a 'we' with them. They and I together work out from our own fragments to an understanding of the whole.

This is why I am not doing philosophy-as-usual. It is the form that would be most comfortable for those privileged white males at the centre. I have to say that in the past I too have found this mode very comfortable (I must have served my apprenticeship well). I am trying to learn to shift, slowly, though too fast for many colleagues. Like Patricia Williams' law students, I sometimes still crave the 'crisp, refreshing, clear-headed sensation' (1993: 13) that academic, formal argument gives me. However I know that much of my intended audience find the academic, dry, formal mode discomforting. Many people in women's studies, cultural studies and education find the normal voice of the academic Anglo-Saxon philosopher positively off-putting: intimidating and alienating. Thus, my deliberate casting of this book outside the ordinary ways of writing philosophy. All of my primary audience should be able to understand it. None should feel excluded – though mainstream philosophers, having least experience of not being the only audience, are likely to feel the most put out.

4 EAVESDROPPERS

In section 3 I discussed the kind of people that I hope to engage in discussion. There are other groups who may eavesdrop and join in if they want.

Margins are not a kind of round table. Some of us speak from more central places than others. It is not only some white males who are privileged. I, like most others, sometimes speak from a place of relative privilege and sometimes from a place of relative disadvantage. Having this double positioning helps me avoid some crass mistakes. I realise, for instance, that good intentions are necessary but not sufficient to ensure open communication. Even with the best of intentions, communication is skewed by structural injustice. Not everyone needs to join in my conversations and I would not be improving justice or rationality if I could persuade them to do so. The dominant universalising voice of reason somehow usually manages to miss this point entirely. It finds puzzling and irrational the laughter of the Others – and their silences, their unwillingness to share their forms of language. The more marginal easily notice the point of silence and laughter.

Patricia Williams points out the difficulty of discussing rights and needs with a white male friend of similar academic background. She says: 'Probably the best Peter and I can do – as friends and colleagues, but very different people – is to listen intently to each other so that maybe our children can bridge the experiential distance' (1993: 150). Meanwhile, black people in the United States need to work together to retain the power of the vision that talk of rights confers: ' "Rights" feels new in the mouths of most black people. It is still deliciously empowering to say. It is the magic wand of visibility and invisibility, of inclusion and exclusion, of power and no power' (1993: 164). Importance is given to the intent mutual listening she advocates as conversation with white people puzzled by such a reaction. But such importance pales into insignificance beside the importance of blacks talking to each other. Justice and rationality would not be improved by white people of good will taking up their time. Spivak says succinctly (1992: 189):

> It is only in the hegemonic languages that the benevolent do not take the limits of their own often uninstructed good will into account. That phenomenon becomes hardest to fight because the individuals involved in it are genuinely benevolent and you are identified as a trouble maker.

There are two such sets of people who might wish to eavesdrop but not to join in my conversations. (I do not include those in positions of relative privilege who do not want to listen, annoyed as they may be by the style or content.) There are those who feel oppressed by me and those who are quite removed from me and whose best interests would not be served by closing the gap because justice would not be better served if they did so. In either case I may wish to understand them – but they may not want to waste their time with *my* concerns – any more than I want to spend my energies dealing with the agendas of white males (especially where feminism is concerned). Thus, if they want to make use of what I say, then I am pleased, but my concern is not – cannot be – to make myself universally intelligible to everyone, including for instance, the peasants in Bangladesh and unemployed young men on housing estates in my home city of Nottingham.

5 THE UNNOTICED QUESTION

I have been discussing how I make myself understood to a range of people by recounting experiences. My problem is that while this seems to help *advance* the argument, it causes problems for the *flow* of the argument. I commented on this in connection with Patricia Williams in section 3, where I said that her long stories contributed to understanding but got in the way of the flow of the argument.

However, mainstream men do not appear to notice the difficulty of making oneself universally understood. Why does it not get discussed in mainstream philosophy? It is an example, after all of a well-known philosophical question: 'What are the limits of intelligibility?' Moreover, it affects anyone trying to write – or doesn't it?

My view is that male writers – those few powerful males who have traditionally had the power to publish books and define what is to count as worthwhile knowledge – think that they can assume that their audience is pretty much like them. They can confidently write 'we' knowing who they are talking to, who will count as 'we', and who will count as 'they'. They build on assumptions of shared experience, shared knowledge and shared culture: from books they have all read to their common experiences of family life. They build on their shared narrowness.

In his recent book, Bernard Williams makes a cursory mention of the question of 'we'. In a footnote he says:

> Obviously it cannot mean everybody in the world or everybody in the West. I hope it does not mean only people who already think as I do. The best I can say is that 'we' operates not through a previously fixed designation, but through invitation.... It is a matter of ... my asking you to consider to what extent you and I think some things and perhaps need to think others.
>
> (1993: 171)

It is true that the general argument of Williams' book is not hard to follow. However, in the details he presupposes a knowledge of Greek tragedy, including the details of plots of myths and plays. Footnotes supporting the points are routinely in ancient Greek without translation. And he calls this an invitation!

Donald Davidson does not even mention the issue but is as culturally specific as Williams in his assumptions about his audience. For example, in his influential article, 'A nice derangement of epitaphs', Davidson assumes that his audience is familiar with a range of cultural figures (Mrs Malaprop, Humpty Dumpty in *Alice in Wonderland*, the Jabberwocky) as well as with James Joyce's *Finnegans Wake* (Davidson, 1986). My Hong Kong and Taiwanese students, who have excellent English and who have grown up in a culture dominated by Britain or the USA would not know these references. Ironically, Davidson's article is, precisely, concerned with the limits of intelligibility.

No wonder there is such alarm among the small band of powerful males at the possibility of losing the Canon or the Tradition. They would lose an array of cultural references which help them frame their arguments. They would have to take seriously the possibility that their own set of references is as partial as anyone else's. Unlike them, the rest of us – the majority – have to address the question of speaking to a disparate audience.

6 CONCLUSIONS ABOUT SPEAKING FOR MYSELF

I have been discussing the need to make myself understood by recounting experiences. I have suggested that those who do not need to do this are in the comfortable position of completely sharing a language with all their audience. For example, a small group of white, middle-class feminists would share a language to the extent that they would have no need to tell long stories. Similarly the group of academically powerful philo-sophers share a language. (The difference is that the philosophers assume that anyone who does not speak their language is inadequate.) However, anyone talking to an audience which does not completely share the same languages will find it helpful to recount stories.

Thus, I need to use stories to make my points. The rest of this chapter contains stories of my own life on which I draw later in order to develop theories. They can be read, now, or, equally well, at the various points in Part II when I draw on them.

7 MEMORIES OF MY OWN LIFE

7.1 Wanting and not wanting to belong, acceptance and rejection

7.1.1 Facts, ideas, people: it's personal connections all the way down

It is easy enough to think of times when I learnt about connections, when I learnt whom I loved and whom I did not. But, in search of counter-examples, I have tried to think of memories which might not involve people and connections. I have found it impossible. I find connections with other people colour and frame every important building block in my remembered, imagined, conscious self.

I am someone who gets on quite easily without other people, who is often happy to be on her own. I was certainly self-sufficient as a child. I was happy playing on my own so I could have the best roles – the prince, the princess, the cowboy and the horse, the knight in shining armour and his evil opponent. But all of these games are ways for a child to work out her connections with different kinds of people. So I have also tried to remember games I played which were not people-oriented. In the garden I marshalled snails into patterns and on the beach I dug endless water channels arranging how the trickles ran into the sea. I was happy not to have to negotiate their logic with anyone else.

Even here the connections with others are an important part of the memory. The snails are remembered partly because of their own pleasures, but partly because in my memory they are mixed up with memories of my grandfather. (Though surely his garden did not have snails? Memory may be playing me false, but this investigation is *not* about facts; it is about memories.) My grandfather loved patterns and numbers and arranging things. I would have enjoyed talking snails with him. The water channels were of interest to my family. I remember discussion of them revolving round my future identity: perhaps, they mused, I was going to be a civil engineer.

To continue with the project of trying to find memories which might not involve people and connections with them, I have tried to think of significant times in my intellectual or cognitive (as opposed to social and emotional) growth when I was a child. I have clear memories of myself discovering things, and making intellectual connections. These memories, too, are imbued with other people.

My view of myself as numerate is one which comes from connections with others. Discovering the secret of the multiplication tables was a private affair. Having understood the principle of tables, I remember lying in bed and finding that I could, by myself, generate the eight times table. I was immensely excited to be able to generate a set of numbers which were impressively big to the 6-year-old I was then. However, such moments are framed by the context. Much more significant in terms of my identity as someone who likes numbers and can understand them is the memory of being good at maths at school, or of appreciation from my family. I remember running in to my parents' bedroom to count to 100, at 6 a.m. and I remember their delighted congratulations.[3] I was one of the few in my primary class who could easily understand it when we started to deal with 'x' rather than with actual numbers. My grandfather delighted me with a simple proof that it is impossible to find the biggest prime number. At 16, when only a few of us in my all-girls' school chose to specialise in maths and science, we told endless stories to ourselves about the group who took maths, and the kind of people we were. We were the ones who enjoyed the puzzle about the existence of imaginary numbers, and we were special, being such a small close-knit group.

7.1.2 Wanting and not wanting to belong: deciding how to belong

When I look back at my teenage self, I notice that I used to tell myself endless stories about my gender. I wanted to be sure that I was a woman, that is, a real woman. I also wanted to be myself. In other words, I wanted to be sure that 'self' was a woman.

I was pleased to be scolded (at the age of 15 or 16) for wearing nail varnish *on the very same day* that I came top in the chemistry exams. The first achievement balanced the second. I was relieved that I was known to be forgetful and absent-minded *as well as* known to be intelligent and capable. (So I could be someone who said 'Oh, silly me!' as well as 'I can manage perfectly well.') I was proud rather than ashamed when my form teacher complained in my school report that I dissipated my obvious leadership qualities in making jokes: I did not want to be bossy and authoritative, any more than I wanted to be invisible and biddable. Many of the stories that the group of us doing maths and physics told ourselves about what kind of people we were, were stories about gender. We kept on commenting to each other how light-hearted and unsolemn we were, and how unlike our imagined image of boys doing the same subject.

Note what did not count in the self-assessment of my gender: my female body – genitals, breasts, periods, and clear heterosexual feelings (an attitude my teenage self experienced as 'natural', as from the body, and quite removed from any social influences). No doubt the absence of any of these would have been worrying, but their presence did not seem to be a comfort. Nor would simply taking on the trappings of femininity do. I wanted the real thing. It was no good simply pretending, as I could have done, by being heavily made up, simpering when I met boys, or acting as if I had girlish ambitions to be a nurse or a secretary, careers thought of as more feminine. On the other hand, I was happy to nurture the right attitudes if I could find a seed for them. I developed an aversion to games and PE, especially as I was worryingly tall and strong rather than small and petite. I persuaded myself that I was frightened of spiders. I was glad that it was easy to give in to period pains by asking to lie down with a hot water bottle in the school sick room.

None of this anxiety was related to acceptance by any group of real people. That was a separate, if analogous, issue, where different things counted, and which led to its own tensions. My problem stemmed from a personal need to do with my construction of self. I wanted to belong to an abstract grouping: real women.

The problem went on worrying me until the end of my teens, when I eventually resolved it (illogically enough!) by deciding that I must be a real woman because I liked and wanted babies. (In fact, in retrospect, I do not think I particularly liked them.) I also decided that there were real innate sex differences, which showed themselves in personality, and the attitude to babies was the key. This resolution of the issue allowed me to go on being myself even if that meant accepting that I possessed a number of apparently masculine attributes. I reasoned that these attributes must be unimportant so far as distinguishing the sexes was concerned, because I had them, and I was a real woman. No wonder I resisted feminism whenever it forced itself on my attention. Its critical questions about sex differences would have threatened the fragile edifice I had constructed.

The whole question raised itself again, years later, at a series of feminist conferences called Girls and Science and Technology (GASAT). No doubt my past anxieties and their resolution contributed to my sharp rejection of the ideas being floated that girls and women were less abstract, less linearly logical and had a characteristic female logic (and it would be much better for science and the future of the world if more scientists were women with their special characteristics). My argument was that such a characterisation of women meant that *I* could not be a woman, and this was plainly wrong. I was sure I belonged to the category 'woman', and it would have to be drawn so as to include me.

I have told this story as a project of belonging. It could also have been told as a rejection of belonging. After all, it would have been simpler for me not to specialise in sciences. I liked English and history just as much as maths and physics. It would have been easier to learn to hide my intelligence and competence altogether, and there was plenty of peer pressure to do so. In fact, to say that I simply expanded and mystified the category 'woman' until it included me is too simple a story.

In truth, I did not value or even *like* women very much. All my friends were men. I was proud of this fact. I remember feeling that if there were a lot of men in a meeting or gathering they validated it as valuable. I was pleased that I could do physics, because it must be hard and worthy if there were so few girls doing it. On the other hand, I was a girl and I used to wonder if I had got into the course only because of being a girl, on a quota.

I did not want to be a man, but I did not quite want to be a real woman either. My actions all showed that my self-definition was of a self different from most women. I had heroes and a few heroines as role models, and a few female friends. I was constructing a self that was a bit of an outsider, that could grow and live in the spaces between the stereotypes.

This self-construction had its analogues in one of the Girls and Science and Technology conferences too. I and a few others spent a very happy evening transgressing the assumptions of the Conference, by listing what we liked about technology – not just clean water and contraceptives, but also fast cars, brightly coloured powerful earth-moving equipment, and computer gee-whizzery. We belonged – we were feminist women actively contributing to a critique of science and technology – but we liked not quite belonging too.

I found there were compromises to be made if I wanted to be, simultaneously, a physicist, a philosopher, a feminist, a woman. In fact I did not want to be all these things, or not wholeheartedly, but the effort of negotiating my way around the contradictions affected the way I was able to set about deciding just what kind of person I would be happy to be.

A turning point for me was attending my first Girls and Science and Technology conference. It was the first time that I had attended a conference at which women were in a clear majority. At the suggestion of the facilitator, the seminar group in which I found myself began the session with introductions. Each of us was to explain why we were at the conference and something about our personal or professional interest in the area. I was very anxious indeed. Now, I thought, I would be found out. My credentials for attending such a conference were shaky, I thought. I was no longer 'in' science. I had arrived at this conference by a circuitous route, having become interested in girls and technology through my interest in the philosophy of emotions and its relevance to education. I would be shown up as an outsider, as a charlatan, even. I was not a real physicist, a real feminist or even a real philosopher.

There was no escape. I explained myself to the other women. I found that they were listening with interest and respect. The facilitator smiled.

'A typical woman's career', she said. The relief of it! Suddenly I was all right. I did not need to pretend. None of the rest of the women was any more typical than I was. Indeed many of them had assumed that they, too, were marginal, with few rights to be there. With that one comment, my shame resolved itself into a kind of self-respect.

Much the same thing happened at the first British Women and Philosophy meetings. We made the same kind of introductions and again I, and others, had the same feeling that we, unlike everybody else, would be odd, marginal, not really there by right. There was the same sense of relief that shame could turn into self-respect. The condition of not being 'normal' was in fact normal – and indeed was a likely result of trying to fit the contradictions of being female into the framework of more straightforward male identities and their associated careers.

Self-respect and re-understanding experience led to new emotions about other experiences. One of these emotions was a mixture of painful puzzlement and bewilderment as previous perspectives became over-turned and I felt uncertainty and a sense of vertigo about how many other perspectives and feelings were about to change too. Old certainties with their alliances were lost and I moved into the unknown, with new alliances to be forged out of new loves and hates, facing new rejections and hoping for different acceptances.

As someone who works in schools, I watch children decide how to belong. They negotiate their own identities through complex mazes of overlapping groups, using their connections of love and hatred to form some alliances and to resist others. I spent some time in a class of six-year-olds in rural Maine in the USA, working alongside the teacher on a collaborative educational project. The children were learning the story of Groundhog day. As was I – I had not heard it before. One little girl refused to answer questions, saying she was Jewish, and therefore her family did not celebrate Groundhog Day. We tried to point out that I, as a British person, also did not celebrate the day, but that we could do so without compromise; it is an American festival, rather than a religious one.[4] At the age of 6 she was negotiating her own Jewishness. Included in that identity was the wish to claim it publicly even if (or, perhaps, just *because*) it made her different from the other children.

On another occasion, I was working with a teacher of 10-year-olds in the inner city of Nottingham. The children were diverse in terms of social class and in terms of their ethnic backgrounds. We were working on a project related to making an all-day trip to Warwick Castle, with its towering stone ramparts, scary medieval dungeons, and plush drawing rooms. I was conscious that when the children were asked to think themselves back in time to an earlier Warwick, only the ones with one or more white British grandparents would imagine that it was their own great, great, great, grandparents that they might encounter. Those with grandparents from the Punjab or the Caribbean, thought themselves into a doubly strange environment, having lost familiar faces as well as familiar surroundings. It was important for us teachers to notice that this useful exercise of the imagination asked for different negotiations of identity and belonging within our group of children born and brought up within a few streets of each other.

We also noticed that imagining that you are anyone who counts in history tends to mean imagining you are a boy. As we designed activities for the children to help them learn history, it was noticeable that it is easier to identify with the people in the history books, the closer you are to being male, white, rich and Christian. For instance, as part of the same historical project, the children designed shields for themselves. I remembered, with pleasure, how much I had enjoyed learning about shields and heraldry as a child. But did it do me any good to imagine that I was part of the male, ruling class, rather than a female member of the peasantry (where my own family must have come from)? And what effect did it have on me to know that many of these shields were used in the crusades, a war of Christendom on Islam? We are asking some children to change sex, class and religion as well as ethnic background as they identify with those who are the primary subjects of history.

On the other hand, part of the pleasure of history is imagining yourself to be very different people, and, for me, part of the pleasure of places like Warwick Castle is exactly that ordinary people are no longer excluded from the beauty and riches of such a place, including all those beautiful heraldic symbols. Another pleasure is seeing the macho warlike world of medieval castles turned into the innocent pleasures of holiday outings. None of the children comes from the nobility. None of them quite 'belongs', but all of them have inherited the right to enjoy this castle, and learn from it. There is room for me, and for the children, to negotiate room for ourselves within the contradictions we face.

7.1.3 Reactions to others: do they belong?

Other people's new-born babies have become a problem for me since I have considered myself a feminist. When I hear of a new-born baby, I, like everyone else, has the impulse to ask: 'Is it a girl or a boy?' But why should this be the first question? Or even the second? What is being said about the salience of gender if this needs to be fixed before anything else? I cannot believe that this is the most important thing about a baby, even if my reactions tell me different. So I try not to ask and I find it very difficult! I still want to know. I have found myself asking 'Have you thought of a name yet?' Who am I fooling? I am hoping they don't say 'Robin' or 'Chris' or some other androgynous name.

Even more worrying is the fact that I find it hard to talk to someone if I do not know their sex. This was brought home to me meeting Ray in a class of 10-year-olds. I was engaging her in conversation, as part of a process of getting to know the children in the class. She was dressed in jeans and trainers. She had short hair. I had no obvious way of knowing if she was a boy or a girl. To my private embarrassment I found that I found the conversation went more easily the moment that I managed to fix her sex, which I did within a few minutes. Plainly I was doing something in my normal behaviour that depends on the sex of the child I am talking to, even though I would claim not to be adding to gender stereotypes by treating the boys and girls differently for no particular reason.

When I tell these stories to the practising teachers who are my education students they laugh with recognition, often adding similar stories of their own. Belonging to the category 'boys' or 'girls' continues to have the salience it has always had, regardless of unisex clothes or gender-bending fashions.

7.2 Feelings, emotions, rationality, politics

7.2.1 Feelings and internal states of commotion

Some years ago I used to spend most of my free time working for Amnesty International. I remember when I first heard of the organisation. As a teenager I was taken to a evening of folk music where the Amnesty candle burned, and someone explained the organisation to us. Later, I joined a local group, and began to write letters, sit on committees, collect jumble, sell Christmas cards and write leaflets. It is obvious I was emotionally affected by the original evening, and that I continued to have an emotional commitment to the aims and ideals of the organisation.

Working for Amnesty did not mean being in a continual state of rage about injustice or pity for people incarcerated and forgotten. On the contrary, my usual state of mind was more likely to have been enjoyment of shared fund-raising activities, boredom at committee meetings, or, occasionally, elation when a newspaper took up a press release, or when a prisoner was let out of gaol. However whatever the occurrent feelings that characterised the work I did for Amnesty, it was the feelings of outraged justice and of pity which remained my motivating emotions.

I have described feelings in relation to my work for Amnesty. If I had wanted to be more precise I would have used fewer, not more, names of feelings. Even as it was, I qualified the names by putting them into context. However, I have found it is difficult to monitor my own speech, so I have spent some time listening out for the way friends of mine used emotion words. Roughly speaking, I found, the more precise the description of a feeling, the less the names of emotions were needed.

One day, I heard about how Mick had felt about organising a big strike when he told a group of us the story. He told us of clashes with the police, the triumph of the strikers after difficulties and the celebrations in the pubs. In the long account only once did he use the name of a feeling. He had been among some reinforcements arriving at the factory gates. As they arrived, 'We felt a little bit proud and a little bit embarrassed.' Otherwise, feelings were conveyed by which incidents he related and the kinds of things he chose to tell us about them. For instance, the man guarding the gate for the employers saw the reinforcements coming, and threw the key over the wall. We did not need to be told he was scared and desperate: the context showed us more precisely what his feelings were than words like 'scared and desperate' would have done.

On the other hand people do also describe their feelings using the names of emotions. When Mary's father committed suicide, her overwhelming feeling was anger, not grief, and she said so: 'I felt so angry with him.' But she also went on to describe what thoughts were in her mind, what had made her angry, what things she was remembering. She needed the concise but imprecise word 'angry', so that we would not misinterpret the more exact feelings she then went on to express.

7.2.2 Feelings named in a culture

When I first went to Europe in my teens I discovered that the Germans and the French named feelings that I recognised but which I could not translate into single English words. Words that I was particularly taken by were *gemutlich* and *sympathique*. The first means something like companionable, cosy and convivial, without quite being any of these. The second is somewhere between empathetic and in accord with oneself. It was like finding a secret code. I felt that I had developed a new maturity in my new-found words, that I had a better hold on the feelings described.

Of course I was naïve in my enthusiasm. The very fact that I learnt them so easily in spite of my rudimentary German and French meant that the concepts are not so foreign to English. Ten years later, living in Iran, I had a lot more trouble with the Farsi word *khejalat*. It veers somewhere between the English words of 'shy' and 'shame'. But these were significantly different concepts to me, from my Western European perspective. I am not sure that in two years I ever quite grasped the concept, though I became better at using it. The emotion expressed by *Gorbaneh shomah* proved a little easier. I am unable to translate it in the short phrases that I used to explain *gemutlich* and *sympathique*. The literal meaning is 'I'll be your sacrifice', but this is simply not a sentence that can be used in everyday speech in English. However, once I started to use it, I found it easy. I was not aware of making the mistakes I made with *khejalat*. I must have been expressing something, but not something that is easy to say in English. Perhaps learning these words required taking part in the day-to-day social interactions typical in Iran?

When I went to stay in the United States for a few months I was surprised to find that feelings were named rather differently there, although Britain and America apparently share a common language. Even though the culture of the United States should have been familiar to me from films and books, it still took me some time to learn to describe and express feelings adequately. The actual words were the same as ones I knew already, but they were used differently. Sometimes I found this deeply embarrassing. It was necessary to send Valentine cards saying 'I love you' to the six-year-olds in the school where I was working. They would have been very upset if I had not joined in this festival. Writing them I felt false. To me 'I love you' is said to an adult, and it has sexual overtones, especially on Valentine's day. I understood the feeling named and it is one I recognise: teachers indeed love the small children in their classes. It is not a feeling so readily expressed verbally in England.

In all these cases I was learning a language. The language that I learnt was the result of some careful teaching by the people I met. Wrong usage was a cause at best for laughter, and at worst, embarrassment. This was why *khejalat* was significant in Iran. Since I am a woman, it was a concept that particularly applied to my own conduct. Indeed, it was clear that the Farsi I learnt was that of a female, middle-class Iranian. I began by speaking like my colleagues in the school where I was based. Since they were almost all men, I picked up men's gestures and intonations. I was soon put right. Friends noted how my pitch changed as I switched from English to Farsi: I had learnt (with what accuracy I do not know) that it is proper for Iranian women to have higher pitched voices than their English equivalents. Similarly, when I picked up some phrases from working-class people, I was soon told that such phrases were inappropriate for me.

7.2.3 Feelings likely for certain groups

When I was travelling across the Middle East I found it hard to explain to natives of the country, or to friends back home, just how wearing I found the continual 'Hallo!' that met me when I walked in the streets. It is something that is harmless, a kind of habitual response by some men and children to passing foreigners, especially if they are female. It was something that was barely noticeable at first. As time wore on it became like a persistent swarm of flies, impossible to ignore and deeply irritating and intrusive. Unless I had experienced the cumulative effect of it, I would find it hard to understand. On the other hand, I find that those who have experienced it are far more likely to know exactly what I am talking about.

Living in the Middle East, I also discovered how much I hated not being able to go for a walk on my own without thought for who might follow me or perhaps, in rural districts, throw stones after me. I continued to go for walks on my own, for pleasure, but I learnt to walk with my eyes cast down, not catching anyone's eye, and in a state of readiness to deal with unwanted encounters. I was in no real physical danger – but I reacted with fear and tension, and my pleasure was reduced accordingly.

I was experiencing something of what it is like to be visible in a society which harasses those who are different. This is an experience which is hard to understand for those who have never been in such a situation. They talk about the importance of understanding the culture, and of what produces such behaviour: they talk about physical danger. Of course I know about these things, but the emotions I describe are not affected by such knowledge.

7.4 Autonomy: personal and political

7.4.1 Dependency and connection

The values I place on dependence and on independence are both experienced by me in everyday life, and yet when I try to explain using the words 'dependence' or 'independence' I find that I speak paradoxically. For instance, it sounds odd when I say that I am dependent on my mother. Yet it is true. This dependence is not the same as it was when I was a child, but it is there, all the same. I like this dependence. I am happy that she is an important part of my life and that I miss her when we are not in touch. Conversely, she is dependent on me, and on the way I am an inextricable part of her life. No doubt, she was also dependent on me when I was a child. Her happiness and purposes in life were partly bound up in myself and my brothers. On the other hand, I am glad that I am independent of her, that I live in my own household. She is equally glad that she is independent of me in her old age, that she lives in her own household. We are both glad that we pay our own way – though we would be happy to provide money if the other needed it.

This is not the only dependence I value. All my life I have been glad when I have found close relationships of love and friendship. In making a close relationship, dependency is embraced. At an early stage of my life with my present partner, we were trying to fill in a form for the electoral register. It required us to fill in who was the head of the household and who were the dependants. 'But we're mutually dependent,' he said, only half joking. We were not trying to get rid of vulnerability and need. We knew it could not be eliminated by contracts or exercise of rights. We make arrangements about our property and know our mutual responsibilities. Such agreements do not touch the emotional dependence which comes from being a part of each other's lives and each other's sense of well-being. Disputes have to be resolved in the light of this. We each know that the happiness and interests of the one are important to the other. On the other hand, I value my independence in this area of my life. Mutual dependence coexists with limits on mutual expectations.

Each of us helps sets such limits, in spite of each having to deal with external expectations and pressures about the proper working of sexual relationships.

My dependent close relationships feel as though they increase freedom more than they diminish it. I can live my life more as I would want to when I have dependent close relationships with a range of other people. If I lived on my own and had no close relationships I would have fewer responsibilities and fewer areas of vulnerability to the actions of others. But the things I want are related to what gives my life meaning: things which absorb me, take my attention, structure my days and weeks, and which form the stuff of treasured memories and dreams of the future. All of these are bound up with those I love. My freedom to do some things is increased if I do not have to consider others. But my freedom to be myself is bound by those others and our ways of leading a life together.

When I discovered the value of women friends, I discovered the pleasures of 'sisterhood' – a relation not much like the experience of being an actual sister to my brothers. It took a bit of time to get used to the idea that women friends were as valuable as men, and then a bit later I realised how few men were as good company or good friends as women. At the same time as finding symbolic 'sisters' I was rediscovering the pleasures of being an actual daughter. When I no longer had to assert my independence so vigorously I was able rediscover our mutual dependence. Perhaps that is why it took me so long to notice other ways of relating, even while, of course, I was participating in them.

It is so easy to miss things because of an idea. The idea of sisterhood stopped me noticing all the usual social relationships I had: very few of them are relationships with equals. I am, at various times, a colleague, a neighbour, a customer, a teacher, a tourist, an employer and an employee. I am also a daughter, a step-mother, an aunt, a sister, and a cousin. I have chosen none of the individuals who fall into these relationships with me. Thus we did not choose each other because we like each other. We have little choice about continuing with our connection, short of drastic steps like leaving the job, moving house, or cutting ourselves off from the family. Therefore the dependencies that we have are not an inter-dependency of equals, of a free association of equal people, who will stand by each other in mutual support. They are the mutual dependencies of non-equals.

7.4.2 *Getting judgements into circulation*

One of the most significant influences on my professional, and indeed my personal, life has come from my connection with the Society for Women in Philosophy. For me, it began with a meeting of a dozen women, mostly strangers to each other, who met up one Saturday in Oxford to see if there was anything to discuss about the relationship of women, feminism and philosophy. At that time, over ten years ago, there was very little women's philosophy visible in Britain. There were a few well-known names. There were a very few published books. When we started a group for a few academic women interested in philosophy we thought it was useful – and enjoyable – to meet. We had little idea of the ways in which such a group would help raise the profile of our work.

Ten years later there is an extensive network of women philosophers, at all academic levels. This has continued to help individuals to make space to discuss their ideas, and to find support. It has also helped to give feminist ideas a wider airing – and an even wider one for the fact that such ideas exist at all. The fact that the organisation exists means that it is easier for outsiders to discover that there are women – or feminist – philosophers in Britain. Publishers know we exist. Some philosophy departments hope to tap student demand for feminist courses, so women academics looking for jobs have put their membership on to their job applications. There is now some recognition of the value and interest of the field, with the result that some men feel that they are missing out on something, and every so often protest at being excluded.

We are only one of a number of women's networks in Britain. It is an uphill struggle to get acknowledgement, let alone debate, from the mainstream. We also all know that the hill has become less precipitous with our existence.

3 Other lives
Learning from their experiences

1 LISTENING TO OTHERS

Like the last chapter, this one begins from a practical question, rooted in a feminist concern for speaking for myself and listening to the personal voices of others. If I am worth listening to, then so are others. If others are worth listening to, then so am I. This presupposes that we are able to speak and listen to each other. The question is, which others do I listen to, and this question itself presupposes the further question, which others is it possible for me to listen to?

In Chapter 2 I discussed these questions from the point of view of myself accommodating my arguments to the audience. I discussed who listens to me and who finds it possible to listen to me. In this chapter I discuss the question from the point of view of myself trying to listen to others.

My wish to listen to others is not simply a kind of liberal impulse to listen to everyone. Rather, it is to contribute to a creation of a theory which is not blind to difference. In part, this is a response to the justice of the charge that most published feminist theory is too narrow, being white, middle-class and Western. It is also a result of the illumination I find from listening to those who benefit from a perspective or standpoint that is different from my own. On the other hand I do not wish to engage in a kind of 'cultural tourism'[1] which fails to open itself to difference while congratulating itself on its breadth of knowledge.

If I have to make efforts to listen to particular others, how do I choose who to listen to? There are two main questions embedded here. The first main question is: '*Who is it possible for me to listen to?* This, itself, is a three-fold question. First, how is it possible to find such others? I do not want simply to rely on chance encounters. Nor do I suppose that I can hear such others easily, drowned out as they usually are by loud, confident, well-educated, male voices. Second, is it possible to understand what they are saying? It may be that I am unable to understand some people, in which case listening is a waste of time. Third, is it possible to understand some people only if they make an effort to speak to me? In the last chapter I commented that I had a particular, if rather vaguely defined, audience. There was a wider audience of those who could choose whether to listen to me – and I would be unconcerned, really, whether I was intelligible to them. They might eavesdrop on me, if they liked. Could I similarly eavesdrop on others? If not, I rely on their efforts, and the question of who I am able to listen to depends on them.

The second main question embedded in the question of who I choose to listen to is: *'If there are a very large number of others who I can find and understand, which few do I choose?'* It is entirely probable that there will be a large number. There are, at a rough estimate, about six thousand million other people from whom I could learn. Even if a sizeable proportion are eliminated because it is not possible for me to hear them, it is entirely probable that it will not be possible to listen to all those that remain. There is not enough time. Thus I have to make efforts to listen to some of them, while not listening to others. Talking of the degree of difference from the dominant white, middle-class and Western minority is only of limited help. It is relatively easy to label other people as members of a group be it women and men, black and white, or some particular hybrids or combinations such as white women or middle-class blacks. It is easy, but it is misleading. First, no individual can be assumed to be *representative* of any particular group, and second, it is wrong to assume that we can identify such groups for any particular individual. Just as I am, each of the others is a person-sized fragment, but neither I nor they know what they are fragments of. I need to decide how to choose among them.

2 FINDING OTHERS TO LISTEN TO

The complexities of the questions I have raised were not apparent to me at first. My first thought was merely that I needed to use the theories and experiences of a range of people. As I said, I was anxious to avoid the trap of only noticing inequality as it affects me adversely, rather than also seeing where I benefit from it. Therefore, I thought, I needed to find people who were different from the generality of those who produce theories and describe their experiences. I did not see them as representative of particular groups – any more than I saw myself as a fragment of any particular, easily identifiable, grouping. However, I thought it important that they came from groups other than the white, middle-class, male, Western, heterosexual, able-bodied minority who see themselves as the norm.

I particularly wanted to focus on black or Asian women (and some men) from the West and on women (and some men) from the rest of the world. I imagine that this is the same impulse that leads to the attempt to be inclusive that is seen in some feminist anthologies with their black and Third World contributors. But immediately a warning bell sounded for me. A high proportion of English language feminist publishing originates in the USA. As an outsider to the USA, I am always aware that the inclusiveness is very partial. Usually, the contributors from other countries have doctorates from the USA – and in some cases are Americans who have lived abroad for a long time. A tiny minority are from other Western countries, and an even smaller minority are from the rest of the world. The contributors are an unrepresentative group of people, who are strongly influenced by the USA.

Examples of recent anthologies show this clearly. Take for example Brodzki and Schenck (1988). There is an explicit attempt to provide a range of texts in 'time, geographical location, and social positioning' (1988: xi) partly in order to escape the situation in which Western women were 'boxed . . . into the basic habits of thought of a culture in which they did not entirely share' (1988: x). Of their eighteen contributors, only two are working outside the United States (in France and England) and one of those has an American Ph.D. The only one who originates from outside the West, Leila Ahmed, who writes on Egypt, teaches in Massachusetts. Similarly the anthology by the Personal Narratives Group sprung from a series of meetings which were structured 'so as to include individuals from different disciplinary backgrounds and different geographic areas of interest in order to encourage cross-cultural and cross-disciplinary dialogue' (1989: 9).

Of their twenty-two contributors, seventeen work in the United States, two in England, one in Canada, one in Italy, and one in Tanzania. All of them originate in the West, although Marjorie Mbilinyi has been working in Tanzania since 1968. Even the book edited by Johnson-Odim and Strobel (1992) which is titled *Women in the Third World* has only one out of the sixteen contributors currently working outside the USA. She is an American woman who has lived and taught in Egypt since the 1960s. Of the rest, at most four, judging by their names, originate from outside the USA.

Two recent anthologies manage a little better: in Lennon and Whitford (1994), of twenty contributors, twelve work in the UK, two in Australia, two in Italy, two in the Netherlands and one each in New Zealand and the USA. Their backgrounds are also more diverse: nine from Britain, four from Italy, two from Australia, one each from Azania, New Zealand, India and Ireland. In Moghadam (1994), of twenty-one contributors, nine work in the USA, four in North Africa, two each in Britain and Eastern Europe, and one each in Finland, Nigeria, Pakistan and Turkey. Their backgrounds are five from the USA, three from Europe and the rest from other parts of the world. However, even in these two collections, at least thirty-seven of the forty-one writers have spent a significant amount of time studying or working in the USA or Europe.

Where are the voices unmediated by an education in the West? Or is it that such voices are addressing such a different set of needs that conversation between us is hard to sustain? Worse, would my attempt to engage with them necessitate my wasting their hard-won time? I needed to learn from these collections and go beyond my first thought.

My second thought was that I must stop and think what I was looking for. This required me to examine what possibilities exist. The possibilities can be broken down into two categories. It should be possible to learn from other people using either (a) their theories or (b) their descriptions of their own experience. I need to know which of these will give me best access to a range of voices. What are the opportunities and pitfalls to be found in each? How do I choose from among them? Is it going to be anything more than a form of cultural tourism?

3 USING THEORY AND THE LIMITATIONS OF USING IT

There can be no doubt that in developing a theory of self, I will be drawing on the theories of others. So why look beyond them? The reason is that looking at theories will not be adequate as a means of gaining access to a wide range of perspectives. There are two powerful reasons for this inadequacy, and I shall consider them in turn. The first reason arises within any given society, whether it is a nation or a cultural group-ing, and the second from the global relations between different societies, again whether they are nations or cultural groupings.

3.1 Theorising for some

The first reason for the inadequacy of just looking at theories operates *within* a society. In any society, theorising is predominantly carried out by a very small, socially defined group of people. In our own society it is made up of white, middle-class males. The reasons for this state of affairs have been well rehearsed over the years. Feminists point out that it is no accident that most theorising has been done by men, by whites, and by the rich. Theorising is an activity which requires time and other resources. This is Virginia Woolf's argument in *Three Guineas* (1938, 1977). It is Alice Walker's argument in her essay 'In search of our mothers' gardens' in the book of the same name (1984). Of course, there are examples of those who have managed to theorise in the most adverse of circumstances – but they are few.

Many feminist theories began in response to the observation that most theories are made by men. Such theories showed the systematic bias inherent in standard (male-produced) theory, usually in the way it left out women altogether. Well-known examples abound. For instance there is the way that social sciences have based their observations primarily on boys and men.[2] Where women were included, male-centred theory made assumptions about value systems, as in interpretations of normal conversations in linguistics which 'proved' women's ways of talking to be inferior.[3]

Later on, feminists began to produce their own theories – and necessarily drew on their own value systems in their production, including in their choice of evidence to look at. They were immediately criticised by men, unused to being ignored. Theory informed by feminism remains a minority interest in the academy.

This is not only a Western problem. If I am interested in, say, women, or any other group of dominated people, the local theories are likely to be inadequate. To take one example, the edited collection by Carrithers, Collins and Lukes (1985) contains a number of scholarly surveys of persons and selves within the thinking of cultures as diverse as Western modern individualism, Southern Sudan, China and the Brahmins of Kashmir. In all these cases the sources quoted are almost all male, and, not surprisingly, the 'person' or 'self' investigated is overwhelmingly male. For instance Mark Elvin's article on conceptions of the self in China begins with a woman's poem, but soon goes on to male poets and finally on to the traditions of Confucianism, Darwinism and Buddhism, in which all the theorists quoted are male.[4]

Similarly, the feminist critique and construct of theory is not just a Western phenomenon. Alternative theory has been created in a number of non-Western contexts by feminist women, although they themselves would not always use the term 'feminist'. To take just the example of the Arabic-speaking world, a number of internationally known women have produced critiques of the masculine biases of their social, political and religious systems.[5] These critiques are well-known in their own countries (sometimes too well-known for the comfort of their governments) as well as in the West. However, as in the case of the West, these critiques remain well outside the mainstream in their own countries.

Where the dominated group are in a small minority, it is even more difficult for them to develop theories as a group, which can be presented in the public domain. In Britain for instance, black and Asian people make up only 5–6 per cent of the population as a whole. For larger groups, such as working-class people, it may still be difficult, as they turn into minorities at university level (or much earlier in their formal education, in some countries). While women are now entering universities in much the same numbers as men, they are still a small minority of the post-graduates who will be well-placed to produce and publish theory. In Britain, people whose fathers are professionals or managers are four times as likely to get university degrees than are people who come from working-class families. Although 35 per cent of the population are working class, there is only a small minority of working-class graduates (Halsey, 1985). Consider: How many African-Caribbean or Asian philosophers are working in Britain? Let alone female ones? Or working-class ones? Or combinations of these? The answer is, very few in relative terms, and very few in absolute terms. Thus it is hard for these groups to produce enough theory-makers for there to be a community which, in Michael Oakeshott's celebrated phrase, talks to itself, and in which ideas feed off each other.

The difficulties do not stop with theory-making. Publicising the theory widely once it has been developed is something else that is easiest for the more dominant members of a society. It is important not to underestimate the significance of networks of academics and publishers, on the one hand, and of prescribed courses and their booklists on the other.

It is probably necessary to emphasise that I am not confusing quality with quantity of theorists. Why, then, do I say that more would be better in the case of presently missing groups, like women? The point I have made is twofold. To summarise: first, theory is rarely, and with difficulty, produced in isolation. Academic life depends on there being like-minded 'critical friends' who can discuss ideas before they are presented to the world at large for further criticism. Second, it is important that the ideas can reach the world at large, if the ideas are to be influential. All these things are more difficult for small minorities.

It is also necessary to point out that I am not suggesting that any individual person is directly affected, in any particular way, by their gender, race or class as far as their theorising is concerned. As I will explain in more detail in Chapter 5, individuals find all kinds of ways round the need to participate in or identify with certain groups who may be willing to accept them, but also may well reject them. However, if gender, race or class is salient within the culture in which they find themselves, individuals will be unable to escape that salience in their own lives, no matter how they choose to deal with it. Thus I am talking about groups of people – who will certainly be made up of disparate individuals. The success of women-only groups (i.e. not *feminist* only) for philosophers, psychologists, and other theory-makers is testimony to the need there is for perspectives to be shared, even though agreement is not reached (see Chapter 2, section 7.4.2). There is no *one* feminist philosophy, epistemology or moral theory, yet feminist epistemologies, and moral theories are more readily produced in women-only settings.

3.2 Abstractions out of context.

Global relations between different societies underlie the second reason that looking at theories will not be adequate as a means of gaining access to a wide range of perspectives. It is harder to understand theories that have developed out of different contexts. Coming to understand the theoretical works of, say, China, or the traditional religious beliefs of, say, Kenya, is even more difficult than coming to understand the theories of one's own society.

In the first place there is the question of different tongues. A secular or Christian Westerner trying to come to terms with Middle-Eastern Islam or the spirit world of Kenya, has to deal in the first place with the difficulty of translation. This is acknowledged for the texts which are central to mainstream theorising. Discussions of the various different translations of Greek are commonplace in Western philosophy. Or, another example, the importance of careful, scholarly translations from one European language to another is taken for granted, as is the difficulty of making a good English translation of, say, Heidegger or Derrida. Scholars working in traditions further removed from our own have fewer such translations to draw on, since there are fewer people competent to discuss the niceties of linking traditions and comparing them.[6] I come back to this point in section 4.1, 'The trouble with translation'.

In the second place, there is the question of having to deal with being able to understand abstractions out of context, something which is even more difficult than translation. Theorising is, necessarily, a process of abstraction. If the context from which the abstraction has occurred is unfamiliar, then the abstraction will be doubly difficult to understand, let alone to consider critically. A British feminist philosopher, Anne Seller, discusses how she came to understand what possibilities she had for dialogue within an Indian women's university and the place of theorising within that dialogue:

> At best such theories [gender equality] provide a platform from which to view the problem. At worst they obstruct rather than facilitate dialogue. I was also beginning to recognize that the more abstract and theoretical our formulations, the more culturally specific they become. Intuitively, I had expected the opposite.
>
> (1994: 243)

It is no wonder, then, that theory is a limited way of getting to grips with a variety of perspectives. If we are looking to a variety of perspectives within a single society it will be hard to find theories which provide it. Moreover, it is no wonder that it is difficult to engage with theories produced from very different countries and cultures, or by people living very different lives. To say that using theory is of limited use is not to say it is of no use at all. Rather, it is to emphasise that other means of engaging with a variety of perspectives also need to be found if difference is to be properly acknowledged in any future theorising.

4 USING DESCRIPTIONS OF EXPERIENCE

Some of the problems of theorising do not occur for descriptions of experience. It is easier to describe experience without first having had an expensive education, or finding a reference group of the like-minded who have had a similar grounding. So it is hardly surprising that while most descriptions of experience come from rich, white men, in the form of autobiographical writing or fiction, there are also plenty of examples of these forms of writing which come from those who are not rich, white and male.

The sector of the population with access to writing is small – but it is much larger than the sector with access to theorising.[7] Consider the autobiographical poetry written thousands of years ago by Chinese women – and recent autobiographical novels written by them today.[8] Or consider the slave autobiographies of the USA, the autobiographical writing by working-class people in the nineteenth century, or the testimonies of Latin America.[9]

Early on in various feminist movements, there has been a move to record and publish the experiences of women.[10] In the previous sections I referred to theorising by women who do not come from the West, using the example of Arabic-speaking women. I continue to use the example of the Arabic-speaking world to look at women's autobiography. I look at Egypt in particular, which shows the range. Early on in the Egyptian women's movement, autobiography began to be written by women as well as men. The first such was Huda Sha'arawi who died in 1947, and whose memoirs were published posthumously in 1981 (Sha'arawi, 1986; Ahmed, 1988). A well-known later example is el Sa'adawi who wrote about serving time as a political prisoner (1986). Life histories have been collected. For instance, Atiya (1988) is a collection of stories from interviews with a number of Egyptian women from various backgrounds. Fiction concerning Egyptian women is readily available written by Egyptians of both sexes (e.g. el Sa'adawi, 1989; Mahfouz, 1990). These books also serve as an example of the interest now generated in women's experiences, by the very fact that I, a non Arabic-speaking English woman, with no special interest in Egypt, or in Arab culture, have access to all of them in English and in paperback.

While descriptions of experience are more plentiful and representative than theorising, serious difficulties remain in using them. The issues are ones of being able to understand descriptions of experience, which are originally told in another tongue, and then, even if a good translation is found, of being able to engage with them (a) at all critically, and (b) so as to have one's own preconceptions criticised and challenged.

4.1 The trouble with translation

I have been reading accounts by and of women in a number of different contexts. To do so I have needed a translation, because most women do not speak English. The translator, in the very act of translation, provides an interpretation. Sometimes even this is not enough. For instance, I found I experienced great difficulty in understanding the life histories of the three Swahili women as edited and translated by Mirza and Strobel (1989). I could not tell what kind of stories they were telling, the reasons they picked out one episode rather than another, and what kind of reaction they were expecting from their audience. What understanding I gained came from reading the commentary from the editors, and thus was so heavily influenced by them, that I felt I was reading an anthropological text rather than an autobiography.

Light is shed on this question by Shostak's discussion (1989) of her own process of writing about Nisa the !Kung woman. Shostak describes the various stages in the final text of Nisa's 'own words'. She begins the descriptions with the initial questions asked by 'that Marjorie Shostak, aged twenty-four, recently married, a product of the American 1960s [who] asked questions relevant to a specific stage in her life' (1989: 232).

She continues by discussing her final editing choices in the transcription of the interviews, which needed to be intelligible to Americans, with their much weaker oral culture, and their impatience with duplication and repetition. The result of her work was that the final account was rejected by one publisher on the grounds that Nisa 'sounded as if she could be "the woman next door" ' (1989: 238). At the time Shostak was elated: her younger self had hoped that she 'would learn from the !Kung what it was to be human' (ibid.). She took the publisher's criticism as evidence that Nisa's 'experiences must reflect something universal after all' (1989: 239). It is now clear to the older Shostak how much the politics of the younger Shostak informed her translation. It is also clear to her that escaping politics in the act of translation is impossible.

The degree to which even literary translation is a political matter is discussed by Spivak. She points out that a translator 'should be capable of distinguishing between ... resistant and conforming writing by women. ... She must be able to confront the idea that what seems resistant in the space of English may be reactionary in the space of the original language' (1992: 186). She says, with incredulity at the naïvety of the 'uninstructed good will',[11] 'And then to present these translations to our unprepared students so that they can learn about women writing!' (ibid.)

Spivak argues convincingly that the comprehension that comes from understanding the context is a 'surrender to the text'. Speaking deliberately in the language of eroticism she says: 'First, then the translator must surrender to the text. She must solicit the text to show the limits of its language' (1992: 181).

This shows the trouble with translation: I cannot have a straightforward translation of Swahili, !Kung or Bengali, because such a thing does not exist. Moreover, even if I understand the sentences at some simple level, that does not help with the import, because I cannot understand the context in which they speak without an interpretation from the anthropologist or other mediator. This requires me to know both the intentions of the translator or interpreter and also something of the context of the original.

It remains possible that a translation is, in fact, impossible. The meaning needs to be conveyed in other ways – for instance by telling stories designed to explain. Even this may not be enough. Joseph Brodsky, the Russian poet, who is fluent in English, has this to say: 'At least it's been my impression that any experience coming from the Russian realm, even when depicted with photographic precision, simply bounces off the English language, leaving no visible imprint on its surface' (1986: 30).

4.2 Engaging critically with others

Descriptions by other people cannot be taken at face value any more than can my own. However, Liz Heron introduces her book *Truth, Dare, Kiss or Promise: girls growing up in the fifties* as if raw experience is the real thing, items of raw data which can then be interpreted. She says: 'But if we are to acquire genuine insights into the versions of femininity we now inhabit, we also need to look at the specific features of our childhood' (1985: 2).

She goes on to draw conclusions from the similarities and differences in the accounts, seemingly taking them at face value. The 'data' include the values and material circumstances of parents, place, region, class and the post-war period. But if we look at this list we see how partial it is. First, ethnic identity was also addressed, but only by black writers. Less obviously, perhaps, all the authors had a similar implicit theory of autobiography. Different forms of autobiography will emphasise different things. Brodsky in the Soviet Union writes autobiography centred on politics, as do the writers of the testimonies of Latin America. Religion is central in nineteenth-century autobiographies written by ex-slaves in the USA.

Heron's contributors would have given quite a different account if they had had different perspectives, or a different idea of autobiography. As I explain in Chapter 2, this issue is addressed for one's own autobiography in the process of re-working. If it is *my* experience, I use it, but it always remains in question. I take the account as provisional and I invite others to do the same. Surely, therefore, it is appropriate to do the same to these autobiographical accounts by other people. However, such questioning is only possible for a reader who thoroughly understands the context. This is why I chose Heron's writing about England to criticise rather than, say, el Sa'adawi's writings about Egypt.

4.3 Learning from others

The question of understanding others across contexts, and in conditions of inequality, is raised by Spivak (1990: 59):

For me, the question 'Who should speak?' is less crucial than 'Who will listen?'. 'I will speak for myself as a Third World Person' is an important position for political mobilization today. But the real demand is that, when I speak from that position, I should be listened to seriously, not with that kind of benevolent imperialism, really, which simply says that because I happen to be an Indian or whatever. . . .'

Such 'serious listening' requires some kind of critical dialogue. It gets progressively more difficult to have a dialogue as social distance between the participants increases. As social distance increases, the likelihood increases that any criticism and interpretation could not be checked out with the original speakers. As it increases further it becomes more difficult to check out interpretation and understanding even with those who have enough in common with the original speaker to bring the necessary understanding to bear. Without such a dialogue a listener is liable to interpret words, gestures and actions through the lens of her own previous assumptions and value positions. The more that there is some dialogue, the more the likelihood of real change and disruption to original assumptions and perspectives.

In the case of listening to those who are at a geographical or linguistic as well as a social distance, it is extremely unlikely that any dialogue does takes place directly between the speaker and the learner. However dialogue is still possible because it can be mediated in a number of ways.

In the case of those from the West trying to understand those from other parts of the world, mediation is provided (1) by those from other parts of the world with knowledge of the West;[12] (2) by those from the West who have some special knowledge of some other part of the world, and who have made a serious effort to engage in dialogue; (3) by those personal contacts which individuals happen to make with each other. Similar sets of mediators exist for those from the dominant minority in a society trying to listen to their own less audible minorities.

In Britain it is relatively easy for white women to make contact with, say British black or Asian women, or with individuals visiting Britain from other parts of the world – and for black and Asian women to meet white women or each other. Thus personal contact is an important source of mediation. Each individual can learn from talking to those few 'other' women who she has dealings with – and whose time she is not wasting. That is, I am assuming an ethical encounter, in which the dealings are of some mutual benefit, and not just instigated for the benefit of the partner in a position of structural dominance. They can help her to take on some of their perspectives, informed as they are themselves by many conversations with others like themselves. This is not, to repeat, a case of asking for 'the black', or 'the African' or 'the white' perspective as if an individual could or should act as an informant for a social group. Rather, in talking to each other about mutual interests, they hear different perspectives from each other, which are partly a result of their being black, or African or white.

Such dialogues depend on mutual interests of some kind. I commented in Chapter 2 on how difficult I find it to understand Spivak. That I try to do so is because we share interests, interests which may be significant in Bengal, but are certainly so in feminist theory, in the West, at this time.

4.4 Cultural tourism

I referred to 'cultural tourism' at the start of the chapter. The word 'tourism' has connotations which summarise the issues that I want to address. Tourism is one of the most obvious instances of cross-cultural interaction. However tourism usually results in a very limited form of interaction. Tourists return to their own place in the world with a sense of the exotic – but their own lives are not significantly changed at all.[13] Typically, tourists are comparatively rich (though not always). The idea of cultural tourism draws on all this.

I recently saw an extraordinary example of cultural tourism: the film, *Aladdin*.[14] Most obviously, we notice the use the scriptwriters make of magic carpets, Arabic styles of architecture, and deserts, while making sure that anyone who *looks* Arab fits the negative American cultural stereotypes of Arabs as untrustworthy, faintly ridiculous, somewhat menacing, tradesmen and princes.[15] But we should also notice the structure of the film script. It re-works an old story from the Middle East, transforming it into a twentieth-century one from the United States in which the two heroes (three if you include the genie) 'just want to be free'. The two young people use this freedom to fall romantically in love, and also to get rich while retaining an aura of a democratic classlessness. What happened to the wonderful role model of Scheherazade as a challenge to woman as victim? At the level of structure, why did they have to make Aladdin a self-sufficient street urchin with a cute monkey, rather than the no-hoper living with his mother of the original? My own overriding impression of reading the *Arabian Nights* as an adult was of the unexpected moral structure of the stories. The heroes and villains were at the mercy of luck: there was no expectation that they would get their just desserts.

The intention in this book is to do better than this. A useful principle in such an attempt is what Meena Dhanda terms 'openness to persons'.[16] She draws a distinction between such openness and the liberal ideal of tolerance: 'of realizing "the relative validity of one's convictions" and yet, standing for them "unflinchingly" ' (1994: 254). She argues that openness to persons requires one person to acknowledge the other, not by 'appreciating the other's point of view' which is often impossible in cases of real disagreement, but, rather, by appreciating that the other is a different person, that is:

one grant there may be a point of view other than one's own. It is not necessary to grant that the other has a point of view, but only that the other may (or may not) have another point of view which I cannot decide in advance.

(ibid.)

The difference between this and the liberal ideal is:

that there is both a greater and lesser confidence than is necessary to make the claim of 'relative validity' and 'unflinching' commitment. In my view, on the one hand, one is completely convinced of the soundness of one's convictions, which is a sign of greater confidence. On the other hand, one is totally prepared to re-evaluate one's convictions, so that one cannot be so resolute as to be unyielding in situations of conflict.

(ibid.)

5 CONCLUSIONS ABOUT LEARNING FROM OTHERS

The purpose of the discussion so far has been to answer the question, Who it is possible for me to listen to? The answer given in the course of this chapter is that listening to others is possible only if the attempt is made to be open to particular others. This means making the effort to understand the context in which they speak. It takes time and trouble. It needs to be undertaken in the knowledge that understanding will be imperfect. It also needs to be taken in the knowledge that the listener may find herself changed by the encounter. This emphasis on time and trouble and on the possibility of change distinguishes 'tourism' and tokenism from genuine openness to persons.

The second question still remains, about which few others do I choose from the very large number I could listen to, since it is plainly impossible to undertake such a serious project with every human being. That is, who *should* I listen to?

In my view there is no easy or comfortable answer here. There is no recipe to follow step by step. On the one hand, a creation of a theory which is not blind to difference requires me to be able to hear those who speak from the margins. As Spivak (1988) says, 'Let the subaltern speak.' On the other hand, the more marginal someone is, if they are on a different part of the margin from oneself, the harder it is to listen to them, and to engage with them. This is a continuing tension. It is impossible to engage with, or even to hear, everyone; but it is possible to listen to some and to engage with a few of those on a different place on the margin.

This is not a comfortable answer, but it can be used to formulate some principles of procedure. Following them is a matter for judgement rather the following of an exact recipe.[17] They are as follows:

Try to hear those who are trying to talk to you from different positions

Expect to learn from those different from you, but don't require them to talk to you. On the other hand, make the effort to engage with them in projects of use to both of you.

Don't try and listen to everyone. This will lead to tourism.

Keep checking to see if you have lapsed into narrowness on the one hand or tourism on the other.

Get on with it.

It follows that the feminist project of listening to each other is a group endeavour, which presupposes overlapping networks of open-minded people. If I engage with some people and you engage with a somewhat different set of people and we talk to each other, then we are able to continually revise and work on narrowness of perspective. We therefore have a kind of network of engagement – something that reminds me of a computer that no one person can now programme. It is a group endeavour.[18] It is important to note that this is not an endeavour to build some edifice which will produce a new Archimedean point or God's eye view. *All* the perspectives are continually changing.

This is an epistemology which will always be tentative and revisable. All knowledge must be provisional – radically so – since it cannot take note of everything all at once. This does not mean that realism is not true though. Thus, this is an epistemology which depends on change and revision. There is no chance at all of 'stability' or a 'God's eye truth'. I will return to this epistemological question in the next chapter.

Inevitably, since I have tried to follow my own principles, I have an idiosyncratic set of sources on which I have drawn. I will refer to them during the rest of the book, but I cannot assume my readers are familiar with them all. Rather than rely on lengthy footnotes, I say something about them here, just enough, I hope, to make the allusions to them in the rest of the book comprehensible.

6 LIFE STORIES

Yasmin Alibhai

Yasmin Alibhai is a journalist and a British Moslem woman who is 'almost feminist, almost agnostic, Eng. Lit., Oxbridge, socialist' (Alibhai, 1989: 47). An article of hers, 'A member no more', written in 1989, at the height of the Rushdie affair, is addressed to 'white liberal lefties'. It explains her reactions to the controversy in the context of her personal life – her 'traditional Asian husband' had just left her. She describes her angry reactions to the stereotyping of British Moslems and to being told that Asian views on marriage had to give way to the 'reasonable' idea that marriages can be broken at will. She describes the effect on all British Asian lives of ubiquitous racial violence, and the lack of protest about it from white liberals. She reassesses her 'oriental identity', her sense of the sacred, and of where her cultural, social and political future lies.

Annie Allsebrook and Anthony Swift

Allsebrook and Swift are English journalists who interviewed street children from around the world in the late 1980s. Their book, *Broken Promise* (1989), is unusual in that the children are allowed to speak for themselves, rather than always being spoken for by adults, however well-meaning.

Nayra Atiya

Nayra Atiya was born in Cairo in 1943. She moved to the USA eleven years later. After teaching at various universities there, she returned to Cairo in her early thirties and this is where she now lives. She was thus both 'insider and outsider' to Cairo society. Over a period of three years she recorded the life stories of five Egyptian women, only two of whom could write and published the accounts in *Khul Khaal* (1988). They earn money as the wife of a garage keeper (helping him with the tasks of running the garage), a charity worker, a housekeeper, a cleaner and a fisherwoman. They speak of their own lives. Their stories range from finding clean water to dealing with marriage, from memories of circumcision to observations on gender differences. They explain what is important to them, describe details of particular episodes and reflect on how to deal with life's problems.

Joseph Brodsky

In his autobiographical essay 'Less than one', Joseph Brodsky (1986) describes growing up in communist Leningrad, where he was born in 1940. He describes his first lie, when at the age of 7 he was asked if he was a Jew, and said that he did not know. He goes on to explain the inevitability of further lies, and the way they bred in him 'an overpowering sense of ambivalence' as he preferred factory life to education within the system; and prison and the KGB to military service. He describes himself as a bookish boy, rejecting the conditions which would give him books, in order to preserve his ability to enjoy them.

Robert Wellesley Cole

In his book *Kossoh Town Boy* Robert Cole (1960) recalls his early, happy years growing up in a well-to-do African, Krio family in colonial Free-town, Sierra Leone, in the early decades of the twentieth century. He set out to write a book which will express the 'cocoon of childhood innocence that basked in that tropical sun'. He lyrically describes the small events of that life, from infancy to secondary school. It is an evocation of childhood, intended for a dual audience: West African and European. The reader is not expected to know about West Africa's peoples, customs, religions, food, or history.

Frantz Fanon

Frantz Fanon's famous book *Black Skin, White Masks* is a work of scholar-ship incorporating psychoanalysis and philosophy. It is written autobio-graphically with anger and bitterness. In his chapter 'The Fact of Blackness', he dramatises the difference between his being black in his home country, Martinique, and being black in France where he emigrated in the middle of this century. He describes the effect of the name-calling he experiences: 'My body was given back to me, sprawled out, distorted, recolored, clad in mourning in that white winter day' (1986: 113). Angry, shamed, nauseous, self-contemptuous, always dangerously highly visible as 'the Negro doctor', rejected and unacknowledged, he resolves to assert himself as a BLACK MAN.

Paul Gilroy

Paul Gilroy's book *The Black Atlantic* (1993) includes his own retelling of the stories of two former slaves, Frederick Douglass and Margaret Garner, and of two black intellectuals, W. E. B. Du Bois and Richard Wright. Both Douglass and Garner began their lives as slaves. Douglass was leased by his owner to another man, Covey, who was to 'break him'. Finally Douglass was pushed beyond endurance and, risking his own death, threatened to kill Covey. This episode was, Douglass affirms, the turning point in his career. Margaret Garner fled from slavery with her four children, her husband, and her parents in law. Trapped and besieged by slave catchers she killed her 3-year-old daughter and tried to kill the other children rather than let them be taken back into slavery. The case became a testing ground for the Fugitive Slave Act in the USA.

W. E. B. Du Bois was born in a small black community in New England during the last century. Moving to university at Nashville, he had to learn how to be a member of a closed racial group with particular rites, loyalties, history, art, philosophy and, most significantly, traditions of music. Although he was criticised by some commentators as being inauthentic, and insufficiently black in his background, Du Bois says he enthusiastically 'replaced my Americanism: hence-forward I was a Negro' (Gilroy, 1993: 116) At the same time, he embraced the culture of Western Europe, of Shakespeare, Balzac, Dumas, Aristotle and Aurelius, against the strand of American black thought which rejected them. At the end of his life he took up residence in Ghana, renouncing American citizenship. There are similar tensions in Richard Wright's life. He was born in Mississippi, in 1908, and moved North, where he developed his career as a writer in clubs set up by the Communist Party. He later moved to Europe and was criticised for losing his vital folk sources. He himself remained deeply ambivalent about folk culture, admiring its creative response to adversity while observing in it the effects of racism.

Satu Hassi

Satu Hassi is from Finland. She used to be an engineer, and is now a poet and a freelance writer. She is also a mother. In an article called 'On Loneliness' written for a European conference on the theme 'Women Challenge Technology' she explains why she left engineering. She describes how she had continually to account for her decisions, first to become a woman engineer, and then to stop being one. She was always the highly visible, odd-one-out on business trips, at presentations, at meetings. She was often taken for the assistant. Her colleagues had none of her own preoccupations with child-care, because their wives 'did all that'. On the other hand neither did she share preoccupations with her only female co-workers – secretaries and clerical assistants.

bell hooks

Bell hooks was born in Kentucky in a black working-class neighbourhood. She is now a world-famous professor at Yale University in the USA. Her books of essays, *Talking Back* and *Yearning*, describe some of the difficulties and the contradictions of achieving her current position, and maintaining it with integrity.

Erica Jong

Erica Jong is a white American woman, most famous for her novel *Fear of Flying*. She is also a poet.

Woman Enough

Because my grandmother's hours
were apple cakes baking,
dust motes gathering,
linens yellowing

& seams and hems
inevitably unravelling –
I almost never keep house –
though really I *like* houses
& wish I had a clean one.

Because my mother's minutes
were sucked into the roar
of the vacuum cleaner,
because she waltzed with the washer-dryer
& tore her hair waiting for repairmen –
I send out my laundry,
& live in a dusty house,
though really I *like* clean houses
as well as anyone.

I am woman enough
to love the kneading of bread
as much as the feel of typewriter keys
under my fingers –
springy, springy.
& the smell of clean laundry
& simmering soup
are almost as dear to me
as the smell of paper and ink.
I wish there were not a choice;
I wish I could be two women.
I wish the days could be longer
But they are short.
So I write while
the dust piles up.

I sit at my typewriter
remembering my grandmother
& all my mothers,
& the minutes they lost
loving houses better than themselves –
& the man I love cleans up the kitchen
grumbling only a little
because he knows
that after all these centuries
it is easier for him
than for me.

(The Raving Beauties, 1983: 119–20)

Jamaica Kincaid

Kincaid's books, *Annie John* and *At the Bottom of the River*, like her other books, are fiction. However they give an insight into a girlhood in contemporary Antigua, the Caribbean island where she was born and grew up. A central theme of the books is the relationship between the mother and daughter, which demonstrates a combination of tenderness, anxiety and repression, familiar to many mothers and daughters, but articulated in terms of Antiguan life.

Marialice

Daphne Patai transcribed the life story of Marialice, one of sixty Brazilian women who told her their stories between 1981 and 1983. At the time of the tape recording, Marialice was 30 years old and a cleaner in a government office, married and childless. Patai comments in her article 'Constructing a life story' that Marialice would not necessarily 'stick to the point' of any question, but, using the conventions of oral narration, rather than those of prose, often used it to speak of what most concerned her. Thus a question about inter-racial marriage led to a reply about her feelings for her mother, and a question about religion led to a reply concerning a phantom pregnancy.

Ved Mehta

Ved Mehta has recounted his life story in a series of books. He was born into a well-to-do Indian family, the son of a doctor. He suffered a meningitis attack when very small, which left him blind. His books describe the family, their life together, his time in a boarding school for the blind in India, and his determination to complete his education in a school for the blind in Arkansas, where he was the only foreign student.

Sally Morgan

Sally Morgan was born in Perth in 1950. She is an Australian who only discovered her Aboriginal origins in late childhood and early adulthood. The effect of the discovery, its confirmation and the family acknowledgement of their own history is described in her autobiographies. The most famous of these is *My Place* (1987).

Grace Nichols

Grace Nichols is a poet who was born in 1950 in Georgetown, Guyana where she grew up and worked. She has lived and worked in Britain since 1977.

In Spite of Me

In spite of me
the women in me
slip free
of the charmed circle
of my moulding

Look at Graceful, eh!
long skirts, legs crossed
all smiles
articulating ethnic attentiveness
'Graceful is as graceful is,'
I mock, but Graceful
just goes on being graceful

And Indiscreet
who can stop Indiscreet
from acting indiscreet
wearing her womb on her sleeve
telling the details of her sullied
secrets. Her moves, her searches
her tiresome cosmic wetness

Obsessional at least
has the good sense
to stay put at home
head tied, cloth soaked in lemon juice,
to keep her thoughts at bay
Obsessional, Obsessional, please . . .

Dissatisfied
is really too dissatisfied.
Since she can't change
the course of the rains
or make it possible for people
to feed their children,
she won't do anything. Not even
crawl out of her dressing gown

Focused, dear, dear Focused
is at the typewriter inside –
busy, remote, impatient –
(especially with telephone interruptions)
Focused wants to be left alone
to delve into life
to come up with life

to serve up life
raw, stewed down or evoked

Reassuring, of course,
will do everything
cooking, cleaning,
urging everyone to vitamins
and a balance of meals

Complexity goes off to be
Aaaaaahhh in spite of me
the women in me ...

                    slip free.

                                (Nichols, 1989: 7–8)

i is a long memoried woman is a sequence of poems which includes these
two:

Holding my Beads

Unforgiving as the course of justice
Inerasable as my scars and fate
I am here
a woman ... with all my lives
strung out like beads

                    before me

It isn't privilege or pity
that I seek
It isn't reverence or safety
quick happiness or purity

                  but

the power to be what I am/a woman
charting my own futures/a woman
holding my beads in my hand

Epilogue

I have crossed an ocean
I have lost my tongue
from the roots of the old one
a new one has sprung

                             (Nichols, 1984: 63–4)

Marge Piercy

Marge Piercy is a white American novelist, probably most famous for her
Utopian novel, *Woman on the Edge of Time* (1979). She is also a poet.

In the Men's Rooms

When I was young I believed in intellectual conversation:
I thought the patterns we wove on stale smoke
floated off to the heaven of ideas.
To be certified worthy of high masculine discourse
like a potato on a grater I would rub on contempt,
suck snubs, wade proudly through the brown stuff on the floor.
They were talking of integrity and existential ennui
while the women ran out for six-packs and had abortions
in the kitchen and fed the children and were auctioned off.

Eventually of course I learned how their eyes perceived me
when I bore to them cupped in my hands a new poem to nibble,
when I brought my aerial maps of Sartre or Marx,
they said, she is trying to attract our attention,
she is offering up her breasts and thighs.
I walked on eggs, their tremulous equal:
they saw a fish peddlar hawking in the street.

Now I get coarse when the abstract nouns start flashing.
I go out to the kitchen to talk cabbages and habits.
I try hard to remember to watch what people do.
Yes keep your eyes on the hands, let the voice go buzzing.
Economy is the bone, politics is the flesh,
watch who they beat and who they eat,
watch who they relieve themselves on, watch who they own.
The rest is decoration.

(from The Raving Beauties, 1983: 83)

Mary Seacole

Mary Seacole was born in Jamaica in 1805. She was of mixed race, having a Scottish father and a black mother (who was a free woman at a time when slavery still continued in Jamaica). Seacole led an adventurous life, travelling to Central America, Europe and the Crimea, making use of her extraordinary medical talents – usually subsidising this work by using her business acumen to open hotels. She became famous for her medical expertise at the front in the Crimean war and for the British hotel she opened there, where she made a living serving the army with supplies and meals. She had previously tried to join Florence Nightingale's project, but she was rejected. Her autobiography, *Wonderful Adventures in Many Lands*, was first published in 1857.

Anne Seller

Anne Seller is an English philosopher. She publishes philosophy which draws on autobiography, including an article written with me. Some of the work in this book was inspired by conversations I have had with her, and so, not surprisingly, her autobiographical writing (which includes 'Greenham' and 'Should the feminist philosopher stay at home?') is also influential on my thinking.

Liz Stanley

Liz Stanley is an English sociologist. In her article 'The knowing because experiencing subject', she describes her reactions to caring for her mother who suffered a severe stroke and was confined to hospital for eighteen months before finally dying. She reflects on her changing relationship to her mother. When her mother finally dies, Stanley thinks first that they are both now free, but a month later, she notices that 'The thing I miss most is the responsibility, the way my life and thoughts were organized around Mum' (1994: 146).

Carolyn Steedman

Carolyn Steedman is English. Her book *Landscape for a Good Woman* (1986) weaves autobiography and biography to give an account of the lives of her mother and herself. Her purpose is critical as well as expressive. She is exploring how to find a place for these stories in history, politics, psychoanalysis and feminism.

Valerie Walkerdine

In her book *Schoolgirl Fictions* (1990), Walkerdine analyses her own struggle with the images of her early childhood in Derby in the 1950s, and the making of her identities as schoolgirl, teacher and academic. The book is a collection of essays, written over a period of years, in which she has analysed mathematics learning in children (the mastery of reason) as well as re-thinking her own early essays in the light of later insights.

Patricia Williams

Patricia Williams is American. In her book *The Alchemy of Race and Rights* (1993) she writes of the contradictions of working and teaching as a black lawyer in New York. She draws on memories of her childhood, and analyses the autobiographical stories that lie behind her own academic work. The book is unusual because she sets out to transgress mainstream conventions of writing by using a mixture of styles which combine informal, personal observations with critical theorising.

4 Theory and experience
Epistemology, methodology and autobiography*

1 INTRODUCTION

One of the aims of this book is to use the subjective experience of women to question the abstractions assumed by mainstream philosophy of mind, by which I mean as found in philosophy developed by white middle-class males from the West. To use 'personal experience' – or 'subject position' – to question philosophy is to do something which in itself questions the knowledge base which underlies the (various) mainstream understandings of self-identity. It draws into question philosophy's own understanding of itself as universal: unbounded by political considerations such as gender, which enter 'personal experience' and which contribute to 'subject position'. In Chapters 2 and 3, I began a discussion of the use of personal experience to improve knowledge, but I left various threads hanging.

In this chapter I pick up these threads, though some of them are more fully followed up in Part II of the book. I address the underlying epistemological questions related to using auto/biographical writing and, in particular, the assumptions that language creates us but is also created by us and that descriptions of experience are always revisable. I also explain further the idea that the epistemology with which I am working is one which depends on change and revision so that there is no chance of finding a stable version of 'the truth', sometimes called a 'God's eye view'.

The argument of this chapter is complex. It picks a path through the numerous suggestions and theories about epistemology and subjectivity presently to be found in feminist thought and practice. At the same time as acknowledging the differences within the suggestions and theories, I argue that there is a sense in which all the epistemological critiques of mainstream theory share commonalities, precisely because they are *feminist* critiques. I develop the argument by showing how these commonalities can act as precepts which any adequate epistemology must respect. I then

* In this chapter I draw on the following autobiographies from the annotated bibliography in Chapter 3: Robert Cole, Mary Seacole, Carolyn Steedman, Patricia Williams.

use these precepts to suggest how methodological principles can be derived from them, if a particular argument about language and the fragmentation of communities is accepted. I then go on to show how autobiographical stories can fit these principles, if a particular view of autobiography is taken. I call such autobiography 'critical autobiography', and give some examples of it.

This is the final chapter in Part I. The chapters that make up this part of the book provide a springboard for Part II, in which I construct a theory of self-identity using autobiography and other life-narratives as well as using more conventional theories.

2 FEMINIST EPISTEMOLOGIES: POLITICS AND SUBJECTIVITY

2.1 Challenges to traditional epistemologies

Feminism has been the source of challenges to traditional conceptions of epistemology. It has been this, in part, by refusing to assume away personal experience (or subject position) and politics. The relevance (and meaning) of these terms remain in question in feminist philosophy, but they are not assumed away but rather argued about. By 'conceptions of traditional epistemology', I refer to the tradition which springs from Descartes, Locke, Hume and Kant (presently to be found in Popper, Quine and Davidson) and their fascination with the possibility of certainty and objectivity. It is an epistemology founded on the quest for certainty and sure foundations.

It is important to note at this point that feminism is not the only source of challenges to traditional epistemology. While various feminist critics were formulating their challenges, traditional epistemology was being brought into question from other directions. Challenges to the tradition are part of a general philosophical move away from the hope of Newtonian or Cartesian certainty and away from a reliance on an objectivity, derived from direct sense experience or reason, which will produce universal truths.

Different challengers to traditional epistemology are often lumped together as if they formed a coherent position, which they do not, any more than traditionalists do. However, commonalities can be found in the viewpoints maintained by the traditionalists and, similarly, commonalities exist among their challengers. The upholders of the traditions argue that the subjective, in the sense of personal, anecdotal and individual, has been thought to detract from the certainty, reliability and usefulness of knowledge. It is of use only in so far as it can be used to generate universals. The adherents of the opposing argument take the view that Western traditions have failed to generate reliable (or useful or ethical) knowledge, just because they do not pay proper attention to the subjective. The dichotomisation between traditionalists and their challengers is only useful as a guide to an area which needs closer attention if it is to be understood.

Closer attention reveals that the Western traditions of epistemology have been challenged from several directions which, unfortunately for those wanting neat categories, overlap with each other. Challenges can be found within the familiar and mainstream reaches of philosophy, such as phenomenology and its heirs, or Alistair MacIntyre's explorations of rationality and justice. The most radical set of challenges comes from postmodernisms, post-structuralisms, and feminist epistemologies which have arisen outside mainstream philosophy.[1]

Different feminisms have made their challenges, in part, by refusing to assume away politics. They have drawn attention to the deep and irreducible connections between knowledge and power. The feminist challenges arise from a perspective which is directly concerned with politics: a perspective focusing on the oppression of women. The politics of taking a feminist perspective seemed straightforward enough in the early days of the new wave of feminism: sisterhood was powerful. Studies focusing on women and girls proliferated. However, the position has rapidly become increasingly complicated. Class, race, nationality and sexuality have combined to make feminist politics increasingly complex and ambiguous. The very possibility of taking any (let alone any *one*) feminist perspective has been brought into question.

It was during the historical period when the new feminisms were formulating their challenges to 'male' knowledge that traditional epistemology was being brought into question from postmodernism and post-structuralism. Such challenges have gained increasing weight and influence in recent decades. These debates have been dominated by European theorists, such as Lyotard, Foucault, Derrida and Lacan. They found their way into English language social theory relatively early and have finally begun to influence the mainstream of English language philosophy (Rorty, 1979; Rajchman and West, 1985; Monk, 1992). Postmodernists and post-structuralists have many disagreements amongst themselves, but they unite in challenging the supposed neutrality of traditional epistemology by arguing that the fundamental categories of 'truth' and 'knowledge' are not only irreducibly complex and ambiguous but are also saturated with politics.

Thus, over the last four decades, challenges to traditional epistemology have been articulated particularly strongly within feminism and within postmodernism and post-structuralism. Indeed, in sharing a common time-span, they have also come to see that they share some common ground. Consequently, there has been an uneasy relationship between the two. The relationship has been uneasy partly because it is unclear how common the ground really is, and partly because the relationship is not a partnership of equals. This uneasy relationship shows very clearly that while feminisms offer challenges to particular traditional epistemologies, and may also challenge others, it is not possible to identify a single 'masculine' epistemology, against which feminine or feminist epistemology could define itself.[2] Equally, it is not possible to identify a single 'feminine' or 'feminist' epistemology by which to judge any others.

2.2 Western feminist epistemologies: disagreements and commonalities

A number of very different, and disagreeing, feminist epistemologies were developed during the 1980s and early 1990s. At the start of the 1980s the idea of a feminist epistemology was still a startling one. Feminist epistemological challenges began by being focused on the masculine bias inherent in 'knowledge as usual', as I pointed out in the last chapter. Critiques were made in several areas of knowledge, notably literature, history, philosophy, natural science and the social sciences. As these critiques deepened and widened, it became clear that the idea of 'bias' itself, and the notion of objectivity on which it was based were in question. The result was a ever-increasing focus on epistemology itself.

Alternatives to the traditional epistemologies were developed. Development was not along a single path. Feminists provided a range of possible epistemologies. It soon became apparent that there is no such thing as a definitive 'feminist epistemology'. For instance, Irigaray provides a critique of the masculine imaginary which generates a rationality which is characterised by the principle of identity, the principle of non-contradiction, and binarism (Whitford, 1988, 1991). She suggests that women's imaginary might be fluid rather than solid, taking touch rather than sight as its dominant organising metaphor (Young, 1990: 84, 193). Lorraine Code, from a position sharply critical of Irigaray's theorisation of sexual difference, argues for epistemic responsibility: knowledge gained by 'receptiveness and humility' and sensitivity to the particular and concrete case (Braidotti, 1991: 190; Code, 1984, 1988). Seller argues from a position very different from Irigaray's with her emphasis on the masculine and feminine. Rather, Seller argues for a democratic epistemology: knowledge based in communities of resistance, in which attention must be paid to every individual's subjective experience (Seller, 1988).

Other examples of feminist epistemologies are provided by Donna Haraway and Sandra Harding who disagree over postmodernism. Haraway, as a postmodernist, embraces particularity and difference. She combines postmodernist and socialist feminist perspectives to argue for 'situated knowledges' in which 'the only way to find a larger vision is to be somewhere in particular' (Braidotti, 1991: 272). Harding, arguing against postmodern fragmentation, proposes a standpoint epistemology in which it is argued that the subjectivity of a researcher, in terms of gender, race and class, is crucial in her research design, and must be taken into account when dividing beliefs 'into the false and probably less false' so that it is understood that there are no 'transcendental, certain grounds for belief of the sort claimed by conventional epistemologies' (Harding, 1991: 8, 169).

It would be possible to continue with this catalogue of different epistemologies. For instance, there is epistemology founded on female embodiment and epistemology deeply influenced by post-structuralism. Overviews of some of these debates can be found in a number of recent books and anthologies.[3]

The depth of disagreement between different feminist epistemologies is striking. Given the range, together with the bitterness and the depth of some of the disagreements, it might be thought that there is nothing common to all the suggestions. Indeed it is usual to note the disagreements and unusual to point out that a common thread runs through this diverse range of feminist challenges to traditional epistemology. After all, the differences are significant practically and politically as well as theoretically. However, there are common threads which can be picked out and it is these commonalities that concern me here.

The metaphor of a 'thread' is intended, partly, to indicate that the agreement is no more than threadlike: the differences are indeed significant. A few threads are not enough to weave a cloth. The commonalities are no basis for a fully worked-out epistemology. They may be enough to be of use in critiques of other epistemologies. Further, they may be enough to develop some methodological principles by which to improve our knowledge, even while it is acknowledged that the knowledge is not fully grounded in an adequate epistemology. No doubt the present relative chaos of numerous epistemologies all claiming to be *the* feminist epistemology will resolve itself, in which case it will be possible to do more. Or possibly, we will resign ourselves to doing less.

I discern three common threads which I will pick out. In the first place, commonality arises because all these epistemologies spring from a concern with the subjective consciousness or the self of an individual. Lennon and Whitford commenting on the recent history of feminist epistemology, say:

> In different ways all of these strands of thought implicate the subject in the production of knowledge. It is argued that it is not simply due to bad practice that masculine subjects have allowed their subjectivity to imprint on their product. Such imprinting is inevitable. Knowledge bears the marks of its producer.
>
> (1994: 2)

None of the feminist epistemologies assumes or argues that the perspective of individual human beings can be superseded by the 'objective' 'view from nowhere' or by a 'God's eye view'. All of them assume that the self, or a particular subjective position, is a starting point – though almost all of them go on, quickly, to point out that individual 'experience', 'perspectives', 'subjectivity' or 'position in a discourse' are only the first step in a collective enterprise of formulating a (feminist, usually) perspective. Thus Irigaray argues for the necessity of fostering a female community in which to discover a feminine subjectivity, different from the one created by males. Code emphasises the importance of self-knowledge, of knowing oneself, but equally she emphasises the necessity of there being an epistemic community of knowers who both come to know women's experiences and participate in a wider dialogue with others. Seller's work explicitly starts with particular individuals in particular situations. Both Haraway's and Harding's epistemologies depend on taking individual perspectives and combining them, politically, into group perspectives.

The difficulties in seeing this common thread are increased by the different language habitually used by different traditions of philosophical thought. For instance, I use both the terms 'self' and 'subjectivity' in order to indicate that I am not intending to choose between them for the purposes of this argument. The terms are each used to mark the different traditions (Anglo-Saxon and Continental European, respectively) which gave rise to them. Even allowing for the extremely significant differences between them, they agree in one important respect: each indicates the particular perspective of an individual.

There is no neutral, non-theoretically loaded, way of describing the particular perspective of an individual. In the case of the Anglo-Saxon tradition, it is more likely to be labelled 'experience'. As I said in Chapter 2 the word 'experience' itself sounds alarm bells for some feminists. Grant (1993) and Lazreg (1994) provide reasons for these alarm bells in their discussions of the use of 'experience' in feminist epistemology and politics. They point out that, too often, subjectivity has precluded engagement with difference and introduced unhelpful individualism or universal sisterhood into theorising. Those of the Continental tradition rarely speak of 'experience'. They are more likely to use the term 'subjectivity', or 'positionality' to indicate the opacity of subjectivity and how provisional it is. This difference originally marked a conceptual difference between the transparent rational self on the one hand and the deconstruction of it on the other. This sharp difference no longer pertains. The assumption I made in Chapter 2 that experience is not transparent or transparently describable is no longer startling to many of those coming from the Anglo-Saxon tradition, while the concept of self has reappeared in post-structuralist writing.

A second connecting thread can be found. It arises because the epistemologies are all *feminist* epistemologies. In their different ways each one has been developed in response to the devaluation, silencing and oppression of girls and women which other epistemologies underpin. Thus, from the start, all these epistemologies have a moral/political stance. To be sure they disagree about the details of values and power, but both 'values' and 'power' are there as organising concepts. For all these feminist epistemologies, politics and values must precede epistemology, because the analysis begins at that point. Facts are not value-free. On the contrary, the argument is that human knowledge is saturated with values, whether or not they are acknowledged. In short, all the various feminist epistemologies unite in turning traditional epistemology (though not all masculine epistemology) inside out. The question about whether values can be derived from facts is seen to be badly formulated. Facts come trailing their constituent values, and cannot be separated from them.

There is a third thread which is the significance of theory and theorising. Even though some feminists have been bitterly opposed to any engagement with male-produced theories and methods of theorising, feminist *theory* must, logically, be predicated on the importance of theorising. If theorising in general is a useless or dangerous activity, then feminist theory itself would be useless or dangerous. Those making feminist theories cannot, in good faith, hold such a view.

'Theory', here, need mean no more than systematic and public reflection on ways of doing things and the assumptions that underlie them. Such reflection can be more or less formalised. However, 'theory and theorising' may also refer to full-blown Theory, the abstractions of academia of the very kind that some feminists have been opposed to. In any of these guises, theory is an attempt to draw together the perspectives of individuals into a better understanding. Differences of viewpoint are taken as a starting point for wider agreement – or for a better informed, deeper level of disagreement. In the last chapter I argued that a powerful source of those critiques – the points of view of others – would provide a never-ending challenge to any one established structure of knowledge. Thus I claim that there is a fourth element which can be added to the commonalities in feminist epistemologies. This element is the claim that there is no possibility of the acquisition or creation of stable, unchanging knowledge. Instead, there is continuing spiralling. A structure of knowledge is subject to criticisms which generate principles, abstractions and new structures of knowledge, which, in their turn, give way before new criticisms to become new principles, abstractions and structures of knowledge, in a never-ending process.

To summarise this section: I have argued that there are four precepts for a critique of any epistemology, which arise from the commonalities in feminist epistemologies, and from my own analysis of dialogue with others. These precepts are as follows: (1) knowledge must be grounded in individual 'experience', 'perspectives', 'subjectivity', or 'position in a discourse'; (2) the factors of power and values cannot be added on afterwards, but are fundamental; (3) theorising is indispensable; and (4) there is no possibility of the acquisition or creation of stable, unchanging knowledge, since all knowledge must be subject to critique from other viewpoints which may fundamentally revise current structures.

I now turn to the question of how to turn these critical precepts into something usable in the construction of knowledge about self-identity.

3 FROM EPISTEMOLOGICAL PRECEPT TO METHODOLOGICAL PRINCIPLE

In this section I make a proposal about moving from the epistemological challenge expressed in the precepts established above, to the establishing of methodological principles which can be derived from them. That is, in Gunew's terms I begin the move from 'critique to construct'. She identifies a paradox of attempting such a movement:

> Feminism as construct is an attempt to move feminist knowledge beyond the stage of being an oppositional critique of existing male-defined knowing, knowledge and theory. The central paradox in this area is the question of where feminist knowledge should situate itself, from where does it derive an authority or legitimacy which is not constructed by the prevailing structures of knowledge?
>
> (1990: 25)

Male-defined structures of knowledge are not just to be found in formal Theory. Even more seriously, they are likely to be found in language itself, which, of course, includes the language of theorising, in so far as this language has been dominated or monopolised by men. To put this another way, a difficulty for formulating a feminist perspective is that theory is inevitably based on experience which is mediated by language – which may already be masculine: the experience can only be formed into a feminist perspective using theory (the prevailing structures of knowledge) – which may also already be masculine. This is a theme that I return to throughout the book.[4] In this chapter I take up this theme by showing how a clearer understanding of language makes it possible to turn the precepts into methodological principles.

In Chapters 2 and 3, I pointed out that there was no sharp distinction to be drawn between those who 'spoke the same language' and those who did not. Individuals are not entirely of one group or another. On the contrary, individuals are fragments of an uncertain number of groups. Thus the distinction between 'feminist knowledge' and 'male-defined knowing, knowledge and theory' drawn by Gunew is seen to be an oversimplification. The critique of currently dominant 'knowing, knowledge and theory' is, to be sure, likely to be a critique of something largely defined by males, but is also likely to be a critique of something that is defined by people who are Western, white and middle class. On the other hand, neither the dominant nor the critical positions are independent, free-standing monoliths. All of us share some viewpoints and disagree on others, and this is so whether we are men or women, black or white, rich or poor.

This is an optimistic observation. It means that it is possible for us to proceed without throwing out everything that has preceded us – and without having to dream up a new knowledge untainted by any oppression. Rather than wholesale destruction followed by having to build from scratch, we are taking part in a process of renewal and re-construction. Whereas dreaming the impossible dream is often a politically useful activity, it is not enough on its own. Rather than only looking for a utopia, feminist philosophy can also proceed by what Spivak has described as negotiation – a practical politics which will bring the present system to crisis, without immediately declaring a total revolution:

> Given our historical position we have to learn to negotiate with structures of violence, rather than taking the impossible elitist position of turning our backs on everything.
> The practical politics of the open end is not like some kind of massive ideological act (the surgical operation) which brings about a drastic change, but I have always emphasised that there have to be both these kinds of things, each bringing the other to crisis.
>
> (Spivak, 1990: 101)

Chapter 2 and Chapter 3 each began with problems related to learning from individuals, taking the politics of discourse into consideration, in order to improve knowledge. Chapter 2 focused on the difficulty of 'I' and 'we': what various kinds of 'we' that 'I' was a fragment of. Chapter 3 focused on the analogous problem of the possibilities of learning from other persons, without labelling them as some particular 'we'. The working principles that I devised depended on notions of language being shared with the audience, more or less exactly. They further depended on the possibility of critical engagement with the speakers, in the teeth of difficulties caused by imperfect translation and lack of knowledge of the context.

Central to the discussion were issues of how language enters into the experience and subjectivity of an individual and, therefore, how each individual has access to a number of overlapping languages. I now look in more detail at these issues. In particular I look in more detail at how far from monolithic is the experience and subjectivity, and therefore the language, of each individual. This discussion will underpin conclusions about the way it is possible to turn the critical precepts into practical methodological principles for the development of knowledge.

The experience and subjectivity of an individual may be influenced by the particular body she is born with. Each human being is born with a body that can be identified (mistakenly sometimes) as male or female, or as being one of a particular race or family (even though neither 'race' nor 'family' means anything very definite). It is possible that the child's developing sexuality, its personality, or its artistic or mathematical abilities are inherited rather than socially constructed. Such suggestions are very often the subject of bitter controversy, as they are thought to be politically loaded. For instance, fears are often expressed that any version of essentialism plays into the hands of sexist and racist elements in a society.[5] Such considerations are irrelevant to showing the fundamental importance of language in framing experience and subjectivity. *Whether or not* there are such 'natural' or 'essential' differences, bodily differences are socially articulated. Social articulations are made through the medium of language (among other media).

In the first place, the psychosocial development of a child depends on the interpretation placed on its body. This is particularly the case with sexual difference. The metaphorical, social or psycholinguistic milieu in which children develop means that bodily sex differences are symbolised into psychosocial ones. There is a considerable feminist literature drawn from psychoanalysis which discusses how it is that a baby develops into a sexed adult with a particular gender.[6]

Over and above psychoanalytic differentiation, there are differences in the social experiences of groups of people, often differentiated by bodily markers, real or imagined, though sometimes by other markers, like markers associated with social class or sexuality. At this level of explanation there is no need for psychoanalytic explanation. It is only necessary to observe society's present perceptions of the salience of differences such as those between girls and boys, or gays and straights, which result in their social differentiation. Different sexes, classes and races are habitually treated differently: men and women, poor and rich, are welcomed into or excluded from different social circles, as are all the complex permutations of 'race': black, white, Asian, Jewish, Irish, Muslim, and so on, endlessly. These are all differences marked and maintained by language.[7] In Iran they taught me to speak like a woman, a process which impressed itself on me only because it was conscious, as the equivalent process in English was not (see Chapter 2).

There is no escaping from this situation by an individual or collective act of will. Even if individuals, or groups of individuals, try to overcome the norms of the society in which they find themselves, they have to use a language which is unequal with regard to the two sexes, structurally and lexically, and with regard to the symbolism of male and female, black and white, rich and poor to be found in metaphors, sayings and literary allusions.

Patricia Williams (1993) remembers how she learnt about race as part of a process of learning language in conversations with other small children, during which she learnt that particular words described her, and were insulting. Strikingly, consciousness of sex and race permeate both Cole's and Seacole's autobiographies, though both of them appear to be far from writing books specially intended for use in anti-sexist or antiracist struggles. Neither of them is able to write from the position of a universal human being. In the act of using language for recording memories of significant events in their lives, they have to explain themselves as female and male, and also as Creole and Krio.

The story is a complex one. A girl will have a different relation to femininity as constructed in terms of her sexuality, her social role and her use of language depending on whether she is identified as black or white, rich or poor. Equally, working-class children will have a different relation to what it is to be working class, depending on whether they are girls or boys, blacks or whites, Muslims or Jews. In Iran they taught me to speak not only like a female, but also like a middle-class Iranian. As a learner, I was not aware which words, inflections or gestures marked one or the other or both together (see Chapter 2). As the stories of Cole, Seacole and Williams show, people are not just of a particular sex, or of a particular class, or of a particular race. They are all these things. For each of these writers sex, class and race combined into inextricable wholes like the eggs and sugar in a cake, rather than being added together in a recognisable form, like the marzipan and icing on top – which can be scraped off. However, it remains true that a variety of cakes can be made from the same eggs and sugar (in combination with various other ingredients), but a cake made without sugar or eggs is a different kind of cake. It also remains true that egg-free, sugar-free cakes can appear very similar to eggy, sugary ones. Williams and Seacole speak as women just as they speak as black people. There are possible lines of connection here between women of different races, American black, Caribbean Creole and myself, British white, even though it remains impossible to extract the part that is 'woman' from each of us.

Sojourner Truth's challenge is perennially relevant:

> That man over there says that women need to be helped into carriages, and lifted over ditches, and to have the best place everywhere. Nobody ever helps me into carriages or over mud puddles, or gives me any best place! And ain't I a woman? Look at me! Look at my arm! I have ploughed and planted, and gathered into barns, and no man could head me! And ain't I a woman? I could work as much and eat as much as a man – when I could get it – and bear the lash as well! And ain't I a woman? I have borne thirteen children, and seen most of them sold off into slavery, and when I cried out with my mother's grief, none but Jesus heard me! And ain't I a woman?

So far I have been emphasising that at every stage of this story of the construction of difference, experience and the ability to articulate it is differentially marked by language. However, it is also important to emphasise the limits of the power of language. Here I will make some assertions rather than arguments, but I take up these points in more detail during the book, particularly in Chapters 9 and 10.

To return to the assumptions made at the start of Chapter 2, language has a considerable power to determine what we see and do, but this power is not absolute. We also create new language, by working on the languages in which we live. Individual experience can be used in creating knowledge in combination with the experiences of others. Groups can develop languages of their own if they share particular psychosocial, social and linguistic experiences. Thus women in a society, for instance, who share particular positions within it can develop a way of talking about this.

Some groups have a greater power to legitimate their own language as the proper one. A particular case here is the language of Theory. It is specialised to those who produce knowledge – these people are usually men. However, as in consciousness-raising groups, as soon as any group of people can develop their own language and legitimate it as a source of knowledge, they can begin to develop ways of speaking about their shared experiences, understand them better, and in the process change the language used to describe them. This in itself will, in its turn, further change the way the members of the group understand their own experiences.

I have argued that language helps to construct persons but in such a way that each of us has been constructed in languages that overlap with those of others. I have further said that groups of people can use and change their language by communicating with those like them. It is now possible to proceed with the move from epistemological critique to construct.

Gunew has made a mistake in her analysis of the difficulty of moving from critique to construct. There is an over-simplification of the gap between the new constructs and the old ones, because it has not been noticed that the languages of the older, male-defined theory and the newer, more female-defined ones are similar as well as different, and, further, that this is bound to be so, since there are overlaps in the languages in which the theories are constructed. The construction of feminist knowledge is as much a process of reform as of revolution. New theory uses old theory as a springboard, the difference being that it is less narrow in its perspectives.

The first precept of the feminist critique was that knowledge must be grounded in individual 'experience', 'perspectives', 'subjectivity', or 'position in a discourse'. This precept also can be taken as indicating that male-defined theory is an abstraction from the experiences and subject position of males. (Or, to repeat the remark from Lennon and Whitford, which I quoted earlier, 'Knowledge bears the marks of its producer'.) The critique says that mainstream theory takes no account of the experiences and subjectivity of others, in that it is assumed by the producers of the knowledge that others are much like themselves and there is no need to listen to their particular viewpoints. There is no need for the argument to stop short once a critique has been made. On the contrary, since we share some, but only some, of our viewpoints both with traditional producers of knowledge, and with those who have been previously marginalised, it is possible to use critiques of traditional views as a springboard to construct new ones. The methodological principle is that the experience of different individuals must be included in any structure of knowledge.

The second precept was that 'power-relations' cannot be added on afterwards, but are fundamental. The analysis of language has shown some of the ways in which power-relations enter into subjectivity, and the description of experience. The argument of Chapter 3 showed some of the complexities of dialogue in situations of inequality and injustice. Thus in re-thinking that experience we have to take account of power and politics. This is possible as long as we notice how power and politics affect our language, how we are positioned in it and how it is used about us, and the effect of large-scale inequalities on communication. The precept turns into a principle that the perspectives of different groups chosen on political grounds need to be taken into account.

Third, theorising is indispensable, whether this means systematic and public reflection or the full-blown Theory associated with academia. In other words, theorising is a term which can be used to describe a communal endeavour to understand each other. That is, it is a way of comparing and discussing different subjectivities and learning from each other – a process of abstracting and ordering one's own understandings. Thus theorising is also about taking abstractions of that process from various sources – this is what I termed full-blown Theory – and using the experience to question it. Taking different perspectives into account is a communal endeavour in which dialogue is used to reflect on experiences and perspectives in order to re-think them. The methodological principle is simply that this is indispensable. It is possible under the same conditions of the previous principles.

Finally, there is no possibility of the acquisition or creation of stable, unchanging knowledge, since all knowledge must be subject to critique from other viewpoints which may fundamentally revise current structures. This precept turns into a methodological principle very simply: continue seeking out different perspectives and do not expect to reach a stable, unchanging state of knowledge. This is possible because it is a continuation of the last three processes.

In short what is needed is a continual process of reflection on experience, but that reflection has to take place in communities. Some communities are as much like each other as possible so that they can develop their own perspectives and language and some of them are made up of people rather different from each other so that they can see the limitations of their own perspectives and language.

To summarise this section: the move has been made from epistemological critique to methodological principles. The requirement of the critique was to include, fundamentally, (C1) the subjectivity and experiences of individuals and groups of individuals; (C2) power and politics; (C3) a dialectic of theory with individual experiences; and (C4) room for a continuing process of change and development in structures of knowledge. The methodological principles are: (M1) knowledge can only be gained using a method which allows for reflection on experience, (M2) using theory, (M3) in a number of different group/political perspectives, which will bring that experience into question; all of which (M4) indicates a never-ending process of returning to old knowledge using the new perceptions and then using the result to re-work the new perceptions.

4 CRITICAL AUTOBIOGRAPHY

The point in the argument has been reached where methodological principles have been constructed. However, general statements of methodological principles are not enough. Actual methods are needed. I focus on one method in particular, the use of autobiographical material, because that is what I draw on for the purposes of this book.[8]

Autobiography is a likely candidate for a technique which is usable within the methodological principles, not only because it focuses on individual experience, but also because it is possible to take politics and theory into account when writing it. However, there is an obstacle. The twentieth-century West has developed a view of autobiography which tends to militate against using politics and theory in autobiographical writing.

4.1 Culturally specific ideas of autobiography

We who live in the late twentieth century and are of the West share a concept of autobiography. Many of us do not realise how specific the concept is to our time and culture. The very word 'autobiography' is a recent one. The word appears in the English language for the first time in 1809 (whereas the word 'biography' goes back to the Greeks).

It is, of course, possible to find what may now be regarded as autobiographies which were written earlier than the nineteenth century and were not named as such by the authors or readers at the time. For instance Augustine and Al-Ghazzali wrote in the fifth and twelfth centuries, respectively. Still, in 1781, Rousseau began his *Confessions* with an explanation (1953: 17):

> I have resolved on an enterprise which has no precedent, and which, once complete, will have no imitator. My purpose is to display to my kind a portrait in every way true to nature, and the man I shall portray will be myself.

It is usually held that Rousseau was right in his belief that his enterprise had no precedent and his *Confessions* are claimed to be the first true autobiography. The reasons for the claim are that Rousseau set out to write about his own personal feelings as an individual, and in doing this he used the (modern) confessional mode. The standard critical view remains that the more personal, confessional and true the autobiography, the closer it is to the ideal.[9]

The confessional mode of modern autobiography is very different from, say, Augustine's 'autobiography' or 'confession'. The word 'confession' that Augustine used in his title has a different connotation from Rousseau's 'confession'. According to Chadwick, for Augustine, 'the very title carries a conscious double meaning, of confession as praise as well as of confession as acknowledgement of faults' (1991: ix).

Foucault provides further convincing arguments that our idea of autobiographical confession is historically and culturally specific, in his series of books on the history of sexuality (1979, 1986, 1988). He notes that confession is increasingly taken as a direct expression of experience, truth and self-knowledge:

> The obligation to confess is now relayed through so many different points, is so deeply ingrained in us, that we no longer perceive it as the effect of a power that constrains us; on the contrary, it seems to us that truth, lodged in our most secret nature, 'demands' only to surface.
>
> (Foucault, 1979: 60)

The narrowness of our view of 'autobiography' is highlighted by current trends in autobiographical writing and criticism, which demonstrate various ways in which autobiography may deviate from the present norm. Attention has been drawn to the fact that autobiographical writing may be focused on political or social considerations, as I mentioned in the last chapter, in connection with Latin American testimonies or American slave narratives. The autobiographer may refer to herself as a fictional being, drawing on myths and stories current in a culture. There may be a movement away from the depiction of a life as linear and unified. This is sometimes the result of the autobiography taking the form of a journal or letters, but it may also be done more self-consciously. Finally, autobiography and biography can be blurred into each other. A blurring of the boundaries occurs when one person tries to write the autobiography of another, trying to write as that person would write, 'from the inside', without interpretation (even while recognising that this is impossible), so that her autobiography can be told. While this can be a literary device, it is also important in life-history work with non-literate people.[10]

4.2 Critical autobiography

I needed to say something about autobiography in general because of the strong association it has for us with one particular kind of autobiography. I use the term 'critical autobiography' in order to refer to the kind of autobiographical writing which conforms with the methodological principles summarised at the end of section 3 (pp. 67–8). The term is needed to distinguish such writing from standard autobiography, because of the strength of the current cultural norms that 'autobiography' should be a personal, confessional, individualistic, a-theoretical and non-political linear narrative of a life. 'Critical autobiography', in contrast, makes use of individual experience, theory, and a process of reflection and re-thinking, which includes attention to politically situated perspectives. Autobiography as simple individual, personal, narrative is just a first stage, and of only limited use, for the purposes of gaining knowledge.

Examples of 'critical autobiography' show how varied the category can be. St Augustine's *Confessions* provide one example. As has already been said, his book does not conform to standard current views of what an autobiography should be. The book is an extended reflection and series of arguments about his own faith and beliefs. The reflection takes place against the account of his life and conversion to Christianity. Thus it is simultaneously a life, a religious life, and a reflection on current theoretical, religious, philosophical issues, which make use of his memories.

It is critical autobiography because it uses experience in order to reflect and re-think, using theory. I would argue that it also includes attention to politically situated perspectives, though not in quite the sense that I have been using the term so far. Augustine, himself, pays no attention to modern political groupings – not surprisingly in the fifth century. He has no consciousness that he talks as a man, for instance, or that he would now be considered a member of an ethnic minority. However, it is political in the terms of the age in which he lived, being written partly in order to locate himself in political controversies and groupings of the time. He himself was in the thick of controversy about his suitability for ordination as a bishop in view of the misdemeanours of his youth and other irregularities of his religious life. The different religious and philosophical groups to which he became attached during his life, like the Manichees and the Neoplatonists, were also political groups, whose typical members were likely to have similar social status (Chadwick, 1991).

Another, quite different, example of a critical autobiography is the book, *Landscape for a Good Woman* by Carolyn Steedman. The book is subtitled 'A story of two lives'. It is the story of her mother and herself and how each of them 'got to be the women they became' (1986: 18). It is also written for a purpose, not just as a personal document of a life. It is self-consciously political in terms of both class and gender. Themes that run through her introduction, 'Stories', explain why she selects the material in the way she does. They plainly show the reasons that I call this a 'critical autobiography'. She is clear that interpretations of the past allow the past to be 're-used through the agency of social information', and continues:

It matters then, whether one reshapes past time, re-uses the ordinary exigencies and crises of all childhoods whilst looking down from the curtainless windows of a terraced house ... or sees at that moment the long view stretching away from the big house in some richer and more detailed landscape.

(1986: 5)

Thus she is using the reflection on the story of two working-class childhoods as a challenge to the 'official interpretative devices of a culture' – and to the dominant academic theories, in particular 'the tradition of cultural criticism in this country, which has celebrated a kind of psychological simplicity in the lives lived out in Hoggart's endless streets of little houses' (1986: 6–7). This is, precisely, use of individual experience, theory, and a process of reflection and re-thinking, which includes attention to politically situated perspectives.

My third example of critical autobiography is different again from either of the other two. Marion Milner's three-volume 'inner journey' (1987: xii) was originally inspired by a desire to find out 'what this soul of mine was really like' (1987: ix). Her three books are an extended 'Experiment in Leisure' (the title of the second book), by which she means an enquiry into what to do with spare time, that is, an enquiry into leading 'A Life of One's Own' (the title to the first book). She uses autobiographical writing, presented as excerpts from, and reflections on, a journal in which she tries better to understand herself and her aims in life. The experiment extends over a lifetime. The first two books were published in 1934 and 1937, but the last, *Eternity's Sunrise*, was written and published fifty years later, in 1987. In the last book she sets out to extend the first two books, by returning to the preoccupations and themes to be found in them. She picks up and re-works ideas using her later experience, contained in journals, to do so. For instance she remarks on

the terms discursive and non-discursive, or simultaneous symbolism, used by Suzanne Langer in her book *Philosophy in a New Key*. It was this that helped me to see that I was basically interested in finding, or creating, the non-discursive kinds of symbols, and that this was really what I was up to in the very first diary in *A Life of One's Own*.

(Milner, 1987: 153)

As this quotation shows, Milner uses academic theories, although she says in the introduction to *Eternity's Sunrise* that it is not a work of scholarship. She is theorising in another sense too, simply by publishing. There was no need to publish these books of an 'inner journey'. That she did so meant that she was inviting others to learn from them and discuss them with her. This, I have argued, is a process of theorising.

She is less politically situated than Steedman, or even, in his own way, than Augustine. However, she shows an interest in gender issues and their relation to her own sex and gender. For instance she says:

> I could see now that I had unknowingly accepted the male assumption that the purpose of life was to have purposes and to get things done. Sometimes I had read criticisms of women's work, usually written by men, maintaining that they should not make the mistake of trying to express themselves in man-made forms but should develop a character-istically feminine approach.... It was only when I had begun to try and observe my own experience that I had discovered that what I had casually assumed of myself, what I had tried to be and felt I ought to be, was something quite different from what I was.... I had come to realize that there are two fundamentally opposite ways of approach-ing experience, both of which are necessary.
>
> (Milner, 1934: 214)

The autobiography I use for the purpose of this book is critical. I have used autobiographical writing not to be confessional or to share a personal account more widely. The writing in Chapter 2 was written specifically to help me in the project of reflecting on experience in order to develop an account of self-identity which would serve the double purpose of both adding to feminist theory and also providing a challenge to the main-stream. In Chapter 3, I use autobiographical writing by others for the same purposes.

5 CONCLUSIONS

This chapter concludes Part I of the book. In Chapters 2 and 3, I began the process of considering the issues surrounding the possibility of sharing experience, and how to present that experience in such a way that it contributes to wider theoretical understanding. This discussion is focused on myself in Chapter 2 and on others in Chapter 3. I also presented some of the experience itself, so that it could be drawn on later in the book.

In this chapter I made a proposal about a way to move from epistemo-logical critique to construct, a proposal that took into account the way that critique began with the perspective of women – and, therefore, from a explicitly political subjective experience. I concluded that 'critical autobiography' (i.e. autobiography which makes use of individual experi-ence, theory, and a process of reflection and re-thinking, and which includes attention to politically situated perspectives) should provide a basis from moving from the false universalisation inherent in mainstream philosophy, towards a situated abstraction.

Part II

Constructing ourselves

5 Wanting and not wanting to belong: acceptance and rejection*

1 QUESTIONS FOR WOMEN: QUESTIONS FOR PHILOSOPHERS

In Chapter 1, I said that self-identity and questions of the self have been central to the women's movement from the first. I also said that the way in which these questions have been framed barely overlaps with the ways that questions of personal identity and the self have been defined in mainstream philosophy. I pointed out that the questions for mainstream philosophy were: The 'I' seems to be unitary?, But can it be?, and, If it is, how? The questions for women bypassed this, focusing, rather, on: Who or what am I? That is, how did I come to be myself? and, Is what I take to be my self, my real self? – and What can I do about it?

In making this distinction between 'mainstream philosophy' and 'women', I am necessarily oversimplifying. By mainstream philosophy here I am primarily thinking of Anglo-Saxon philosophy, represented by Williams, Parfit, Nagel or Dennett, which draws on a line of thinking traced through Descartes, Hume and Kant. Other lines of thinking, mostly originating in Continental Europe, such as postmodernism, critical theory and also communitarianism, have a greater overlap with the questions asked by women, though the two sets of questions are still different in focus.

In this section I look more closely at the questions asked by women and the politics which are associated with various answers. I also say more about the questions of the philosophers, in particular saying where they overlap with the women's questions.

2 SELF-IDENTITY IN FEMINIST THINKING

The questions Who or what am I? – and What can I do about it? need unpacking. I explain them further in this section, by focusing on how self-identity has appeared in feminist theorising. In feminist thought, concerns

* In this chapter I draw on the following auto/biographies and poems from the annotated bibliography in Chapter 3: Annie Allsebrook and Anthony Swift, Robert Cole, Satu Hassi, bell hooks, Jamaica Kincaid, Ved Mehta, Sally Morgan, Daphne Patai, Marge Piercy, Mary Seacole, Carolyn Steedman, Valerie Walkerdine and Patricia Williams.

with the self have been approached from two apparently different directions. First, there is the problem with finding (or creating) oneself: often expressed as finding a real self or a self acceptable to itself. Second, there is the problem with making the subjective experience of the self intelligible. This second problem is usually expressed as a problem of dealing with the experience of a fragmented and changing self. I take each one of these two concerns in turn, finally pointing out that underpinning both of them are similar issues.

2.1 Real selves and the shrouds of conditioning

I begin with the problem of finding oneself. The experience of sex discrimination may be the experience of oppressive material structures. The violent husband, the difficulty of finding child-care, biased immigration laws and regulations: these are all examples which quickly spring to mind. Such conditions may appear to have little to do with finding oneself. However, alongside such material structures – and interacting with them – are habits of mind, in both men and women, which help keep the structures in place. In a woman they may be lack of self-confidence, a de-valuing of her own needs and desires, or even a lack of knowledge about her own needs and desires. These habits of mind can be just as oppressive as the material structures which are so much easier to identify.[1] Walkerdine explains how her 'ordinary childhood' left her constantly trying harder in a never-ending competition to evade failure and loss. She still feels caught in the habits of being a 'steady, reliable worker' and of fantasising about escape from the suburbs into sophistication and glamour. Kincaid gives us a fictionalised account of the constrictions inherent in the habits of mind of a mother, shown by the way she tries to bring up her daughter. She gives her daughter, not her son, the warm bath water, and it is her daughter, not her son, who must learn to be rigidly respectable or risk public shame. Getting rid of these habits of mind can be conceptualised as 'finding oneself'.

These problems were all raised in the 1960s and 1970s, when the Women's Movement was getting going again in the West. At first, the way to deal with oppressive habits of mind appeared to be relatively straightforward, if difficult in practice. If your self-confidence is down, then it needs building up. If you don't know your needs and desires, then you need to develop processes (such as consciousness raising or psychoanalytic procedures) that allow you to get in touch with them. If you undervalue yourself, then you need help to reflect about it and you will see that you should value yourself more. If what has stopped you doing all this before was patriarchy, then patriarchy needs to be tackled systematically.[2]

Underlying the rationality of such processes was the assumption that something was getting in the way of the active core of being. The active core could be essentially female or it could be an androgynous core overlaid by various kinds of conditioning. If the active core is essentially female, then, as Daly put it, the need is to get women unwinding the shrouds of conditioning so to get at the real wild, untrammelled, lusty self underneath (Daly, 1979, 1984). On the other hand, if it is androgynous – a core, with needs and desires, which can be set free – then the shrouds of conditioning would be concealing un-gendered persons, needing and wanting to realise their full human potential. The first supposition led to the politics of radical, separatist feminism, and the second to liberal, reformist feminism.

Oddly, these two opposed forms of politics draw on a very similar understanding of self. Both of them depend on a core self with needs and desires to be met. The only difference between them is that in one case the core self is gendered – essentially female or male – while in the other it is not. The theory that the self is essentially gendered paved the way for a version of identity politics. In this version, identity politics claims that the needs and interests of each woman is determined by her identity as a woman, and that those women who claim different needs and interests are in a state of false consciousness (fembots, as Daly (1979) called them). The opposing (liberal) idea that the self is not gendered, claims that the core is individuated by its particular needs and desires, but that these needs and desires are much the same for both sexes. There is no need for identity politics here, because there is no male or female, only persons – so as soon as the playing field is levelled, everyone can go ahead and realise their own ambitions, meet their own needs and have perfect freedom to become unequal individuals.

This wasn't the end of the story of course. Neither the essentialist female, nor the thorough-going liberal has survived into the 1990s as a viable theory or politics. The reasons for this are related to the second problem to be found in feminist concerns with the self: the problem of making the subjective experience of the self intelligible. However, the answers to the second problem have contributed to new ways of answering the first problem of finding oneself, too. Making the subjective experience intelligible helps in 'finding oneself' – a phrase now understood as meaning 'finding a self which is acceptable to itself', rather than 'finding a real, core self'.

2.2 Subjective experience: fragmented selves and selves that change

A number of feminist philosophers have discussed the subjective experience of self and the implications of such subjectivity for an understanding of self-identity and feminist politics. The subjective experience of the self as fragmented has been discussed by Grimshaw (1988). Grimshaw argues that the incoherence of reason and desire is revealed in the operations of fantasy and that it is truer to many women's experience of the effects of patriarchal oppression than is a unified active core self wholeheartedly fighting patriarchy. She argues that women take into their own selves and value what in some ways they reject. She discusses the contradictory feelings many women have about romantic fiction which they may reject as appealing to traditional femininity, at the very same time as they enjoy it. In a series of articles Flax has also discussed subjectivity and fragmentation, arguing that: 'The unitary self is an effect of many kinds of relations of domination. It can only sustain its unity by splitting off or repressing other parts of its own and others' subjectivity' (1993: 109). Thus she holds that only a politics founded in an acknowledgement of multiple selves can be emancipatory. She argues that (mainstream) philosophers have been able to ignore fragmentation only because they rest their distinctions on a prior, gender-based, division of labour. Thus they distinguish a (higher) rational self from a phenomenal embodied self, and they also emphasise the asocial, isolated qualities of the self rather than sustained, intimate relations with others.

The experience of the self as one of change and development is discussed by Almond (1988). She argues that the physical facts of menstruation, conception, pregnancy, childbirth and menopause generate a series of moral problems related to identity and self-concept for women which are different to those experienced by men who do not go through such changes. Benhabib (1992) also discusses the importance of change and development in a theory of the self. She notes how male philosophers are likely to follow the example of Hobbes in discussing men as if they were mushrooms, sprung fully grown from the ground. Against this view, Benhabib argues that a self can only be understood as constituted intersubjectively, in interaction with others in a process of becoming. She further argues that the logic of even looking for liberation from oppression requires that this interaction is not understood as a simple constitution of the self through discourse. Although women's 'own sense of self has been so fragile, and their ability to assert control over the conditions of their own making so rare' (1992: 16), central to the task of caring for others is the requirement that individuals are understood to be capable of action and asserting control. Thus owing to the gender divisions of labour, women, unlike men, are more likely to notice the existence and significance of childhood and child-rearing to conceptions of self and subjectivity. Men tend to believe in the mushroom theory of men, but women are less liable to make this mistake.

The theory of the essentially female subject paved the way for one version of gender identity politics. The consequences of accepting and working within a fragmented and changing self turned into another version. This newer version did not need to suggest, as the older one had, that the needs and interests of each woman is determined by her identity as a woman, nor that those women who claim different needs and interests are in a state of false consciousness. The underlying assumption of the newer version is that a self is made and makes itself in the changing circumstances in which she lives, and in a direction strongly affected by her own understanding of herself. Circumstances include those which arise just because of gender. In other words, we collectively make ourselves, but not in conditions of our own choosing.[3]

Views about core and neutral selves are changed if the arguments of this section are accepted. If the self is constructed, then whatever the truth about essential femininity, the self is more than its core. It is at least partly constructed by political structures, including that of gender. Thus there are new possibilities of answers to the questions Who or what am I? – and What can I do about it? The answer lies at least partly in understanding the path that led to the self, and re-constructing it accordingly, within the constraints that surround us. Both Walkerdine and Kincaid take this view. Walkerdine's analysis shows that part of the reason for her explicit descriptions of the constraints surrounding her, is to re-work them. Kincaid would not be able to write critically, and also from the inside, about the way a mother tries to shape the gender of her daughter, unless she had both accepted some of that identity but also re-constructed it.

In all the feminist analyses related to concerns about self-identity and its politics, there is an underlying and continuing theme (with different theoretical and political answers). This theme is a concern with agency and control. In the first set of problems – the finding of the real self – the concern is that agency and control have been stifled. In the second – the subjective experience of a fragmented, changing self or set of selves – the concern is to discover how agency and control are activated collectively and in context. Before I turn to consider the construction of self in section 2, I compare these analyses with standard, mainstream philosophical ones.

3 SELF-IDENTITY FOR WOMEN AND THE QUESTIONS OF PHILOSOPHY

It is now possible to see that there is, in fact, some overlap between feminist concerns with the self and the classic questions of Western philosophy about selves and persons. The line of thinking for the standard account begins with Descartes' famous sentence. His argument was that the central certainty from which all else flows is the *cogito*: 'I think, therefore I am.' From this basis he argued for a unified self, a knowing subject, that is transparent to itself, and for clear rational thought as the source of control, and autonomy. Hume, the empiricist, proposed a different answer to the question of the nature of a self. His self was an empirical self, derived from sense experience and the memories associated with it, but this self remained a problem for him, because he was unable to find a satisfactory answer to what might be 'the uniting principle' he was searching for. As he says in the appendix to Book I of the *Treatise*, he finds the problem intractable.[4] Kant's resolution of the question went beyond either rationalism and empiricism, in his 'transcendental deduction' of the categories which organise our experience, if we are to have any experience. He thus distinguishes between the empirical and transcendental self, arguing that it is 'the unity of apperception' which makes for a unified self. The appearances of the self are not the same as the 'thing in itself' which is the self. However, through the application of reason it is possible to discover, not only that we have a self, different from what we perceive of ourselves, but also what we should do, and how far we are able to do it. Thus, autonomy is exercised through reason.

In modern Anglo-Saxon philosophy, the possibility of discovering a unifying principle for personal identity remains of central interest in the philosophy of mind. There have been a number of widely discussed articles about the significance of bodily continuity and memory in terms of brain transplants.[5] Derek Parfit (1984) has produced influential discussions of the role of memory and psychological continuity in individuating persons.[6] Nagel (1979, 1986), among others, has investigated the philosophical implications of psychological experiments on people who have split brains.[7] All of this discussion is concerned with answering the unity question, and therefore unity tends to be assumed when possible answers to questions of control and agency are suggested.

Feminists are not so concerned with establishing a principle of unity, though they are interested in the nature of fragmentation. However, there are some overlaps between Anglo-Saxon philosophy and feminist concerns. They are to be found in the view that control and agency are crucial to selves, and an interest in what constraints there are to exercising either of them. Also, less obviously perhaps, common to both perspectives is an interest in the place of memory – 'how I got to be like this'. However, on the whole, feminists seeking philosophical help with their questions will find the results of the search is rather disappointing.[8]

There is another set of philosophical traditions which also springs from the arguments of Descartes and Kant. These traditions include critical theory and communitarianism. They are more concerned with action and the significance of context than the one I have just described. Benhabib usefully summarises the approach of critical theory:

> This tradition substitutes for the spectator model of the self the view of an active, producing, fabricating humanity, creating the conditions of an objectivity by forming nature through its own historical activity. . . .
> The historical and psychoanalytic critique of the Cartesian ego sees the task of reflection neither as the withdrawal from the world nor as access to clarity and distinctness, but as the rendering conscious of those unconscious forces of history and society which have shaped the human psyche. Although generated by the subject, these forces necessarily escape its memory, control and conduct.

(1992: 207)

Questions of context also arise in communitarian accounts of identity. For instance, Charles Taylor says:

> Consider what we mean by 'identity'. It is 'who' we are, 'where we're coming from.' As such it is the background against which our tastes and desires and opinions and aspirations make sense. If some of the things I value most are accessible to me only in relation to the person I love, then she becomes internal to my identity.
>
> (1991: 34)

Taylor's summary demonstrates that he holds a much more apolitical view than the one described by Benhabib. His view is about individuals in their communities, but is not about political individuals. Indeed Taylor is remarkably uninterested in questions of gender. It barely appears in his analyses. On the other hand, the mainstream of critical theory acknowledges social structures like those of gender, but, compared to communitarianism, pays less attention to the personal.[9]

There is clearly an overlap between these concerns and those of feminists, but the focus remains different. The issues are seen as urgent in political and personal terms by feminists, and thus the questions are posed with a particular focus on both the personal and the political, a focus which is not that of the various theorists who provide conceptual tools with which to address the feminist questions. Benhabib explains this:

> Identity does not refer to my potential for choice alone, but to the actuality of my choices, namely to how I, as a finite, concrete, embodied individual, shape and fashion the circumstances of my birth and family, linguistic, cultural and gender identity into a coherent narrative that stands as my life's story. . . . The question becomes: how does this finite, embodied creature constitute into a coherent narrative those episodes of choice and limitation, agency and suffering, initiative and dependence?
>
> (1992: 161)

These circumstances of 'linguistic, cultural and gender identity' are precisely those which are collective as well as individual. They are precisely those which are perceived as shaped by oppression while being constitutive of the selves of those who would fight that oppression. Indeed, they are precisely those which explain how the political becomes the personal.

Postmodernism is another set of theories derived from the tradition which stems from Descartes and Kant. It too overlaps in its concerns with those of feminists. However it is not easy to discuss briefly partly because it is so hard to agree on what postmodernism is, and partly because there is such bitter dispute about the nature of the relationship between feminism and postmodernism.[10] Fragmentation and change are of central interest to postmodernists. So are the demise of grand theory and the death of the subject. However even though many feminists find a lot of these ideas, particularly those about fragmentation and change, congenial and useful, some of the ideas cause concern, in particular the death of the subject and the demise of grand theory. Many warnings have been made about the dangers of taking up these ideas too enthusiastically, lest agency and enlightenment ideals of liberation are lost just at the point they seemed to be in reach of women.[11] But on the other hand, a rigid fear of such ideas can close minds. Flax (1993) describes being bitterly attacked by feminists for holding postmodern ideas.[12]

4 CONSTRUCTING A SELF

At the end of the section on women's questions about selves, I said that the underlying assumption of the newer versions of identity politics is that a self is made and makes itself in the changing circumstances in which she lives and in a direction strongly affected by her own understanding of herself. I pointed out that a number of issues and themes were central to this assumption. They include: (1) agency; and (2) control; (3) the subjective experience of a fragmented, changing self or set of selves; and (4) the significance of bodies and material conditions. I agree with Benhabib that the central question becomes: 'How does this finite, embodied creature constitute into a coherent narrative those episodes of choice and limitation, agency and suffering, initiative and dependence?' (Benhabib, 1992: 162). This question can be more simply formulated as a number of discrete questions: Who or what am I? That is, where did this self come from? (If I was made in context, what context? What influence did gender have?) Why does it feel as it does? (Why should I experience myself as I do?) Where is it going? (How should I exercise agency? What control do I have?) What should happen to it now? (Where do I want to go now?) So an account of the construction of a self needs to show how social circumstances, material circumstances (including embodiment), change and growth all come together to make a self.

These are not only feminist questions. They are also crucial questions for any groups of people who regard themselves as dispossessed and oppressed. Thus they appear as questions for other liberation movements, which, of course, are often themselves overlapping with women's ones, in that women are often members of other dispossessed and oppressed groups.

In this section I shall give an account which enables us to understand how to answer the questions of self-identity which have arisen within feminism and other liberation movements. I begin by considering material circumstances and then go on to investigate social ones as they appear under the conditions of change and growth which are the conditions of being human beings living in space and time.

4.1 The material and the social: some distinctions

I need to discuss the material as distinct from the social because I want to discuss the way in which embodiment or material circumstances enter the self, without reducing the material to the social.[13] I want to hold on to the significance of embodiment and material conditions. First, if the self is not a blank tablet – that is, individual differences are to be explained other than through individual social circumstances (and I need make no judgement on the question at this stage) – then it will be partly constructed of material (anatomical) circumstances, Second, I want to make sure that the body and its material circumstances do not get over-looked. Thus they act as a corrective to the emphasis on discourse which has been so influential – and led many people to think that language is all there is. I shall argue against that view later.

Examples will help explain the distinction I am drawing. We need to explain the relative excess of ambition in an individual, with reference to her perceptions or reasoning about her circumstances, needs, desires, values or participation in language. However, we can explain the excess-ively tall poppy without any such reference. Similarly, we need to explain the solidarity of a trade union with reference to the members' perceptions or reasoning about their circumstances, needs, desires and values. How-ever, we can explain the ability of trees to grow taller and stronger in forests, without any such references.[14]

Examples of the material include the landscape, and the weather. The landscape or the weather can be described as 'threatening' or 'welcoming' – and they often are – but geologists and meteorologists have no need of such concepts. The material also includes anatomical features of the individual human being: two legs, hair on the head, and a capacity to develop a human language. Examples of the social include families, governments, careers and pleasures. To take just the first of these, the family: 'the family' is notoriously difficult to define without reference to perceptions and understanding. Cross-cultural research has to make use of markers such as 'shares a cooking pot'. To work out just who shares a cooking pot in any particular society, reference has to be made to understandings of kinship, bonds of need and networks of responsibility and the language which underpins and references them.[15]

Once the distinction between 'material' and 'social' has been drawn the interaction between them can be seen. Material and social factors are each the result of the other. Landscape and weather have been affected by people and their societies. Anatomies are the results of human abilities to provide health care, or the suitability of nutrition in childhood. Con-versely, societies are the products of their circumstances. Remote moun-tainous places shape societies which are different from those found by the sea shore near natural harbours.

I need to put in a word of warning about the scope of what I am doing here. In drawing a dividing line between the 'material' and the 'social' I am drawing on common understanding rather than solving at a stroke some of the great questions of philosophy about reality: mind, body, language, and other minds. All I am doing is making broad judgements about what to put on either side of the divide, with the caveat that the exact placing of the divide may be an arbitrary one, or it may be decided by metaphysics which need not concern me for my purposes.[16] All I want to establish is that there is a range of factors affecting the self and that they include bodies and material circumstances and that they also include people and language.

4.2 Material circumstances and the self

People grow up in particular bodies and their selves and subjectivities develop accordingly, as I said first, in Chapter 4, p. 63. Moreover, psychological factors may have material causes in the brain, or elsewhere (from hormones, or in the nervous system). It may well be the case that each human being is born with a unique set of psychological characteristics, such as a tendency to introversion or extroversion or with a special capacity for kindness, anger or patience. There is some evidence that some people are born with extraordinarily great talents for music or mathematics, so it is entirely possible that others have extraordinarily little talent in either direction. Anatomical factors include sexual differences (which are genital but which may also be psychological) and racial characteristics such as eye colour, hair colour, eye shape and colour of skin. They also include material abilities, disabilities, and individual attributes such as having perfect pitch, 20/20 vision, diabetes, cerebral palsy, particularly long legs, or a particularly short neck.

All of the material circumstances of bodies have a significance for the self in interaction with the social. Gender is significant in every society, but the way in which it is significant varies. The ways in which a particular ability or disability may or may not be significant depend on the society in which it is found. For instance, blind children's different selves are affected by the society in which they find themselves. The self Ved Mehta (1985) describes is as much affected by the fact that he is a middle-class Indian boy from a loving family as it is by his blindness. Racial characteristics are often significant but what counts as a racial characteristic varies in different societies. Mehta's visible Indianness began to be significant for him when he went to school in the USA.

In all these cases – gender, disability, race – the self is formed by an interaction of the material and the social. The self that is Ved Mehta is one which is as marked by his perseverance, his intelligence, his sex, his racial characteristics and his blindness as it is by the particular social interactions of family, friendship and society in which he found himself.

Equally it is as marked by the social interactions as it is by the material circumstances in which such interactions take place.

Just as people grow up in particular bodies, people grow up in particular places and their selves and subjectivities develop accordingly. The environment is where we live, grow and develop. As the Green movement has shown us, the quality of the air, the water, the earth and the sky affect us today in the industrial, urban West as they did through the centuries of agricultural, rural living. Further, we find ourselves in particular landscapes. We may find ourselves born in the city or the countryside, or in houses built on stilts on the ocean, like the children of the sea gypsies of Thailand. Babies are born and grow up deep in the forest, in high-rise blocks of flats, among the mountains or in leafy suburbs. Increasingly, we find ourselves migrating across continents from one of these environments to another, with consequences for our continuing development of self, as possible activities and interactions are affected by the environment in which they occur.

4.3 Social circumstances and the self

Just as I needed to discuss material circumstances in order to talk about the effects of material circumstances on the self, so I need to discuss social circumstances. I have described social explanation as requiring reference to perceptions or reasoning about an individual's or a group's needs, desires, values and participation in language. Social circumstances are many and various. We form relationships at work and at home, with our families, and with strangers through books, films and music. In order to bring some order into this, I shall draw some distinctions: first, in the kinds of connections that can be made; and second, in the kinds of groups in which those connections can be made.

The most important of the social circumstances defining selves are found in our relationships with other people, as individuals or as social groups, rather than in other perceptions and understandings which are unaffected by relationships. In Chapter 2, section 7.1.1, I explained my own memories of the significance of relationships. Steedman (1986) describes how it is the reactions of others to the social class of her parents which fixes for her what it is to be of the working class. The street children of Recife, talking to Allsebrook and Swift (1989), want first and foremost to feel cared for and respected, even though their material and intellectual needs are great. Elsewhere in Brazil, Marialice, a desperately poor woman living at a time of crisis in the economy and a drought in the backlands, puts human relations at the centre of her narrative concerning herself.

Further, the most significant of the relationships are ones of love, resistance, acceptance and rejection.[17] This is a core assumption with which I build a theory of the self in this section. I have explored this

assumption in Chapter 2, Section 7.1.2. It is also exemplified in the
stories I have just mentioned: Steedman, the street children of Recife,
and Marialice. The assumption is in direct contrast to the assumptions of
the 'men as mushrooms' theorists (see p. 78). They persist in talking
of unsocial selves who then proceed to act socially if they want, or of
political social atoms who choose to contract in.

4.4 Connections

I am taking it that love, resistance, acceptance and rejection are connections of belonging, deciding whether to belong and of being given or
refused permission to belong. I am focusing on just some aspects of these
feelings. Thus, love is wanting to belong with an other or others, or with
a particular social group. In contrast, resistance is not wanting to belong
with an other or others, or with a particular social group. These relationships may not be reciprocal. Thus love is also wanting an other or others
to belong with oneself or with one's group. Resistance is its opposite.
Acceptance is the result of some degree of love by others: being allowed
to belong with an other or others. Rejection is the result of resistance on
the part of others: not being allowed to belong with an other or others.
Again, feelings may not be reciprocal. Acceptance is also allowing an
other or others to belong with oneself or one's group, and rejection is
not allowing an other or others to belong with oneself or one's group.
   The term 'group' is a slippery one. People can think of themselves as
individuals, as members of small face-to-face groups, and as members of
large groups where they could not know the other members personally.
There are two kinds of such large groups. First, there are those defined
by structures of a society – gender, race, class, sexuality and age. There
is no choice about being a member of such a group. Second, there are
those defined by membership, where individuals choose to belong, or feel
that they belong. This kind of group is sometimes called an 'invisible
college'. An invisible college may be defined by gender, race, class, sexuality and age, in so far as an individual identifies as a member, but they
can also be defined by religion, music, work, shared values and intellectual
interests. Gender, like other structures of society, appears in this invisible
college only if the individual finds it significant. Finally, the largest group
of all, if it can properly be called a group, is everyone else – the general
public. People interact with strangers of no particular significance to them,
in the normal course of everyday life.[18]
   These groups begin to affect us from the day of our birth. The complexity of the connections increases as a person moves from babyhood
to adulthood, because the number of ways in which groupings can be
made increases. Connections of love, resistance, acceptance and rejection
are made in a number of arenas, such as family, neighbourhood, school
and work. In babyhood the connections can only be made through indi-

vidual personal contact, but the possibilities widen as a person moves through childhood into adulthood. This movement is often portrayed as a process of moving into ever-widening circles. This is misleading. Wider society makes its presence felt from the beginning, in the simplest of individual connections.

To make this account less general and less abstract, I now use it to consider a baby, born in Britain, growing up into an adult and developing its own self-identity. A baby is (usually) born into a family – by which I mean adults and, probably, other children – with whom she develops close relationships. The baby may be loved and accepted wholeheartedly by everyone. However, sometimes love is conditional upon certain conditions being met. A small child may gain the impression that she has to be 'good' in order to feel loved and accepted. While all children – and adults – need to accommodate themselves to the wishes of others some of the time, a requirement to do so all the time leads to what are described as feelings of being inauthentic, or of a loss of a real self. Many psychotherapists agree that children may develop various defences to this situation, which distort their self-identities. Alice Miller describes one of these mechanisms, the experience of the introjection of the threat of loss of love as follows: 'I must always be good and measure up to the norm, then there is no risk; I constantly feel that the demands are too great, but I cannot change that, I must always achieve more than others' (1987: 27). She goes on:

> Accommodation to parental needs often (but not always) leads to the 'as-if personality' (Winnicott has described it as the 'false self'). This person develops in such a way that he reveals only what is expected of him, and fuses so completely with what he reveals that – until he comes to analysis – one could scarcely have guessed how much more there is to him, behind this 'masked view of himself' (Habermas).
>
> (ibid.)

The account, so far, has been of small face-to-face groups. Gender implications have not been mentioned. These, too, appear from the first. Within the family the implications of belonging to wider groupings such as gender will make themselves felt to the child. The first question: 'Is it a boy or a girl?' is a crude demonstration of this – what could it mean otherwise? Can a mother or father not pay attention to the sex of their offspring? I cannot imagine it. The rest of the world certainly does pay attention to it, as research conclusively shows. How this is made felt will vary with other factors. In Chapter 2, section 7.2.2., I describe some of my own experience about this. Jamaica Kincaid (1981) gives a vivid picture of being a girl, rather than a boy, in a Caribbean island. Walkerdine (1990) describes how important to her was a photograph of herself dressed as a bluebell fairy, and the importance of this image for her own thinking about herself.

As I said, being categorised by gender is not necessarily to belong to an invisible college. It occurs regardless of the child's understanding of gender markers and appropriate behaviour. All children will learn, very quickly indeed, that they are seen as sexed and gendered beings. In most cases, they also actively try to belong, working out what membership means – that is they join the 'invisible college'. This means negotiating the different messages that come from parents, siblings, television, friends, grandparents, neighbours, books, videos, and the general public. These are messages about connections: reactions to love and resistance and messages of acceptance or rejection. The strength of gender (and other memberships) for a child will depend on the particular mixing of these messages.[19]

Soon enough, connections beyond the immediate family increase in complexity. As the social network of a child widens, possibilities for forming different groups increase. She discovers people she knows in a number of different ones. Some of these small groups are structured by larger groups and there are now likely to be more of these larger groups. Even if gender was not given much salience at home it will be important at school. Social class, race, disability and sexuality (only dimly understood at first, through jokes and insults, later of crucial importance) will make their presence felt more strongly. Reasons for belonging to one group or another, or being positioned in or out of groups, will increase in complexity. A child has to make more, and more complex, decisions about belonging – about where her loves and resistances lie – and decisions related to acceptance or rejection. Patricia Williams (1993) describes discovering as a small child that she was 'coloured' (insultingly, from her white friends) as well as Negro (as her family had told her she should be proud to be). Steedman (1986) describes learning what members of the middle classes thought of her working-class parents.

Decisions about love and resistance need to be distinguished from decisions about acceptance and rejection. Decisions about love and resistance come from the individual herself, related to her own understanding of the individuals and groups concerned. Such decisions are productive of conflicts such as: 'I want to belong to two groups but I think they conflict'; or, 'I want her to belong to my group but she is a member of a conflicting group'. This occurs at the level of friendship, if it is impossible to be friendly with two groups of people simultaneously. It also occurs at the levels of invisible colleges. These may be colleges related to structures in society. For instance, a child might think that real girls cannot play football. Invisible colleges may also be unrelated to political structures. For instance, either sex might think that bookish people can't be good at dancing. In Chapter 2, section 7.1.2, I described similar dilemmas in my own case. bell hooks describes how she has to make a careful decision about whether it is possible to hold on to her identity as a black woman at the same time as taking a serious interest in postmodernism. This is a dilemma related to political structures. On the other hand, Cole excluded himself at a young age from training for the church on the grounds that he was not saintly enough. This dilemma was not related to his status as black, as Krio, as relatively rich, or as a member of a colonised people, although he discusses the effect of all of these in relation to other parts of his life.

Decisions about acceptance and rejection can be distinguished from decisions about love and resistance, although there is an overlap in some cases. They overlap because, if A wants B or B's group then A accepts B; if A does not want B or B's group then A rejects B. Similarly for B's acceptance of A. Thus far, decisions about love and resistance are the same as decisions about acceptance and rejection. However, there are two reasons for there sometimes being a difference between them. First, A only has the power to accept or reject B into her group on the basis of her own feelings and wishes, if she is in agreement with her group in this respect. Second, decisions about acceptance and rejection of A or B may depend on factors which they took as unimportant for the decision, and indeed may be due to factors which were relatively unimportant in the construction of their identities up to that point. I shall say more about each of these reasons.

Some people are more likely to find that their own feelings and decisions coincide with those of the group. This is less likely for those whose own acceptance is at risk. The group may be ambivalent about some of its members. Acceptance may be conditional. So it is not surprising that girls (and marginal groups in general) are less at ease with their feelings in their chosen groups. Moreover they have more decisions to make, since they do not automatically belong to so many of the groups they wish to join. Girls find that they have to choose between being real girls and a number of other attractive groups, only some of which will easily accept them. Boys are not exempt from such dilemmas. Both girls and boys may feel ambivalent about their chosen roles as masculine or feminine.[20] The ambivalence can then be stamped out of consciousness, or worked out and resolved over a life-time. Consider two black woman, Mary Seacole and Patricia Williams, who decided to join groups where they were in a minority among men and whites. They could have decided to act as though sexist or racist stories told in their presence were insignificant, as if they were honorary men or 'coconuts'.[21] However, neither woman would condone offensive stories. Mary Seacole remained ambivalent all her life about her position. Patricia Williams says that she has spent her life 'recovering from the degradation of being divided against myself' (1993: 120).

Sometimes there is no choice about rejection or acceptance, whatever the feelings and decisions of the individual concerned. Rejection is total, even if the person makes strenuous efforts to join a group of his or her choice. Alternatively it may be hard for someone to leave a group she dislikes, even if she wants to. She continues to be recognised as 'one of us', whatever she says. Rian Malan (1991) describes his easy acceptance by right-wing Afrikaners in South Africa, in spite of the years he had spent living and working with people of other races and other political persuasions.

There is another, second, reason that decisions about love and resistance are the not same as decisions about acceptance and rejection. It is that factors that lead to the acceptance or rejection were not, until that point, taken as salient by the individual concerned. For instance, small children may have joined the invisible college of gender – but have defined it as a broader church than it is. If gender becomes the reason for acceptance or rejection it becomes crucial to the construction of identity even if it was not so salient before. Childhood may be the time that a person discovers that her sex, class or race are significant factors in her acceptance or rejection from groups she want to join. Other people may not discover this until adulthood. I explained my dawning realisation of the ramifications of being a girl in Chapter 2, section 7.1.2. Similar discoveries are described in accounts of childhood by Kincaid (1981), Steedman (1986), Walkerdine (1990) and P. Williams (1993), in the contexts of race, class, and different national cultures, as experienced by girls. Alibhai (1989) explains how she underwent a bitter discovery of race/ culture membership, as an adult, when the Rushdie affair was at its height. Satu Hassi narrates her story of learning, as an adult, that there was a difficulty in being both female and an engineer, in a article she called, significantly, 'On Loneliness' (1986). A different kind of difficulty about women being taken seriously as academics by colleagues, is described in Marge Piercy's poem, on p. 53, 'In the men's rooms'.

4.5 Dealing with acceptance and rejection

I have been focusing on particular cases of love, resistance, acceptance and rejection. It is the *processes and results* of acceptance and rejection, on which I now focus. Choosing or being chosen to belong to a group – or not to belong – starts a process. It is not just that love and resistance are met with acceptance or rejection. Acceptance and rejection themselves provoke love and resistance.

Acceptance in a group strengthens the bonds. It is often thought that this is only true for marginal groups. This is not so. Where there is privilege the bonds are drawn the more tightly – or how else would it remain privilege? Consider the boy deciding to act masculine. He has chosen a group where he belongs. He then works to maintain this group membership, strenuously distinguishing himself from the non-masculine by excluding others. Masculinity is important to boys, even when they feel at home in it. Notice, for instance, how many of their jokes and insults to each other depend on gender.[22] The upper-class girls in a school studied by Elizabeth Frazer were more conscious of their class position than were the girls from the nearby state school, many of whom were working class (Frazer, 1989). It is for this reason that the experience of belonging or not belonging is essential to the self-identity of the person concerned, whether or not the factor which gives access to the group is one that she had previously thought significant.

If someone has been rejected – or has rejected herself – as a result of attributions of race, class, gender or disability, she finds it necessary to construct a new identity which accommodates the rejection. It is some-times possible to deny the attributions, becoming an honorary male, or a coconut, for instance. Alternatively, the wish for membership itself can be abandoned, and the attributions made correspondingly more powerful in the new self-identity. As Hannah Arendt said, 'If I am attacked as a Jew I must defend myself as a Jew' (Young-Bruehl, 1982). This is a process born of rejection and not to be confused with freely choosing such a group because she feels at home in it, however happy she feels later with her new group. In the long run, the created self-identity changes through a process of accommodation. Mary Seacole was unable to join the Florence Nightingale contingent in the Crimea, in spite of her obvious suitability. She never lost her disappointment and anger at the discrimination she faced, even though her resolution of the problem was a resounding success for her, personally. There are various strategies which help the process of successful accommodation. I want to focus on politicisation, taking note of plurality as I do so.

Plurality comes about because of the effect of overlap and multiple choices between groups. As I have continually emphasised, social class, race, sex, sexuality and disability all come in multiples and combinations. This plurality gives space for manoeuvre as well as cutting down choices. Rather than the image of an ever-tightening noose, an appropriate image is a multiplicity of threads which can make webs of different shapes and sizes. Given that the individual faces contradictions whatever she does, she has a certain freedom to negotiate her own way of resolving them.

Such space of manoeuvre is affected by the processes of politicisation. For the rest of this section I focus particularly on politicisation, as a way of dealing with rejection which depends on the individual coming to an understanding that not only do communication and belonging extend beyond the immediate social circle, but also that the public social circles can be used as a basis for improving the situation.

Such a process can start in the very young. A child may identify with 'girls', for instance, or, as she grows older, with 'the working class' or 'Muslims'. In other words a process of politicisation is begun, based on a politics of identity. This identification can then be used as part of a process of re-constructing the self in ways that are not wholly defined by the excluding groups, and which in turn affect the self-identity of both excluders and excluded.

As the child grows older and understands what is happening, the process becomes more powerful. The connections which individuals make with groups of other people enable them to characterise their experiences, and in the process to alter the experiences they have. I describe the power of this in my own life in Chapter 2, section 7.1.2, and also in section 7.2.4. Thus individuals are enabled to understand the power of loving and resisting in the creation of identity, and to transform it, individually and collectively.

Sally Morgan's life was transformed when she discovered the reasons for her previous exclusion. As a result she discovered and embraced an identity which included being an Aboriginal woman. It is instructive at this point to consider North African Muslim women intellectuals, like Mernissi and el Sa'adawi. They need to negotiate the exclusions of 'Third World' and 'Muslim', as well as gender in their construction of self-identity as international writers. Being a woman, of the 'Third World', or a 'Muslim', is not the same in terms of self-identity in North Africa as it would be for the same individuals if they were to migrate to Britain. For those who have migrated, their continuing construction of self-identity in the face of acceptance and rejection has had to adjust to new inclusions or exclusions. It is apparent from their powerful, influential writing that North African Muslim women intellectuals have made their own spaces. Compare this to the attempt of many Westerners to portray Muslim women as victims of their culture and needing to be Westernised if they are to be liberated as women. That is a space which they all reject.

It has to be said that this process of the politicisation of otherness is uncomfortable, however cosy it looks from the outside. In this country, Michele Roberts has fictionalised the process in her novel, *The Book of Mrs Noah*:

> The Ark of the Women is the Other One. The Salon des Refusees. Des Refusantes. Cruise ship for the females who are only fitted in as monsters: the gorgons, the basilisks, the sirens, the harpies, the furies, the viragos, the amazons, the medusas, the sphinxes.
>
> Where shall we go, the women who don't fit in? Those of us who are not citizens but exiles? Those of us who are not named as belonging, but as outcasts, as barbarians?
>
> (1987: 19–20)

She goes on to describe the initial, uncomfortable, meeting of the women on the Ark:

> Here I am, returning to a nice warm womb full of the nourishment and sweetness of women, a fine safe place in which to grow and change, and what do I find? Not only disagreement and conflict (Women's groups? Give me a coffee morning any day) but also untruths.
>
> (1987: 57)

How could it be otherwise, when what they had in common was rejection, rather than a shared wish to be nourishing and sweet?

5 CONCLUSIONS ABOUT THE CONSTRUCTION OF A WEB OF IDENTITY

I have offered a proposal for a theory of self-identity which takes into account the material circumstances of particular bodies marked by sex, race and sexual pleasures, growing up in material circumstances such as riches or poverty. It considers the way these interact with social circumstances over lifetimes which begin with babyhood and go through the changes of a long adulthood. Thus it provides a basis for answering the questions women ask about self-identity: I pursue these questions in the next few chapters.

In summary, the proposal is as follows. Self-identity is to be understood as a kind of web, the construction of which is partly under guidance from the self, though not in its control. Thus it is marked by competing constraints and influences which overlap and fuse. The theory is one which affirms that the creation of identity is a collective affair in which each person has a valuable contribution to make. It is thus highly individualistic, in the sense that it values the individual, and does not hold that some are dispensable, or more dispensable, than others. Each individual creates her own identity, although she is constrained by circumstance in doing so. Equally it is highly communalistic and political. It states that the individual can only exist through the various communities of which she is a member and, indeed, is continually in a process of construction by those communities. It emphasises that the concept 'community' must be understood to include both those it is possible to know personally and also the wider society and its political categories. Indeed, politics are inseparable from the construction and maintenance of the self. The experience of acceptance and rejection, and the reaction to them cannot be understood without reference to the structures of power in the society in which the self finds itself. The proposal is that self (the self, the individual) is constrained by overlapping, various communities, each of which is itself changing. Such plurality is the norm, not the exception.

6 Feelings, emotions, rationality, politics*

1 INTRODUCTION

The subject of this chapter picks up two themes from the previous chapters: the epistemological significance of experience and women's perspectives of Chapter 4, and second, from Chapter 5, the way that inclusions and exclusions – acceptance and rejection – shape self-identity, in the context of structures of power such as gender, social class or race. The first theme appears as a logical dilemma for feminists about how much trust to place in emotion. The second theme appears as the significance of the way that different groups of people come to understand themselves in terms of their emotions and rationality. The two themes interweave to create a theory of a politics of emotion and of a politics of rationality.

1.1 A logical dilemma for feminists

The epistemological significance of experience and women's perspectives was discussed in Chapter 4. It was pointed out that a difficulty for formulating a feminist perspective is that theory is inevitably based on experience which is mediated by language – which may already be masculine; and that the experience can only be formed into a feminist perspective using theory – which is already masculine (See Chapter 4, section 3). It was argued that this difficulty could be resolved by using the methodological principles summarised in Chapter 4, section 3: reflection on experience, using theory, in a number of different group/political perspectives, all of which indicates a never-ending process of returning to old knowledge using the new perceptions and then using the result to re-work the new perceptions.

In Chapter 5, section 2, it was pointed out that a significant source of feminist theorising has been found in particular feelings and emotions, and, related to this, the experience of embodiment. Grimshaw and, to a

---

* In this chapter I draw on the following auto/biographies and poems from the annotated bibliography in Chapter 3: Yasmin Alibhai, Joseph Brodsky, Frederick Douglass (in Gilroy, 1993), bell hooks, Marge Piercy, Mary Seacole, Anne Seller, Carolyn Steedman, and Valerie Walkerdine.

lesser extent, Flax, both focus on feelings, while Almond, Flax and Benhabib all discuss the significance of embodiment. In all these cases 'feelings' are shown to relate to 'reason', thus giving a source of understanding, insight and knowledge. Indeed feminist activists and theorists have trusted feeling, as a source of knowledge, refusing standard accounts of the dichotomy between emotion and reason as a masculine distortion. Anne Seller (1985) writes of the 'concrete reality of Greenham', of trusting emotions of fear and anger, while refusing an emotion/reason split. Walkerdine's writing about the mastery of reason is rooted in passions which she also expresses in poetry and autobiographical writing.

The question arises whether feminists are right to trust feelings. There is a logical dilemma for feminists about the use of feeling and emotion which is closely related to the difficulty about the use of experience. This dilemma lies in the fact that on the one hand feminists might say: 'emotion gives feminists access to truth, and in such a way that we see that the dichotomy of emotion and reason is a false one' but, on the other, 'reason, including its manifestations in language, is a masculine tool of oppression'.

The dilemma is clearly put by Miranda Fricker:

> The socialisation of our emotional faculty therefore produces an interdependence between what the cognitivist views as the separate components of sensation and judgement comprising an emotion, and this interdependence allows us, indeed obliges us, to theorise emotions not dissected but whole. But by the same token it also opens up difficult questions about the 'freedom' of our emotions. How far have feminists been right to lay their trust in emotions – reason being suspect as a possible tool of oppression – if like reason, those very emotions are produced and interpreted in the terms of the patriarchy? This question becomes all the more vexed if we consider that emotions are inextricably linked to beliefs, beliefs which presuppose linguistic concepts and rational structures. This being so, perhaps emotions are as deeply entrenched in patriarchal conceptual organisation as are the reasoning processes which structure belief.
>
> (1991: 16)

I return to this important question at the end of section 2.

1.2 Exclusion: gender stereotypes and emotion

The second theme from previous chapters which is picked up in this one is the way that exclusions – acceptance and rejection – shape self-identity. In order to discuss it further, I shall introduce the word 'stereotype' here. One effect of exclusion is to stereotype the excluded groups. In the case of women one of those stereotypes is woman as embodied and emotional.

I introduce the word 'stereotype' with some caution because it is subject to misunderstanding on two counts both related to believing a stereotype true. First, a stereotype is not believed by everyone – but since it is recognised by everyone, it is powerful even for disbelievers. For instance, everyone in Britain understands mother-in-law jokes and knows about wicked stepmothers, whether or not they believe the relevant stereotypes. What mother-in-law or stepmother can entirely escape them? What son- or daughter-in-law or step-child has been able to ignore them entirely? To pick another stereotype, what schoolgirl has not feared identification with the stereotypes of 'slag' or 'drag'?[1] Second, when a stereotype is believed to be true, counter-evidence makes little impact. Thus it is more than the series of associations which come with any word. It is an ossified version of those associations, resistant to amendment in the face of counter-evidence. So a stereotype is still held to be true, no matter what is believed about individual women and men, and whatever individuals believe about women and men in general (Haste, 1986; Haste and Baddeley, 1991).

In social psychology, stereotypes have been characterised as a subset of the general cognitive process of classifying and categorising features of the world presented to the agent. Human beings employ categorisations to introduce order into the chaos and confusion of the world as it presents itself. Some of the categorisations harden into stereotypes. This process is helped by the fact that most stereotypes are ambivalent and that many stereotypes held by members of a stereotyped group hardly differ from those outside it. One stereotype of woman is that she is more emotional than man. This is an ambivalent stereotype: it is not all bad to be emotional. It is also a stereotype held by many women. I discuss the truth of the stereotype later in the chapter, at the end of section 2.3.

It is possible to isolate the main factors in the process of categorisations which have this effect. These factors are the 'primacy effect', the perseverance of belief, and the search for confirming rather than disconfirming evidence for theories and schemas. Nisbett and Ross say:

> The primacy effect refers to the way early encountered information serves as the raw material for inferences about what the object is like. . . . Theories about the nature of the object are revised insufficiently in response to discrepancies in the later-presented information.
>
> (1980: 172)

The 'perseverance of belief' and the 'search for confirming rather than disconfirming evidence' are self-explanatory. People tend to hold on to beliefs, even if they have been given good reason to discard them. They do so, in part, by recognising the relevance of confirming cases more easily than that of disconfirming ones. Even when disconfirming cases are noticed more (since surprising events attract attention) the confirmatory ones are more likely to be retrieved from memory.[2]

Feminists have identified various dualisms in Western thought which map on to stereotypes of femininity and masculinity. They have pointed out that the stereotype of woman is that she is unreasonable, illogical, irrational, intuitive, close to nature, innocent, childlike, emotional, dependent, passive and oriented to the personal and private. This stereotype of woman is very different from that of rational, active, independent, and unemotional man whose sphere of action is in the public world away from family and domesticity.[3]

According to the stereotype, the relationship to the body is very different for the two sexes. Women are in thrall to their bodies. Their lives are interwoven with their reproductive capacities: their face is their fortune and their biology is their destiny. By contrast, male pride in the body is pride in control and performance. Men may even view their bodies as highly efficient, 'well-tuned' machines. An example of this male view of the self is shown by another source of male pride, sexual prowess, a concept which depends on sexuality being thought of in terms of the performance of feats of strength and endurance. In short, women are 'in tune with', 'in harmony with', 'close to' or 'part of' their bodies; men are in control of them.

The race and class dimensions of the argument should be noticed alongside the gender ones. The stereotype for black people, 'primitives', and the working classes are startlingly similar in relation to emotions and bodies, to those of females, though they also have important differences. In the West there is a long history of both scholarly and popular thinking which claims that black people, so-called 'primitive' people, and the working classes are closer to feelings and nature and are more emotional than white, so-called 'civilised' and middle- or upper-class people.[4]

In the next section I consider how inclusion and exclusion, encompassing their effects seen in stereotypes, contribute to the construction of emotion.

2 EMOTION AND POLITICS

2.1 An explanation of feeling and emotion

Reason and emotion are different – or so says common sense as expressed, for instance, in the assumptions of the media. However, it is now commonplace in analytic philosophy to view the dichotomy between reason and emotion as mistaken. The mainstream view is that emotions are rational, cognitive, and related to logic and understanding. Little emphasis is placed on occurrent feelings and experience, or on consciousness, though some of the mainstream would hold that some affect, or desire, or both, is necessary for an emotion to be properly called an emotion.[5] No sharp division is drawn between emotion and thought, affect and cognitions, emotional feelings and intellect, passion and reason. On the other hand, a sharp distinction is drawn between sensation and emotion, physical and mental, physical laws and socio-psychological laws. The breaking down of the distinction between reason and emotion dichotomy masks a new distinction still related to the body, which considers both reason and emotion of the mind rather than of the body.

The mainstream account of the rationality of emotion rests on a related view about mind and action which emphasises the rationality of persons. A person's actions are taken to be the (rational) result of her beliefs and desires. These beliefs and desires are ascribable over time by third parties who observe the behaviour of the agent and discuss and describe it. The states called 'belief' or 'desire' are not open to immediate introspective knowledge and need not correspond to any internal event or entity at all. When philosophers wanted to rehabilitate emotions as valuable – educable, worthy of attention – they emphasised the rationality of emotions. Emotions were differentiated from non-intentional states like moods and feelings, thought to be more bodily than mental. My own view of emotion goes further than the mainstream account. It questions not only the division between reason and emotion but also that between feelings and reason, so, in the end between bodies and minds. Distinctions can be drawn, but not in the way that is usually thought.

In the mainstream view of emotion, much is made of differences between 'emotions', 'moods' and 'sensations'. However, the clarity of division is illusory. Making such a clear division depends on using a narrow range of examples in which emotions are easily seen to be rational, fitting into the action, belief and desire framework. Further, the mainstream has a need to establish that some feelings (emotions) have intentional objects while others (moods, or sensations) do not.[6] Establishing this depends on drawing on just a few examples of moods and sensations, and ignoring others. Finally, for the mainstream argument to be able to distinguish mental and physical, it needs to establish that sensations and moods have feelings which are occurrent. This distinguishes them from emotions which need not have occurrent feelings.

The preferred examples of emotion for thorough-going cognitivists such as Bedford, Kenny or Solomon are 'fear' or 'anger', rather than 'love' or 'pity'.[7] Fear or anger are easily seen to be rational. They are contrasted with moods and sensations, like cheerfulness and pain. The argument goes as follows. First, emotions, like fear and anger, are rational, whereas moods and sensations, like cheerfulness and pain, are not. Second, the point is made that fear and anger have intentional objects, unlike either cheerfulness or pain. Finally, neither fear nor anger need be accompanied by occurrent feeling. Both emotions may be expressed by avoidance of situations which stir up the feelings. In contrast, it is claimed that cheerfulness and pain are accompanied by occurrent feelings. Interestingly, Oakley (1992), includes love easily in his theory, since he says that feelings and desires are as necessary as cognition for something to count as emotion. He interestingly redefines feelings as including psychic feelings (i.e. not of the body), and focuses on romantic, sexual love rather than other kinds.[8] Thus he is easily able to include affect and desire. He has a lot more problem with care and its relation to emotion. He counts 'concern' as a simple feeling, along with 'longing', 'tenderness', 'concord' and 'exhilaration'.[9]

It is interesting to notice how these arguments about the definition of emotions depend on the examples used. Love is fitted in as an emotion with difficulty by the theorists who emphasise cognition over feeling.[10] Kenny (1963), who thinks that feelings have some importance, includes it among his examples, but only as a motive for altruism.[11] He holds depression to be an emotion rather than a feeling in spite of the fact that 'We are often unaccountably depressed on days when everything seems black' only by arguing that the objects for this emotion are 'the things which seem black' (Kenny, 1963: 61–2). This is unconvincing. 'Everything seems black' is not a description of things, but a way of talking about a kind of backcloth to whatever comes to mind, as is a mood, or a feeling of pain. On the other hand for Oakley, whose account of emotions is one in which desire and feeling is introduced, depression is an emotion because of its effect on desire and its affect, and in spite of its unpredictability. But in that case, what reason could he give for leaving out care, concern, longing and so on from the list of emotions?

'Sensations' present similar problems to 'emotions'. Theorists trying to categorise them have considered a narrow band and, not surprisingly, the complexities of the category are lost. Pains and hungers are described as if they had no context, for instance. But pain and hunger always have a context. Both of them vary with the meaning they have to the individual experiencing them. This conclusion gets support from medical descriptions and psychological research into pain in which there is evidence that pain varies with the meaning it has to the sufferer. The pain of battle wounds, the pain of amputated limbs, the pain of torture or the pain of an injection are not explicable only in terms of physiology – though they are not independent of physiology either (Melzack, 1973). The same is true of hunger. The hunger of famine is not the same as the hunger of anorexia in terms of motivation, behaviour or the conscious experience. Mary Seacole describes her hardships in Central America and the Crimea with humour and pride, as a source of her sense of self-worth as she chose to undergo them, herself (Seacole, 1984). Frederick Douglass describes how different his physical pain became when his determination to be free outweighed his wish to die (see Gilroy, 1993).

Occurrent feelings are no easier to put into water-tight categories. Pains and hungers are described as if it were clear when an experience or feeling is conscious or occurrent. This is a mistake. The boundary between conscious or unconscious feelings is as unclear for bodily feeling as it is for emotional ones. Familiar examples come from vision and hearing, where we can become directly and fully attentive to sights and sounds of which we had been not fully conscious previously, for instance in a 'double-take'. Hunger is more often a disposition to act than a conscious state, and even when it is conscious it is intermittent. Sartre has pointed out how the consciousness of sadness comes and goes according to circumstances unrelated to the reasons for the sadness (1958: 61).

The attempt to provide hard categories for emotions, feelings, moods and sensations is a procrustean exercise. For each of the categories there are serious problems, which are pointed up by the difficulties the various theorists have about individual emotions. Love is taken to be an emotion by nearly everyone who speaks English, and should need no special pleading, whether it is sexual love, love of children or parents, love of friends, love of work, love of wisdom or any other kind. Even the relative inclusivity provided by Oakley's account has its problems as he struggles to include as emotions some states of a person that still fall outside his schema, while eliminating others that seem, on the face of it, not so different. In short, as Amelie Rorty says 'Emotions do not form a natural class. A set of distinctions that has generally haunted the philosophy of mind stands in the way of giving good descriptions of the phenomena' (1988: 104). If emotions are not a natural class, what function do emotion words have? And what is the function of the word 'emotion' itself, if it does not refer to a natural class? In brief, the answer is that emotion words refer to widely recognised patterns of behaviour and action that people want to discuss, explain or simply to mention. Words like 'emotion' or emotional are used for a wider set of patterns and qualities – and get their meaning in opposition to other words like 'rational' or 'bodily'.

The names of individual feelings and emotions are used as an imprecise gesturing at a pattern of internal states, thoughts, reasons/understanding and behaviour.[12] For some named pattern to be called an emotion it is likely to include more than one of these. However, there is little agreement about individual cases. The names need to be imprecise since the patterns named are so many, changing and overlapping. When more precision is wanted, the speaker includes descriptions of what is important or relevant in the situation, and also reports on the content of the thought, on sensations and on both real and imagined behaviour. Which factors enter into a description of a feeling depends on what interest is served by discussing them. For instance a description of anger is very likely to emphasise reasons and actions as central and important, and states may also be mentioned. ('She was angry because. . . . ' 'I saw red.' 'He went icy calm'.) Descriptions of 'pity' or 'being in love' are more likely to emphasise the perception of the situation and the occurrent feelings. A description of pain is more likely to be about internal states, but it may also include a description of the part of the body affected, or of the thoughts which accompanied it. These thoughts may well relate to the reasons for the pain being there at all: illness, bullying, torture, or testing oneself for endurance. In the case of torture, as many reports from Amnesty International make clear, the reasons are an intrinsic part of the pain. In Chapter 2, I described various examples of explanations of feeling which illustrate the points made above, about the relative need for the names of feelings and for description using internal states, thoughts, reasons/understanding and behaviour.

It is possible to make use of words in the language which make fine distinctions between different emotions. Instead of saying 'angry', it is possible to say: 'furious', 'wrathful', 'annoyed', 'cross', 'mad', 'irritated', 'resentful', 'displeased', 'raging', or 'peeved'. None of these on their own will give a complete picture of a particular episode of emotion. The value of emotive language is that it adds to such a description: words like 'hypocritical', 'slimy' or 'jumped-up' describe the emotion of the speaker as she feels about a person, as well as acting as descriptions of character and value-judgements about her.[13] Similarly, strong emotions can be described and expressed in works of art. Picasso was expressing and describing his feelings about politics and women in many of his paintings. Vonnegut's *Slaughterhouse 5* is an expression of horror at the destruction of Dresden. Zameenzad's novel, *My friend Matt and Hena the Whore* expresses complex emotions about war and famine in the Horn of Africa.

I have been discussing the use of emotion words. I now turn to the use of the word 'emotional'. 'Emotional' does not refer to particular states. It is a judgement about actions, reason, perceptions, or internal states which gets its force in its implicit contrast with 'rational'. Fear is an emotion which may be rational. Likewise, swerving a car to avoid an accident, comforting a crying child, kissing someone you love: none of these actions is normally described as emotional. They may be thought to be quite in accordance with rational behaviour. However, each of them is an action which depends on emotion. All of them are likely to involve the experience of occurrent feelings. Conversely, a person who always avoids cliff edges out of an exaggerated fear of heights is exhibiting emotional behaviour without the occurrent experience of fear.

The difference between rational and emotional behaviour is to be found in the word 'exaggerated'. The word is needed to make the avoidance of the edges of cliffs seem emotional rather than rational behaviour. A person who constantly wants to walk too close to cliff edges might also be judged to be acting from emotional reasons such as bravado or suicidal tendencies.

So where did the emotions and feelings – all the named and unnamed but recognisable patterns of human behaviour, in all their variety – come from? How did they come to be as they are for adult human beings? To answer this question I shall consider babies, their bodies, and their social lives as they grow and mature. I shall then go on to discuss a politics of emotion: how far emotions and feelings are constructed politically, and how they may help self-change in a liberating direction.

2.2 Learning about feelings

All human communities seem to have concepts which are very closely related to our general names of feelings, like fear, hostility, surprise and happiness.[14] On the other hand, as I have been saying, emotion names are general and imprecise, and although it is possible to make finer distinctions, precision is achieved in particular cases by re-description. Some feelings appear to be missing altogether in some communities, or to be particular only to one community. We in the English-speaking world do not have the emotion word the Japanese call 'amae', though since it is not hard to explain in English, it is possible that we have the emotion – the pattern. The Japanese use the word 'amae' to express the secure and comfortable feeling of belonging, acceptance, being able to presume on others (Rowe, 1988: 47). It has positive connotations, like its root, which means 'sweet'. We also do not have the emotion word which the Gururumba people of New Guinea call 'being a wild pig'. It is unlikely that we have the emotion either, though we have emotions close enough to it for us to be able to find the Gururumba comprehensible. A person becomes a wild pig when he (typically a young man) has been bitten by a ghost. When a person is in this state he performs acts like looting, shooting arrows at bystanders and running off into the forest. He returns in his normal state, not remembering anything of the 'wild pig' behaviour (Averill, 1979). In Chapter 2, I describe the difficulties I had with the concept of *khejalat* in Iran, and how I tried to match it against the concepts I knew which were somewhat similar.

From the above observations, it seems likely that feeling or emotion words have their origins in something objective but are modified by the understandings of a particular community. An analogy may make this point clearer. Kinship terms, such as 'mother', daughter' and 'aunt', have a basis in biological relationships, and they are not hard to translate in a general and imprecise way. However, finer distinctions and exact translations are more difficult because the significance of various kinship relations, whether biological reactions or not, varies with the structure of the society. In Ghana, no linguistic distinction is made between the words 'step-daughter' and 'daughter'.[15] In Iran, the father's brother is *'amu'*, a different word from the word for the mother's brother, *'dat'*: how then would a translator of an English autobiography into Farsi translate 'uncle' in cases of kinship, let alone when 'Uncle Ron' might be an affectionate name for the neighbour?

If it is right that there is 'an origin in something objective', how does that 'something objective' turn into the particular culture-bound emotion, especially when emotions are felt as spontaneous and real, not as bound by convention? In answer, I can tell a story about babies making sense of their bodies and feelings as they grow up in a society, because the learning process starts with young babies. New-born babies probably cannot have the feelings familiar to adults such as love, anger, sympathy, malice and boredom because these emotions are too complex for babies, dependent as they are on understanding and language beyond the reach of a young baby. However, even very young babies have feelings related to the adult ones, which can be generally recognised by their parents from the reactions which accompany the feelings. At a very early stage, the baby can notice the results of her reactions, and is able to identify some feelings too. (She knows that she is hungry rather than bored or lonely.[16]) Thus perceptions, memory, and learning together combine to enable her to have desires for action. These themselves lead to new feelings and to new judgements. The process is a protracted one. The adult use of emotion words and the adult understanding and expression of feeling is a sophisticated one requiring several levels of learning.

I can tell a more detailed story in terms of one particular emotion to show what I mean. Consider the particular example of anger. It is an emotion with a gender inflection, but not too obviously so. Moreover, it is not named in all cultures. From the time that babies begin to act on the world and notice that it has an effect on them too, they realise that they do not always get what they want. This arouses feelings of frustration and hostility. I use the clumsy phrase 'frustration and hostility' in order to keep vague about the exact feeling, while gesturing in a general direction.

Babies learn to label some of these feelings 'angry'. No doubt quite other feelings also get so labelled. Feelings related to what adults call frustration, hostility, and the like, result in various well-known kinds of behaviour: crying, turning the head away, and throwing the body about. Just as parents both ask and tell a child what she likes and wants, they also both ask and tell her what she feels. The telling is partly deduction. No doubt parents often get it wrong, but they are right often enough for their child to get a general notion of 'angry', probably somewhat confused with incipient ideas of what it is to be upset, tired, bad-tempered and hungry. As in wanting or liking, the child is more often treated as the ultimate authority about her feelings. This is usually, but not always, because parents also try to persuade their children into feelings which are desirable or appropriate. Children learn that there are occasions when they should not be angry, and occasions when it is politic not to show anger even if they feel it. Many girls learn that they should neither be angry nor show anger as much as boys.[17]

I said that there are several levels to the learning process and I have described one of them. I now turn to others. Children and babies also notice the emotions of others. To return to the example of anger, children learn what other people do and how they look when they are angry. Both sexes learn that gender influences ways in which adults typically express their anger. Children of different classes and races will be learning slightly different lessons about all this. All this occurs at the same time as they are learning to identify and act on their own feelings. Sentences like 'She did it because she was angry,' are learnt and accepted. So is 'Don't go and disturb her now. She's very angry.' Through such sentences as these, a child gains a general idea of how other people react in anger. A common response to a person's anger is to attempt to find the reason for it, and then to attempt to find a remedy. Another is to anticipate the result and do something about it. This encourages children to learn that the reasons and results of anger are usually of more consequence than the quality of the feeling. All these lessons include lessons on the proper behaviour and feelings for each gender. Part of learning the reasons for anger is learning what ought to count as reasons for anger. Anger thus begins to get defined more in terms of its reasons and results than its occurrent feelings. The reasons help to define the resulting behaviour. However, the feelings were essential to getting the process started.

Different lessons will be learnt about other emotions and feelings. For instance there are emotions where the quality of occurrent feeling is of more interest than the reasons behind it. They include sexual attraction, personal likes and dislikes, and cases where we feel pity, wonder or horror but can do nothing about it.

There are more sophisticated levels of describing and expressing feelings which children learn as they grow older. Patterns of perception, motivation, and feeling quality are not, and cannot be, exactly matched to the names of feelings. Different languages conceptualise slightly different ones, and it is possible that we all have feelings that we do not succeed in conceptualising at all. However, we are not bound by the language we grow up with and its vocabulary of emotion words. If there is too wide a gap between an expected pattern of sensations, internal states, reasons, thoughts and behaviour and a word which could describe the pattern, then the components of it can be described in explanation and no special word has to be given. This is not easy to do well, although the attempt to do it is a common subject of conversation and literature.

In some languages there is no word which can be used to translate the English 'anger'. Solomon (1978) argues that the language of the Utku people of Canada is one of these. As a British woman, if I were living among them and trying to explain myself, I could not rely on a shared understanding of behaviour patterns related to anger and the feelings that accompany them. I could not give a simple expansion of the phrase 'I am angry'. However I could describe a pattern, noting that it would be necessary to assess whether the listener had the same kind of reactions as myself or, alternatively, had shown an imaginative understanding of a range of other people and their feelings. A shortened version of this process is necessary when talking to people who share one's own language, precisely because of the imprecision of names of feelings.

There are still further levels of learning about feelings and language. When we are puzzled by our own behaviour we can use emotion words to try and increase our self-knowledge and also our self-control. In other words, we ourselves can carry out the persuading and deducing that parents do for young children. For instance, a person may notice that her actions do not cohere with what she remembers feeling. It is then possible to conclude: 'I felt sleepy but I was not', or 'I felt angry with her, but I was not really. I now realise that I was disappointed in myself.' It is difficult to be sure we have got this deduction right, especially when the feeling is one which we would not want to admit, like jealousy or malice. It is even easier to make a mistake if adults have consistently misidentified patterns in the children they are bringing up. If a boy has learned that boys do not feel pleasure at sweetness and softness – are not soppy – then he is likely to make mistakes about his reactions to young animals or soft toys. It is also easy to make mistakes when an emotion is unfamiliar. As so many films and songs testify, young adults make mistakes about sexual feelings.

This account of learning to describe and refer to feelings is one in which the learning is a long drawn out process, involving several levels of sophistication. It is a possible story which is consistent with the complexities of adult language and understanding. It is also consistent with the possibility of broadly understanding the feelings of other people across cultures, ages and historical time, even though the feelings are altered and vary in detail.

2.3 A politics of emotion

At every stage of the account of how emotions come to be felt and understood there was an emphasis on the importance of the contexts in which individuals come to understand their own behaviour and patterns of response. Many of these contexts are those in which political structures like gender are important. As I explained in Chapter 5, in connection with the construction of self-identity in general, contexts are provided by small-scale face-to-face groups and by larger groups which include 'invisible colleges' and the political structures of gender in a particular society. In this section I focus further on ways in which feelings and emotions will vary according to politically relevant factors. I will look at feelings and emotions which are named in a particular culture; which are thought appropriate for those within a culture; which are thought more appropriate or likely for certain groups; and which are more likely for certain groups.

I have already given examples of feelings which are not named in English. It is important to note that such differences also exist within the subcultures of what is often taken to be a single culture. Thus the feelings which are named in the culture depend on which particular subculture is considered. In Chapter 2 I discussed the German word *gemutlich* which names a particular feeling which is not named directly in English. Although 'the West' includes both Germany and Britain, the 'subcultures' marked by the English and German tongues name different feelings. I found the same is true for the USA, another country of the West, as I explained in Chapter 2. For the obvious reason that males and females talk the same tongue, gender differences in the *names* used for feelings are not so marked as differences related to race, nationality or even social class where dialect plays a part.

Within any particular culture, or subculture, some feelings and emotions are thought appropriate while others are recognised but incur disapproval. There are differences between nationalities. In Chapter 2, I discussed the concept of *khejalat*. In Britain a tendency to feel shy or ashamed is tolerated in little girls and boys but it is considered to be something to grow out of, apart from the relatively few occasions where modesty is called for.[18] This was not the case in Iran for girls, as far as I understood it. There are also differences between social groups within a culture. This is more complex, and I turn to it next.

Some feelings and emotions are thought appropriate or likely for those within a culture only if they are members of certain social groups. Many of these groups are politically structured. Thus some feelings are thought particularly appropriate in girls or in boys, but not in both. Earlier, I remarked on the gender differences related to feeling anger and feeling soppy. In Chapter 2, I described my efforts to feel the proper things I thought that girls should feel. Complexity arises because it is important to know just who is assessing the appropriateness. There is the official line and there are the different views of the members of subgroups. Consider, for instance, being macho and the feelings associated with it. It is a useful example because it is so clear that approval and disapproval for its different manifestations are inflected by class, culture and gender. As bell hooks explains, for someone moving between social groups (in her case between black, working-class and white, middle-class, academic groups in the USA) there is a continual requirement to adjust to different views of appropriateness.

Finally there are some feelings and emotions which are more likely to arise within particular social groups than within others. Few white women have felt the terror of racial violence experienced by so many of the British Bengali women, even more fearful of leaving their own homes than of staying in them (Mitter, 1986). In Chapter 2, I described the feelings related to being a visible minority in the street, something I hardly ever now experience in the normal course of my life. Brodsky describes growing up in communist Leningrad, continually trying to out-smart the system; bell hooks describes her reactions to being taught by a professor who subjected his students to racist and sexist jokes; and Carolyn Steedman describes watching her mother having to cope with the health visitor looking down at her on account of her poverty. All of these are experiences peculiar to those who are in some way marginalised.

The conditions I have described for the construction of emotion and feeling explain why it is useful to speak of 'a politics of emotion'. The phrase refers to two aspects of politics. First, political structures are, inextricably, part of all aspects of our emotions: internal states, thoughts, reasons and behaviour. Second, the fact that emotions are political in the first sense, can be used with political intention to understand and change situations which need changing.

This first sense of 'politics of emotion' has been the focus of the argument so far. Since individuals come to have, express and understand their feelings through a process which is mediated by political structures, the emotions themselves are different for groups differentiated politically. There is a similarity here with the politics of identity. Each individual creates an identity for herself constrained by, but not determined by, politics. Similarly the feelings of an individual are constrained, not determined, by political structures.

The second sense of 'politics of emotion' needs more explanation. Emotions are spontaneous and can surprise the person who feels them. However they are not reflexes and can change as a result of new understandings. They can also be used. If people feeling similar things get together, they can work for political change, including for changes in how they feel. The process is a complex one because both the construction of an emotion and its political effect come about in language communities and political communities which are overlapping. This complex overlapping produces all the complications of fragmentation which were discussed in Chapters 2, 3, and 4. It also contributes to the possibility of mutual understanding and political alliance, as I argued in Chapter 4, section 3. That there is this second sense of politics is the answer to the dilemma of trusting emotion. The dilemma is allied to the dilemma in Chapter 4 which was also solved by the application of the methodological principles of Chapter 4, of a continual process of critical reflection on experience.

The ways in which a politics of emotion, in the second sense, can be created are followed up in the rest of the book, particularly in the next chapter, where I consider self-esteem and self-creation. An example of the second sense is provided by the stereotype of woman as emotional which was remarked earlier, in section 1.2. The stereotype of woman as emotional provides an interesting example because it so clearly shows both the political construction of particular states of emotions and also how such constructions can be used politically. As I pointed out earlier, there is an ambivalence about the stereotype of woman as more emotional than man. It is not all bad to be emotional. It is not good (at least in the eyes of most women) for anyone, men or women, to be quite unemotional. As girls grow up they need to deal with this stereotype. Many of them learn it and take it to themselves, though there are some who tough it out. (Either way they deal with it; it is not possible to ignore it.) So it is neither surprising that the stereotype is held by many women, nor that many women are emotional. They have learnt to be so.

The stereotype has implications for feminist politics. In Chapter 5, I discussed the various political implications of views about female difference. They have been greatly influenced by this emphasis on emotion. Between them, they demonstrate many ways of starting with women as we have constructed ourselves, and going on to re-understand and re-work our changing responses to how we find ourselves to be. Among the radical feminists, Daly (1979, 1984) and Griffin (1982) both engaged in a re-valuation of emotion. Another result of this self-construction is women's (and feminist) trust of emotions over reason which I mentioned earlier. Celebrating women's expressions of emotion is one consequence. Anne Seller describes how the fence at Greenham became the focus of emotion: it was decorated, encircled, painted, climbed, cut and pulled down. Madhu Bhushan (1989) describes political action in India that relies on traditional forms of women's emotional expression in order to bring about change in the conditions of life for women.

At the same time, the manner in which women are constructed as being emotional has itself been the object of reflection. Part of this has been the considerable literature which explodes the myth that men are not emotional. Critiques of masculinity indict it as being characterised by anger, violence and rape, that is, as dangerously emotional. Another critique has focused on the male use of women as the emotional Other. These critiques lead to the many analyses which argue against there being a dichotomy between emotion and reason.

The dilemma of whether to trust emotion is seen to have a more complex answer than whether to give way to impulses and ignore the promptings of reason. Rather, reflection on the gender inflections in emotion – including the tendency to trust it – leads to a politics which is based to some extent on having similar feelings and which relies on the possibility of change in those feelings.

3 A POLITICS OF RATIONALITY

I have established a politics of emotions in two senses. As a corollary there is a politics of rationality.

Philosophical explanations of rationality tend to fall into one of two groups. One of these groups pays particular attention to action, motivation and the explanation of conduct. This group tends to come up with explanations in terms of means and ends. Roughly, for this view, an action is rational if, given the beliefs of the agent, it fulfils her intentions, desires and projects. The rationality of an agent is expressed in the calculation of means to ends. The rationality of beliefs depends on how they are caused by her actions in the world. The other group is more interested in belief, logic, argument and language than in action. At its simplest, this view has a criterion of rationality which is little more than logical consistency: it is not rational to believe both p and not-p. In the analytical tradition, the understanding of rationality in this second group is described as coherence of beliefs in a community sharing a common language. In this view, it is logically impossible for anyone outside the community to assess the rationality of its members' beliefs.[19] In the traditions of Continental Europe, discussions about rationality are centred on the structure of language and the construction of arguments and stories. Lacan and Irigaray are examples of those who pursue this track.[20]

In my view, an adequate account of rationality combines both positions. In what follows I outline an account which is in two stages, corresponding to the two groups. The second stage is a development of the first. The first stage deals with what I call 'animal rationality', because it is something which is possessed not only by human beings but by other animals as well. The second stage, which develops from the first, deals with what I call 'language-dependent rationality', and is confined to human beings as the only animal with language. Taken together, the two stages form an account which explains why judgements of rationality are systematically gender-biased.

Animal rationality is closely related to definitions in terms of means and ends. It is the ability to perceive and understand situations and to deal with them accordingly. While it is not necessary to be a language user to exercise animal rationality, language helps. Reflecting on a situation, considering it and deciding what to do, are all made easier by the use of symbols.[21] A very simple action may involve the straightforward taking of a means to an end. The exercising of a choice necessarily means that the individual agent has feelings and preferences about the situation and is using some assumptions about salience, and causality.[22] For instance, if a person is hungry, she goes and finds food to eat. That is, she views some features of a situation as salient (e.g. hunger), uses the category of cause in the understanding of experience (e.g. 'food removes hunger'), and acts accordingly. In less simple cases, such as creating a friendship, the effect of the action alters the situation before the end is accomplished. Ends and means may both change as a result of feedback during the action. In the case of creating a friendship, the exact end in view could not be clear from the beginning, nor could the means to achieve it. Each friendship is different and needs to evolve from the circumstances of the relationship.[23]

The concept of animal rationality is too general to capture the richness of human rationality. The use of language produces different rationalities. I call the second-stage development of animal rationality, 'language-dependent rationality'. In order to understand language-dependent rationality it is first necessary to consider *ascriptions* of rationality. Since perceptions and understandings of a situation vary, and so do purposes within it, rational beings are likely to reach a variety of conclusions about any given situation. To reconsider a previous example. A hungry person may *not* go and find food to eat. Her reasons may be found in her desires and feelings. For instance she may be dieting, busy, observing a religious fast, looking forward to having a meal out later, or all of these together. The reasons may be found in her perceptions of the situation. She may believe any food available is unpalatable or bad for her. She may believe there to be no food available. In general, the exercising of rationality means that the individual agent has feelings and preferences about the situation. These may be various and conflicting. It will be impossible for anyone else to tell if the action of finding food is rational unless these factors are known. In general, *ascribing rationality* as opposed to just *being rational* depends on having some understanding of the understandings, perceptions and purposes of others, and on having some understanding of the complexity of their preferences. These are not necessarily prioritised, as models based on unity of consciousness seem to assume.[24]

The ascription of rationality presupposes an understanding about what the significant features of a situation are and the ways it ought to be dealt with. Therefore, an observer needs to know the agent's feelings and perceptions about a situation. For human beings, an important way of communicating this information is through language.

Communication allows room for some agents to persuade others to alter their perceptions and understanding or to be persuaded themselves to do so. Any group of language users will be likely to reach some agreement about appropriate perceptions and proper understanding, for instance about when fasting or eating are thought the proper response to hunger. Agreement about what is rational depends on agreement about the relevance of perceptions and about ways in which situations should be dealt with. Thus the criteria for rationality depend fundamentally on agreement about understanding of a situation, and the perceptions and desires the agents have about it. Since there is agreement, the rationality underlying the ways that an agent acts is dependent on the communities of language users of which she is a part. These rationalities I call 'language-dependent rationality'.

I have used terms like 'an agent' or 'language community', but it is clear that the judgements I have been referring to are ones that would vary between different social groups just as emotions do. Anyone who has become influenced by a new set of ideas will have become sharply and often uncomfortably aware of shifts which come about as a new set of perceptions and understandings are accepted. Feminists, for instance, are familiar with them. In Chapter 2, I draw attention to some of the tensions I felt, and how my own perceptions changed as I came to see myself as feminist. Marge Piercy describes a similar experience in her poem, 'In the men's rooms'. So does Yasmin Alibhai in her article about her reactions to the Rushdie affair.

It is now clear that there is a politics of rationality, in two senses related closely to the two senses of the politics of emotion. In the first sense political structures are inextricably part of what judgements are made about rationality. For instance, women are thought to be 'less rational' because of judgements which are validated by one sector of the community dominated by males. In the second sense, understanding the political underpinning of rationality, and its basis in a common animal rationality and ability to use language, leads to the possibilities of change both in ascriptions of rationality and in what is counted as rational. I take this up again in Chapter 8, section 4.3, where I discuss the ways that different judgements are validated by a new community and got into circulation.

7 Emotions of the self
Self-esteem and self-creation*

In the last chapter various emotions were discussed and it was shown how an apparent paradox involved in finding a politics of emotion and rationality had been resolved. In this chapter I look particularly at emotions related to the self, in the cases of self-esteem and self-creation. They are examples of the resolution of the paradox: for each case I show how it is possible to generate a politics of emotion in both the senses that were distinguished in the last chapter.

I look at self-esteem as an example of an emotion of the self which is of great interest to women. At the start of Chapter 5 I pointed out that an early and continuing issue for women has been concern with feelings of inadequacy or a lack of self-confidence. I take up this theme as I describe how self-esteem appears in mainstream theory, going on to make comparisons with an explanation derived from the theory of self-identity in Chapter 5. In conclusion I draw out some of the implications for feminist political priorities and actions.

Second, I look more generally at the emotions which surround the creation or construction of a self, showing how the politics of emotion has affected mainstream accounts of self-creation, distorting the account and making them inhospitable to women and other marginalised groups. I derive a different account using the theory of self-identity in Chapter 5 and point to some of the conclusions about political priorities and actions which are followed up in Chapter 8.

Political implications can be longer or shorter term; they can be related to what it is possible to do tomorrow and next year, or they can be related to what might be done during the next couple of decades or even further into the future. The political implications I draw for self-esteem are relatively short term, after an argument that focuses on relatively concrete issues. In contrast, the political implications I draw for self-creation are relatively long term, after an argument that is more abstract.

* In this chapter I draw on the following auto/biographies and poems from the annotated bibliography in Chapter 3: Yasmin Alibhai, Robert Cole, Frederick Douglass (in Gilroy, 1993), Frantz Fanon, Margaret Garner (in Gilroy, 1993), Satu Hassi, bell hooks, Sally Morgan, Grace Nichols, Marge Piercy, Mary Seacole, Anne Seller and Patricia Williams.

1 SELF-ESTEEM

1.1 Achievement and 'mastery' (Nozick, Rawls and humanistic psychology)

Nozick and Rawls both discuss self-esteem as part of a more general investigation of political philosophy. Both philosophers write within the tradition of liberalism, a tradition which is hospitable to the notion of 'self-esteem', since, for liberals, individuals derive their motivations and satisfactions from themselves, rather than from, say, their given roles in the society. For both philosophers, the idea of self-esteem is entirely bound up with achievement.

Nozick takes self-esteem to be derived from achievement, in the context of competition 'People generally judge themselves by how they fall along the most important dimensions in which they differ from others' (1974: 243). He argues that increases in the numbers of people with high self-esteem could only come about from a fragmented society which had a variety of dimensions. In such a society there are more winners. However, he argues that as soon as such a society loses fragmentation, greater agreement about goals will lead inevitably to a general decrease in self-esteem as more people are clustered along a single dimension and there are fewer winners.

Self-esteem depends on achievement for Rawls, too.[1] To use his own term, he is discussing 'mastery'. He equates self-respect with self-esteem:

> It is clearly rational for men to secure their self-respect. A sense of their own worth is necessary if they are to pursue their conception of the good with zest and to delight in its fulfilment.... Self-contempt leads to contempt of others and threatens their goods as much as envy does. Self-respect is reciprocally self-supporting.... Persons express their respect for one another in the very constitution of their society. In this way they insure their self-esteem as it is rational for them to do.
>
> (1971: 178–9)

Indeed he regards self-esteem as 'perhaps the most important primary good' (1972: 396). The connection with mastery and achievement is made explicit:

> One who is confident in himself is not grudging in the appreciation of others.... They call upon their educated endowments and arouse in each a sense of mastery, and they fit together into one scheme of activity that all can appreciate and enjoy.
>
> (1971: 441)

Rawls has a more optimistic view than Nozick about the possibilities of increasing self-esteem. He says that any well-ordered society will include a variety of communities and associations in which achievement and mastery can be exercised, and which may respect each other. He comments:

> To be sure, men have varying capacities and abilities, and what seems interesting and challenging to some will not seem so to others. Yet in a well-ordered society anyway, there are a variety of communities and associations, and the members of each have their own ideals appropriately matched to their aspirations and talents. Judged by the doctrine of perfectionism, the activities of many groups may not display a high degree of excellence. But no matter. What counts is that the internal life of these associations is suitably adjusted to the abilities and wants of those belonging to them, and provides a secure basis for their sense of worth of their members. The absolute level of achievement, even if it could be defined is irrelevant.
>
> (1972: 441–2)

Another influential school of thought about self-esteem is humanistic psychology which is strongly indebted to the work of Carl Rogers. This school of thought derives from the Romantic rather than the liberal strain in Western individualist thought. It, too, has a concern with achievement, but from a different perspective. Rogers places emphasis both on the giving of 'unconditional regard' to individuals so that they may set their own goals in life, and also on the role that individual empathy plays in the process. Here the focus is still on achievement in the sense that the focus remains on what a person can *do* – although in this case the goals individuals achieve are their own, set by themselves. Individuals need to have enough self-esteem (Rogers prefers to speak of 'self-concept') to allow them to strive for achievement. Thus the relation between self-esteem and achievement is that achievement depends on self-esteem rather than the other way about. Rogers approvingly quotes the following teacher's description of an 'experiment' using his methods:

> I firmly believe that the gifted children were the ones who benefited most from this program. . . . Their achievement was amazing to me.
>
> I found that the children who had the most difficulty learning also made great progress. . . . It seems to me that when their self-concept changed . . . these slow learners became fast learners. Success built upon success.
>
> (1983: 52)

Later, commenting on another teacher's adoption of his methods, Rogers says:

> For a mathematician to be striving toward the establishment of love and trust as the basic elements in his classroom is so 'far out' as to be almost unbelievable. Yet a human climate fosters learning in mathemat-

ics, in philosophical issues such as concerned his seminar, in 'hard' sciences, as well as in psychology and the humanities.

(1983: 104)

1.2 Self-identity and self-esteem

There has been an enormous amount of interest in investigating self-esteem empirically. Individualist theories like those of Nozick, Rawls and Rogers have been used to explain the empirical data that have been collected about self-esteem.

Much of the research has concentrated on investigating the relationship between self-esteem and other factors. A puzzling pattern emerges from this research. Why is it that girls, black people, disabled people, members of the working class – all of those I described in Chapter 2 and Chapter 3 as marginal – have less self-esteem in comparison to boys, whites, able-bodied people and those who come from the middle-class?[2]

The standard answers to this puzzle all depend on explanation in terms of achievement. They fall into categories, of which there are two main ones. In the *first category*, the answer is that low self-esteem is caused by low achievement so it is necessary to work on the achievements. There are two versions of this first category. In one version, low achievement on the part of these groups is the result of institutional sexism, racism, homophobia or class prejudice, of the kind which reduces the chances of certain groups gaining competencies. The other version of the first category is strongly reminiscent of Rawls's 'variety of communities and associations', and Nozick's fragmented society: different groups have different aspirations which are not acknowledged as achievement, or rewarded by society. In the *second category* of answers, low self-esteem causes low achievement and so it is necessary to work on the self-esteem. Low achievement on the part of various out groups is to be explained by their low self-esteem, which, in turn, is to be explained by their personal problems, which are themselves the result of the unfortunate circumstances of their lives.

There is a *third* possibility – that achievement and self-esteem are both by-products, so to speak, of other factors, including race, gender, and class, which contribute to the creation of a self-identity with a particular self-esteem and set of achievements. It is the argument of this chapter that the reasons for the puzzling pattern of low self-esteem in those who are 'marginal' are best found by approaching the issue of self-esteem through the theory of self-identity which was developed in Chapter 5.

There are two themes in the theory of self-identity which are particularly important for understanding self-esteem. They are: (1) social relationships; and (2) authenticity. These themes signal the way the theory explained in Chapter 5 is different from other mainstream strands of theory about self-esteem. I consider them each in turn, in relation to achievement.

1.2.1 Social relationships of belonging and achievement

In Chapter 5, I explained the fundamental importance of social relationships for the creation of self-identity. It was argued that self-identity is the result of a continuing process of negotiation both over the giving of love and acceptance, and also over the dealing out of resistance and rejection. In the examples given in Chapter 5, belonging (or not) depended on a range of factors, only a few of which were related to achievement. Acceptance came from being one of a family, or a community, being the 'right' sex, class or colour, sharing values, pleasures and attitudes, or being a colleague. Only a few of these are affected by achievements. All of them affect the person's evaluation of him or herself. Being loved or rejected or being in a position to love or reject others affects how lovable a person seems to herself – or how worthy of rejection. Thus the social relationships an individual makes are *both* the source of self-identity, and *also* the source of the evaluation of the self by oneself.

The theory shows that the aim of improving self-esteem by concentrating only on achievement is fundamentally flawed. There is more than one kind of group with which an individual has to interact. There are a number of different ones both within the small scale and within the larger groups identified in Chapter 5, section 4.4. The individual belongs easily to some of them, and is rejected by others. She can try to enter ones where her acceptance is difficult, and she can try to reject others who want to include her. I drew attention to examples of all of these in Chapter 5. The consideration of groups where a person belongs – is loved and accepted – stands on its head the idea that achievement leads to self-esteem. Achievements and attributes are valued because the individual is valued, not the other way around. In so far as achievements are valued and competition exists it is within a context of the person being valued anyway.

People who believe themselves lovable regardless of any particular achievements will be able to value whatever it is that they can do. The logic goes: 'I am loved and valued, therefore what I do is good,' rather than 'What I do is good, therefore I am loved and valued.' This observation relates to the psychoanalytic perspective summarised by Alice Miller which I quoted in Chapter 5, section 4.4, where it was remarked that a child who believes that love is conditional on achievement will be placed in the double-bind situation in which no achievement can be good enough.

Anyone who has to move out of a group where she belongs in order to join in some other group will be losing self-esteem unless she is easily accepted in the new group. The lucky ones will not be asked to make this choice and will remain comfortably in more than one group. The more obvious the rejection, or the more stringent the conditions of acceptance, the worse the consequences for retaining self-esteem. The power of rejection and what it does to your own self-esteem – regardless of achievement – is expressed with bitterness by those, such as Seller and Fanon, who explain the difficulty of not allowing rejection to have a long-term effect on their self-esteem. Other examples of this were given in Chapter 5, where Alibhai, Hassi, hooks, Seacole and Williams were all mentioned.

1.2.2 Authenticity and achievement

Closely related to the first theme of relationship is the second theme of authenticity. This theme appears as a result of the requirement on a person to adjust her actions and reactions in order to be acceptable in a group. This requirement is often called 'passing'. A focus on trying to pass is a focus on group membership other than on social relationship.

Having to 'pass' means *at the least* playing down aspects of oneself. By 'playing down', I mean acting as if aspects of oneself do not exist, or are utterly irrelevant (see discussion in Chapter 5, section 4.4). Worse, given the exclusionary nature of groups, it may mean going beyond 'playing down'. There may be a further requirement to join in the very actions by which those aspects of oneself were excluded. Typically this means acting as though the aspects left out are causes for shame or ridicule. Consider women joining in the sexist jokes of male-defined groups. There may be even more repercussions. Passing in one group may affect membership of other groups. Indeed it may also mean not truly belonging to any group any more. Half belonging in one may disqualify you from belonging in ones where you originally fitted. Bell hooks describes her changing relations with her own working-class family after she has 'made it' in the academic world. Other examples are to be found in Chapter 5, section 4.4, where Alibhai, Hassi and Piercy were all mentioned. My own experience of this is to be found in Chapter 2, section 7.1.2, where I describe some of my own resolutions to the dilemmas of not quite belonging to more than one group.

The experience of acceptance being conditional, and having to pretend that bits of oneself do not really exist, leads to feeling inauthentic. It becomes necessary to pretend to feelings, attitudes or views – or even a personal history – that you do not have, or to hide those that you do. The pretending and the hiding lead to a feeling of being inauthentic, which has already been briefly described in Chapter 5, section 4.4. There it was noted that while all children – and adults – need to accommodate themselves to the wishes of others some of the time, a requirement to do so all the time leads to what are described as feelings of inauthenticity, or a loss of a real self.

In effect, people in a position where they have to 'pass' or be rejected are asked to make decisions about their own authenticity. They choose which goals to aim for, depending on who they think they are. If the goal requires them to leave part of themselves behind, then in choosing it they choose inauthenticity. If they choose not to try and achieve that goal, they abandon that part of the self that wanted it, and again they choose inauthenticity. At this point feelings can be hidden – to the point of self-deception, as I describe of my teenage self in Chapter 2, section 7.1.2. (I have been describing *subjective feelings* of being inauthentic. I say more about authenticity in Chapter 10.)

It is now possible to see that feelings related to authenticity have a clear relationship with self-esteem. If part of oneself is left outside the circle when one joins a group, that part has been de-valued by the group. Further, if the person has to behave as if ashamed of parts of themselves, or to actively campaign against them, then the person is acting as though she agrees with the group's evaluations. This is dangerous for self-esteem.

Danger can be overcome. There are ways of dealing with the dilemmas posed by difficulties of authenticity which do not damage self-esteem in the long term. But they are very hard. Easier ways are more dangerous. One of the most obvious strategies – and one which looks easy – is to pretend. However, pretending is not as easy as most people think. There is plenty of evidence to show that for many people pretending turns into the 'real thing'. In so far as pretence is impossible, self-esteem must be damaged. Worse, you may be at least half-convinced yourself, while the rest of the group is not. Marge Piercy's poem (see p. 53) is an example of someone fooling only herself about her honorary manhood. Moreover, even if pretence is continued, it too is dangerous in its consequences. The consequences are real enough both in the results of one's own actions and in the reactions of others.

Children at school provide good examples. Sue Lees (1993) describes the difficulties faced by adolescent girls in British schools. There is no way that a girl can express her sexuality, without taking into account the reactions of her peers. These reactions are most obviously expressed in the terms of abuse which follow any girl that steps out of line. She always risks being called a slag – or, if she is Asian, of harming the family *izzat* (honour). A slag is, in origin, a term used to describe a girl who 'sleeps around' or is 'an easy lay'. However, as Lees shows, it is used imprecisely in the extreme: 'A look at the actual usage of "slag" reveals a wide variety of situations or aspects of behaviour to which the term can be applied, many of which are not related to a girl's actual sexual behaviour' (1993: 40).

Lees suggests that the attention is more usefully focused on the *presence* of the category rather than on the criteria by which it is drawn. She argues that the crucial point about the label is it is used as a deterrent to nonconformity, a constantly present threat, which can only be dispelled by 'going steady': 'The term "slag" functions as a pressure on girls to submit to a relationship of dependence on a boy, leading eventually to marriage' (1993: 53).

There are a number of ways of reacting and resisting. Girls can conform, resign themselves to being harassed, or avoid boys altogether (in each case risking having to pretend what they want): they can also resist (again in each case risking having to pretend what they want). Girls resist the label 'slag' by using humour or by fighting. Or they can try subverting it by appropriating it.[3] What they cannot do is behave as if the label does not exist. All of the strategies girls adopt have clear implications for their feelings of self-esteem and authenticity about themselves as sexual beings, or, indeed as girls undefined by heterosexuality.

It is not only girls that suffer from gender demarcations that affect their feelings of authenticity. In Britain, African-Caribbean boys seem to face more problems than their sisters with regard to achievement, self-identity and self-esteem.[4] Their expression of black masculinity constitutes a threat to their being free to be good at school work. David Gilborn provides some evidence of the kinds of decisions about authenticity which have direct consequences for their future self-esteem. In his study of a multi-ethnic school he follows the school careers of two African-Caribbean boys, Wayne and Paul. Both of these boys were thought to be intelligent by the staff, but only Paul passed his exams. Both boys were identified as troublemakers early in their careers at the school. Paul decided to change direction. By the time he took his exams Paul, unlike Wayne, 'did not emphasize his ethnicity through any displays of dress or demeanour, for instance in styles of walking or speech. This undoubtedly avoided further conflict with staff' (Gilborn, 1990: 62). Wayne, like Peter, accepted the need to gain qualifications, but, unlike him, identified his ethnic origin as the single most important factor in his experience at school. Eventually he was expelled before he could take his exams. Each of these young men appears to have made serious compromises with his authenticity as a result of his choices in school. They also must run risks with their self-esteem. Wayne would have found it harder to preserve his evaluation of himself as a clever, capable boy, and Paul as a 'real' black man.

For all I know, both boys were in fact very sophisticated about the choices, and certainly with support they could have managed to be so. Paul could have found other ways of proving his black manhood. Wayne could have found other ways of proving to himself that he was clever. I don't know. Certainly there are children who manage this. In Chapter 5 I talked about politicisation which is a way of becoming sophisticated about such choices and their implications. In Chapter 2, I described some processes of politicisation in my own life (section 7.1.2). Sally Morgan's discovery of her Australian Aboriginal family history (1987), not only explained herself to herself, but also allowed her to take politically based decisions about the course of her life. Grace Nichols' poems in *i is a long memoried woman* (p. 52) is another articulation of the process of politicisation.

The argument of this section goes against the arguments of both Rawls and Nozick. They argue that greater achievement is the key to greater self-esteem. I show that this is too simple a view. Achievement is important, but only if it is understood within a wider context.

I share Rawls's interest in the different groups and communities which make up a society, and in which people can find self-esteem. However it is puzzling that he apparently fails to notice that these groups are more complex than he seems to think. It is even more puzzling that he does not seem to notice that groups stand in political relations to each other. He uses the words 'communities and associations', so possibly he is thinking of face-to-face groups, or of organisations with relatively small numbers, like golf clubs, the freemasons, or sewing circles, though he may be thinking of something larger and more nebulous like 'philosophers' or 'American philosophers'. Once the complexity of groups is noticed, the full extent of their political significance can be seen. It is no accident that sewing circles are not a source of influence in the same way that golf clubs or the Masons are.

My position is closer to the Rogerian one that self-esteem is enhanced by unconditional positive regard. However, my position diverges from the Rogerian one when wider social groupings are considered. I have argued, against the Rogerian model, that political groupings are at least as important as unconditional regard on a one-to-one personal basis. Rogers' intensely personal theory only considers one-to-one educative relationships. However, I have argued that self-identity is created and constituted by social groups personally unknown to the individual. Self-esteem is dependent on this part of self-identity as well as on the parts formed through individual contact.

1.3 The politics of self-esteem

In Chapter 6, section 2.3, I identified two senses in which emotions are political. In the first sense, political structures are inextricably part of all aspects of our emotions: internal states, thoughts, reasons, behaviour. Self-esteem is political in this first sense, because the individual's history of emotions of love and resistance helps to explain the origins of her self-esteem. These emotions of love and resistance will have been affected by her gender (which itself varies according to race, class, age, sexuality and nationality) as I argued in the previous section where I showed how the emotion of self-esteem is constructed.

The politics of the construction of any individual's own self-esteem are not easily seen by the individual herself. The politics arise from a lifetime's patterns of exclusion and inclusion and reactions to exclusions and inclusions. The political factors underlying some of the reactions and choices are only dimly felt. Moreover, once choices have been made, they become more or less invisible, especially to the dominant groups. They have no need to notice those whom they have excluded except in so far as to make sure that they remain on the outside. Thus, for the included, patterns become set and any pretences that were necessary become self-fulfilling.

We are now in a position to see why self-esteem is for the masters. We can further see why it is harder for those masters to notice factors unconnected with achievement in the construction of any individual's self-esteem.

It is more likely that the masters have a high self-esteem. They are included in rather than excluded from groups where they desire to be: the power to exclude others is itself characteristic of being in the master's position. Thus they have had to make fewer compromises, and their self-esteem has not been risked by such compromises. Exercising the power to exclude is crucial. Insiders are likely to remain as insiders through the perpetration of, or at best through collusion in, systems of harassment and bullying. There are a number of well-known reactions to finding oneself part of such a system. There are those who enthusiastically endorse it, taking for granted the use of pain and embarrassment in order to keep their group exclusive. In an astonishingly open article, Nicolson gives some insight into how the English class system works, based on minute observation of newcomers and relentless ridicule and condescension of those people whom old Etonians would consider were not of the right sort in social class terms (Nicolson, 1993). There are other ways of dealing with the self-knowledge of means of exclusion. In the next section I describe Rorty's self-reflections on 'temptations to be cruel' in the pursuit of self-creation.

What of those insiders who do not want to be part of systems of violent exclusion such as harassment and bullying? There is no doubt that there are plenty of people who collude through fear, rather than conviction or enjoyment. They are right to be fearful. Think of those with the bodies and background to be masters, but who do not collude or perpetrate the systems. They do not do well. They are known as poofters, wimps, lefties and Paki-lovers; hen-pecked and chicken. Since this is the case, then those who have joined in out of fear will have made compromises which endanger their self-esteem. They are already in a position to listen to those who have made greater compromises or who have been excluded altogether.

It is now easy to see why it is harder for the masters to notice factors unconnected with achievement in the construction of any individual's self-esteem. Once safely in a group, with outsiders excluded, of course it does indeed appear as if achievements lead to esteem. The bosses only have experience of being in groups where they belong for other reasons, and no experience of 'passing'. So achievement then becomes the differentiating factor.

I have arrived at an example of a resolution to the dilemma posed at the beginning of Chapter 6. Self-esteem is political in the first sense in that it is constructed, in part, by political categories like gender. However, it can be political in the second sense, too. That is, both it and the emotion surrounding it can be used with political intention to understand and change bad situations, including aspects of an individual's own self-esteem. The resolution to the dilemma comes from taking note of two feelings: self-esteem and a feeling that something is amiss with one's own self-esteem. Trusting this combination of feeling leaves space for the issue to be noted. It is at this point that the second sense of 'political' becomes significant.

There are two ways in which self-esteem can be political in the second sense. In the first place, just being aware of the political influence is already empowering. Further, as the phenomenon is understood, the emotions will themselves change (for instance, self-esteem may rise).[5] Even children can be helped, as part of the policy of a family, a school or a community, to understand the power of collectivity in the creation of their own identities, and the extent of their own power to choose how far to identify with any particular group. It is a process which can start in the nursery, since it is clear that children not only identify themselves in gender and race terms at an early age, but do so in individual ways. In Chapter 2, section 7.1.2, I described some small children working this out for themselves. Cole's (1960) descriptions of himself growing up in Freetown in West Africa show him working out his own class, religion and tribe, in relation to his neighbours and school mates who reflected all the complexity and pluralism of Freetown. Significantly, he is equally concerned to place himself as black rather than white, growing up as he is in a colonised country. In more recent times, Patricia Williams (1993) tells chilling stories of how she was placed by others as black when she was growing up in the USA. She tells these stories in the context of her own successful resolutions of such attempts to undermine her. None of these children is conditioned by their identifications, but all of them have worked out individual responses to it.[6]

Beyond just *noticing* the political, there is a range of practical political implications. These are specific to particular situations, as is usual with practical politics. Any practical politics must always be embedded in particular contexts and histories of actions. One example which is from education, but which has wider implications, is the question of dealing with sexist and racist abuse in secondary schools.[7] These incidents may be dealt with through equal opportunities policies or through policies on bullying. Either way, it is important that the school notices that the difference between personal insults and sexist abuse is a serious one. Both are wrong because they demonstrate a lack of respect for other people and hurt them. However, sexist graffiti or name-calling are also objectionable because of the difference they can make to whole sections of the school community and their ability to be themselves. In particular they may affect the choices that groups of children make about the curriculum, and about behaviour in class. The effect goes beyond the victim and his or her friends and enemies. The behaviour of all children who identify with the target of the insult – or who fear they might – are affected by the name-calling.

Secondary schools are a specific example. They point to another area for political organisation, which is related to the difference between individual bullying and racist or sexist attacks. There is a continuing debate in Britain about the issue of specific policy guidelines and laws related to sexist and racist attacks. The implication to be drawn from the argument of this book is that racist and sexist abuse of all kinds is of a different order of seriousness to other abuse. Think of the Bengali women I mentioned in Chapter 6. Think of the gender inflection of domestic violence and its particular relation to cultures of masculinity or femininity in different races and classes. The political implication here is the higher priority that should be given to eliminating sexist and racist abuse and violence compared to individual violence, even though both are wrong. The emphasis given by women writers to male violence and by the ethnic minority press to racial attacks is wholly justified.

2 SELF-CREATION AND EMOTIONS

I have been looking at a particular emotion of the self, self-esteem. I now turn to examine a set of emotions associated with a particular perspective on the self. I show how the set of emotions which surround the creation of a self (or its construction or discovery) are as political as the emotion of self-esteem. As with self-esteem, I show how the theory of self-identity developed in Chapter 5 offers a challenge to mainstream philosophical arguments about self-creation. The challenge is made by focusing on the different emotions made central in both accounts. The mainstream accounts of the emotions of self-creation are such that they are positively off-putting, as well as misleading, to those who do not welcome their masculine bias. This has a further significance in the context of developing a feminist theory of the self, since it has implications for the accounts of autonomy and authenticity to be considered in the rest of the book.

It may be useful to recall here that questions of self-creation have been at the heart of the enquiries of this book. These are questions of how women can find themselves, understand their capacity for action, and assert control over their own lives without losing themselves (see Chapter 5, section 2). Thus it is all the more important to understand how these matters have been presented and explained in such a way as to exclude women, and to show how this state of affairs can be put right.

2.1 Cruelty and domination

In the discussion of the construction of self-identity in Chapter 5, emotions such as love and resistance were paramount. In mainstream theories of the construction of self, it is noticeable that more attention is given to another set of emotions – cruelty, humiliation, domination, pride and shame.

Consider a recent example to be found in Rorty's arguments in his book *Contingency, Irony, Solidarity*. Rorty examines what he considers to be a central paradox about self-creation. He claims that those 'in whom the desire for self-creation, for private autonomy, dominates (e.g. Heidegger, and Foucault) still tend to see socialization as Nietzsche did – as antithetical to something deep within us' (Rorty, 1989: xiv). He compares them with others 'in whom the desire for a more just and free human community predominates' and who are 'inclined to see the desire for private perfection as infected with "irrationalism" and "aestheticism" ' (1989: xiv). A central argument of his book is that: 'There is no way to bring self-creation together with justice at the level of theory' (1989: xiv).

The problem he is addressing here is not simply one of theoretical elegance, or of an academic desire for a universal theory. The problem, as he sees it, is that there is a significant, inherent conflict between the two sets of theories. For Rorty, the demands of justice include the imperative to be less cruel and to act on the desire that suffering will be diminished. On the other hand, he holds that: 'our attempts at autonomy ... may make us oblivious to the pain and humiliation we are causing' (Rorty, 1989: 141). Further, he says: 'Tendencies to be cruel [are] inherent in searches for autonomy' (1989: 144). Rorty is somewhat ambiguous about the tendency to be cruel. Sometimes he seems to be presenting the tendency as the result of lack of attention to others, and sometimes as the result of lack of empathy or caring for others. Sometimes he goes much further, talking as if the attempt at self-creation encouraged cruelty, or required it. He talks about 'the temptation to be cruel', and the 'tendencies to cruelty inherent in searches for autonomy' (ibid.) He further argues that Nabokov is to be praised for 'helping us to see the way in which the private pursuit of aesthetic bliss produces cruelty' and, similarly, that Orwell 'helps us get inside cruelty, and thereby helps to articulate the dimly felt connection between art and torture' (1989: 146).

Rorty's view of the conflict between autonomy and justice is derived from his view of self. He develops his view against what he calls the traditional view that human beings have beliefs and desires and that 'there is a core self which can look at, decide among, use, and express itself by means of such beliefs and desires' (1989: 10). Beliefs are criticisable if they fail to correspond to reality and desires are similarly criticisable if they fail to correspond to the essential nature of the human self. This traditional picture of the self is 'divided into the cognitive quest for true belief, the moral quest for right action and the aesthetic quest for beauty' (1989: 142). In contrast, Rorty argues for a self which recognises that it does not *have* beliefs and desires but *is constituted by* them and may, if it is autonomous, create them. He follows Nietzsche in this, stating that: 'the whole idea of "representing reality" by means of language and thus the idea of finding a single context for all human lives, should be abandoned' (1989: 27).

Instead, like poets, we should know ourselves by creating ourselves: 'The process of coming to know oneself ... is identical with the process of inventing a new language – that is, of thinking up some new metaphors. For any literal description of one's individuality ... will necessarily fail' (ibid.).

Rorty goes on to interpret this Nietzschean framework in Freudian terms. He admires Freud for showing the individual and particular roots of human motives, contrasting him with philosophers who would make them more universal:

> Freud shows us why we deplore cruelty in some cases and relish it in others. ... He shows us why our sense of guilt is aroused by certain very specific, and in theory quite minor, events, and not by others which, on any familiar moral theory, would loom much larger. ... Terms like 'infantile' or 'sadistic' or 'obsessional' or 'paranoid,' unlike the names of vices and virtues which we inherit from the Greeks and the Christians, have very specific and very different resonances for each individual who uses them.
>
> (Rorty, 1989: 32)

For Rorty, the importance of this is that the Freudian framework gives us a way of understanding how it might be that each one of us can weave idiosyncratic narratives (case-histories) which amount to individual projects of self-creation. A further importance of Freud's framework is that it shows that the justice perspective is only one possible alternative to a self-creation perspective. The framework itself is morally neutral between these two strategies for dealing with the network of beliefs and desires with which our particular upbringing has landed us. He says:

> Freud stands in awe before the poet, but describes him as infantile. He is bored by the merely moral man, but describes him as mature. ... He does not see the need to erect a theory of human nature which will safeguard the interests of the one or the other.
>
> (Rorty, 1989: 35)

Rorty builds on this last point. He emphasises that the implication of this framework is the absolute split between individuals' ways of coming to understand their situations (what Rorty calls their 'impresses') and the possibility of universal or antecedent realities which they might be expressing or articulating. The most that can be achieved is 'the accidental coincidence of a private obsession with a public need' (1989: 37). He expands on this as follows:

> The difference between genius and fantasy is not the difference between impresses which lock onto the world and those which do not. Rather, it is the difference between idiosyncrasies which just happen to catch on with other people – happen because of the contingencies of some historical situation, some particular need which a given community happens to have at a given time.
>
> (ibid.)

This highly individualised picture results in two double-binds for women. In the first place they are asked to choose between self-creation and the pursuit of justice. In the second they are asked to behave like stereotypical men if they want to achieve self-creation.

The first double-bind is the one which says that there is a choice to be made between self-creation and the risk of cruelty and being unjust. As I have said before, self-creation in the sense of self-discovery and self-understanding (which is Rorty's sense) has been central to the women's movement. However, Rorty's analysis would mean that as women begin the task of self-creation, they would necessarily each behave as badly as those who have prevented them achieving self-creation in the past. Thus the motivation for one project conflicts with the motivation for the other. This is not a coherent political project. So far, Rorty would agree. The incoherence is one he himself points to.

As the analysis proceeds the project goes from being incoherent to becoming actually incomprehensible. The reason for this is that in the highly individualised account that Rorty gives there is no clue why certain groups (such as women, but also including black, poor and disabled people) have suffered more cruelty in the past. Further, his framework makes it impossible to understand how any such group has formulated its own needs. Indeed Rorty would say that they could not have done so. If Rorty's theory is right, it means that it is simply a waste of time to start the project of righting wrongs by finding a voice and a metaphor expressive of the perspective of such groups. Discourses (and poets who are the generators of metaphor and language) come from those who are not suffering. Thus there is no possibility that the oppressed would have a 'voice'. The most that can be done is to persuade the oppressors to stop being oppressive, using empathy rather than reason. This would free the victims, who can then seize the opportunity to seek the private joy of self-creation by becoming poets themselves:

> Victims of cruelty, people who are suffering, do not have much in the way of a language. That is why there is no such thing as the 'voice of the oppressed' or the 'language of the victims.' The language the

victims once used is not working any more, and they are suffering too much to put new words together. So the job of putting their situation into language is going to have to be done for them by somebody else. The liberal novelist, poet, or journalist is good at that. The liberal theorist usually is not.

(Rorty, 1989: 94)

Rorty's position is, I suppose, that the women's movement should disband itself, and wait for liberal men to come to their rescue. This would, surely, be an extraordinary thing to do: the movement has already developed a multiplicity of strong and persuasive voices of its own. They were created and discovered precisely in the process of becoming a set of collectivities. Rorty has no way of explaining such a phenomenon.

The second double-bind concerns the stereotypical images of men and women within Western society. The emotions of cruelty, domination, humiliation, pride and shame are highly gendered, as has been argued by large numbers of feminists, both in the context of pornography and violence and in the context of sexuality. A recent and highly influential example of a well-worked-out analysis is to be found in Benjamin's *The Bonds of Love* (1990). She is particularly useful here, because, like Rorty, she draws heavily on Freudian theory. She also draws on Hegel's allegory of the master and slave, which I come to next.

Benjamin argues that the underlying structure of male domination and female submission is to be found in the way those apparently neutral universal structures of our society, individuality and rationality, are constructed as masculine, and arise out of a desire to evade dependency, and to dominate the Other who might threaten independence. She argues that the infant's struggle against dependency on the mother, which is a struggle to individuate, 'can turn into ideal love of paternal power. This process of defensive idealisation marks the entry into a gendered reality' (1990: 222). Paternal power is constructed as desirable both because it is an escape from dependency and also because the struggle in which it is established lets both partners find recognition. In her chapter called 'Master and slave', Benjamin argues that in sadomasochistic fantasy we 'can discern the "pure culture" of domination' (1990: 52). 'Subjugation takes the form of transgressing against the other's body' (1990: 55), and the submission of masochism is a 'search for recognition through an other who is powerful enough to bestow this recognition' (1990: 56). In this fantasy, both partners are fascinated by the exercise of paternal power: as adults they not only repeat but also work out the conflicts of infancy in their sexual relations. Thus, Benjamin shows, cruelty is constructed as masculine, even though women both can be and are cruel, and men both can be and are submissive.

Rorty's is by no means the only example of an influential theory of self-creation based in cruelty and domination.[8] Hegel's allegory of the master and slave story is another well-known and influential example of the importance of domination in coming to be a self. In this story, Hegel argues that the emergence of self-consciousness arises from a struggle in which the self resolves the difficulty that it both requires another consciousness in which its own being will be acknowledged or recognised, and also requires that it is possible to negate the other to show that it is fettered to no determinate existence:

> Self-consciousness exists in itself and for itself, in that, and by the fact that it exists for another self-consciousness; that is to say, it *is* only by being acknowledged or 'recognized'. . . . the detailed exposition of the notion of this spiritual unity in its duplication will bring before us the process of Recognition.
>
> Self-consciousness has before it another self-consciousness; it has come outside itself. This has a double significance. First it has lost its own self, since it finds itself as an *other* being; secondly, it has thereby sublated that other, for it does not regard the other as essentially real, but sees its own self in the other.
>
> It must cancel this its other.

(Hegel, 1931: 230)

This negation can either be achieved through the death and destruction of the other, or by making it part of oneself, by making it a slave. The result of this is that there is a life and death struggle between the two consciousnesses. The struggles may result in the death of one. A better outcome, which allows both parties to survive and which leaves each with recognition, leaves one in a state of subjection to the other: one has the self-consciousness of the master, the other of the slave.

The outcome is not good either for master or slave. The master is assured both of recognition and of the enjoyment of the fruits of the labour of the slave. However, the master is not independent at all. It is a 'dependent consciousness that he has achieved' (1931: 237). The slave, meanwhile, gains a self-consciousness, but the fear of death which has led to his bondage 'is his chain, from which he could not in the struggle get away, and for that reason he proved himself to be dependent, to have his independence in the shape of thinghood' (1931: 235).

In the long run, the slave's predicament is the better one. In his work, undertaken at the behest of the master, his consciousness comes to itself: 'By serving he cancels in every particular aspect his dependence on and attachment to natural existence, and by his work removes this existence away' (1931: 238). Thus, it is not surprising that Hegel argues that a period of slavery is 'a necessary moment in the education of all men' (1971: 175). Arguing from the examples of Athens and Rome, he says that a period of servile obedience is necessary to the attainment of freedom and rationality.

Paul Gilroy (1993) uses Hegel's allegory of master and slave to examine both gender and race dimensions of 'double consciousness' and emanci-patory politics.[9] Gilroy argues that Hegel's account of master and slave is deeply flawed, and, indeed, misconstrues the process by which oppression is overcome and self-consciousness realised. Gilroy argues that a slave is also able to realise his or her self-consciousness (become a consciousness for itself) by taking freedom by risking death, without enslaving the former master, and without working for him with a 'quaking, isolated will, and the habit of obedience' (Hegel, 1971: 175). In Hegel's scheme, slavery is a condition of modernity: 'It points directly to an approach which sees the intimate association of modernity and slavery as a fundamental conceptual issue' (Gilroy, 1993: 53).

Only through work and servile obedience will the slaves come to rationality, freedom – and modernity. Gilroy grimly quotes Hegel's com-ments on black slaves:

> Want of self-control distinguishes the character of the Negroes. This condition is capable of no development or Culture, and as we see them at this day, such they have always been. The only essential connection between the Negroes and the Europeans is slavery.... We may con-clude slavery to have been the occasion of the increase in human feeling among the Negroes.

> (1993: 41)

Gilroy suggests a way of challenging Hegel's story, using life stories of two slaves to do so. He considers the autobiographies of Frederick Douglass and the story of Margaret Garner. The challenge issued by the lives of Douglass and Garner is the challenge of 'the turn toward death' – the willingness to die and to kill one's children rather than face the horrors of slavery. The stories have a strong gender inflection. Douglass emphasised the importance of violent resistance, and was rebuked for doing so by Sojourner Truth, herself no weak, mild woman. Garner, on the other hand, risked her own judicial death by turning her violence against her own much-loved daughter, saying that her child would never suffer as she had. Gilroy quotes a commentator at the time as saying, 'The faded faces of the Negro Children tell too plainly to what degra-dation female slaves submit. Rather than give her little daughter to that life, she killed it' (1993: 67).

Gilroy poses the question of what we are to make of 'these contrasting forms of violence, one coded as male and outward, and the other, coded as female, somehow internal, channelled towards a parent's most precious and intimate objects of love, pride and desire' (1993: 66).

His answer is that in both cases the stories construct a conception of the slave subject as agent. The self-consciousness is not achieved either through mastery or through slavish obedience to a master. On the con-trary, the slave in both cases refuses to be either slave or master, but, nevertheless, acts in self-consciousness. Thus, Gilroy argues, the stories of

Douglass and Garner offer a completely different perspective on Hegel's story:

> The repeated choice of death rather than bondage articulates a principle of negativity that is opposed to the formal logic and rational calculation characteristic of modern western thinking and expressed in the Hegelian slave's preference for bondage rather than death.
>
> (1993: 68)

Moreover, the self-consciousness that is articulated owes a great deal to African and black cultural forms. This is an assertion of self-consciousness, freedom and agency that is opposed to the freedom and rationality of modernity for which Hegel argues. Gilroy goes on, in the same passage, to explain the ways in which slaves, including those who had risked death and survived, created their own consciousness through black cultural forms, including through autobiography. He comments that Garner had said she would rather go singing to the gallows than be returned to slavery. Douglass joined the tradition of writing a slave narrative. Both forms of expression, comments Gilroy, exemplify how 'The presentation of a public persona becomes a founding motif within the expressive culture of the African diaspora' (1993: 69). This is, as Gilroy argues, a direct challenge to modernist forms of universal reason, in which difference is not recognised, and the personal is subsumed in the universal.

In this section I have been looking at the emotions surrounding self-creation, first considering standard accounts by Rorty and Hegel which emphasise emotions of dominance and cruelty and which leave little space for explaining possibilities of self-creation by those women and men, both black and white, rich and poor, who are not in a dominating position. I have shown why there is a motive to mount a challenge, by showing the double binds which Rorty's view imposes on members of liberation movements. I gave an example of such a challenge to Hegel's story which takes account of gender and race. In the next section I go on to explain how my own theory presents a challenge which draws on Gilroy's analysis, and goes beyond it.

2.2 The politics of emotion and self-creation

My account of self-identity is an account of self-creation: it is an account of the self making itself, but not in conditions of its own choosing. The conditions it faces include the material and the political. In this section I will focus on self-creation as it appears in my account of self-identity, and compare the emotions that appear in it with those that appear in Rorty's and Hegel's accounts.

In the first place I place human relationships at the centre of the account of the construction of self (while emphasising the importance of material factors, in themselves and for what is made of them socially, in language and in relationships). The human relationships I place as central are those of love and resistance, acceptance and rejection. It is clear that the related feelings include the cruelty and domination, pride and humiliation, which are central to the mainstream accounts of Rorty and Hegel. Relations of resistance and rejection build on these feelings. However, my account also includes the emotions of care, sympathy and affiliation, which are needed for the relations of love and belonging. Thus my account starts with a broader view of the raw materials out of which selves can be spun.

In the second place my account is one which implicitly draws public/ private distinctions in quite a different way from either Rorty's or Hegel's. Gender, race and class politics are there at the ground level in the construction of the self. From the earliest interaction any or all of these may be present to the growing person. Rorty, on the other hand, seems to see only persons, who have no gender or race, playing with language. He introduces any of these political concepts only in so far as they produce victims, for whom the more fortunate must create sympathy. Thus for me, but not for Rorty, the public sphere is not separate from the private one of self-creation. The human relationships in which the emotions are worked out are relationships in which gender, race and class are embedded.

Hegel also draws a sharp distinction between the public and private. Feminists have a hard time with Hegel's master–slave account and its use in discussing gender. On the one hand, Hegel makes it quite clear that this is a story taking place in the public arena where women have no place. According to Hegel, women's rightful place is in the private domain of the family. On the other hand, the master–slave story has proved helpful in the analysis of gender relations for many feminist theorists, including Assiter, Lloyd and Benjamin.[10] Similarly, as I have shown, Gilroy shows that it is not about a universal 'man' but about Western – white – men. Still, Hegel himself, like Rorty, discounts gender and race in his account of coming to self-consciousness, drawing the private/public distinction in such a way as to let him assume that he is referring just to individuals constructed in such a way that race and gender are irrelevant to their self-creation. He simply excludes whole races and the female sex.

My account has yet a further difference from the mainstream one. Not only does it take the perspective of groups other than the dominant ones. It also takes note of the fact that the line between the dominant and the dominated is rarely easy to draw. Few people, I have pointed out, fall on either side of this line. The negotiation of various kinds of exclusion and inclusion – of cruelty and love – needs to take this into account.

Thus there is not one set of emotions surrounding self-creation for one group and another set for another group. However, some emotions will be more salient for some groups than for others. It should not be surprising, then, that the emotions which surround self-creation in the stories told by men and women or by whites and blacks are emotions which are themselves highly gendered, even though they are recognisable by other groups too.

Emotions such as love, affiliation, cruelty and domination are themselves emotions which have overtones of gender. They have overtones of the other forms of political domination, too, as Gilroy argues so convincingly. Cruelty and domination are the emotions which are most associated with the male and the overlords – people who are, in the West at least, white and rich. Love and affiliation for the dominant groups are brought about by the exercise of cruelty and domination, as other groups are excluded. The story is different for the Others. Indeed, there are a number of different stories for different Others. This variety is pointed up in the different stories of Margaret Garner and Frederick Douglass. Sojourner Truth disagreed with Frederick Douglass over the use of violence. In a public meeting she responded to his call to violence: 'in her deep peculiar voice, heard all over the hall: "Frederick, is God dead?" ' (quoted in Gilroy, 1993: 64). Gilroy argues that this difference is a 'symptom of important differences in the philosophical and strategic orientations of black men and women' (ibid.). This variety is not recognised in the mainstream. The philosophical account of the construction of self, as seen in both Rorty and Hegel, is an abstraction from the viewpoint of the most dominant groups.

We can now see that Rorty's double-binds have arisen from mistakes. They are the result of seeing narrowly, using blinkers, from the perspective of the master. Justice is not separate from self-creation because it is part of human relationships which are inextricably entangled in that creation. If men are unable to see the falsehood of their felt individuality and singularity, it is because they are in a dominant enough position simply not to notice the social networks of work and care, and indeed, justice, which underpin it. Blinkers were put on horses so that they would not get distracted by all that was going on away from the street ahead. The street, however, depends on the existence of its margins. As Benhabib says:

> Aesthetic modernism has always parasitically depended upon the achievements of modernity in the spheres of law and morality – insofar as the right of the moral person to pursue her sense of the good, be it ever so fractured, incoherent and opaque, has first to be anchored in law and morality before it can become an everyday option for playful selves.
>
> (1992: 16)

Further, all human beings – not just the privileged few – create themselves using particular voices drawn from interactions with their fellow human beings to do so. Blinkers make this harder to see.

In conclusion, I have been drawing attention to how the politics of emotion has affected how self-creation can be viewed. It has been a very similar argument to the one I made for the emotion of self-identity. Of course the empirical evidence is missing. Self-identity is more concrete – so it is possible to collect some evidence empirically, in a way that is not possible for the more abstract self-creation. However, it is possible to see that the mainstream views about self-creation, like those of self-identity, favoured the masters. The views are couched in such a way that women are uncomfortable with the conclusions, and indeed are put in a double-bind where a choice has to be made between self-creation and being a woman, especially a feminist woman. Thus the politics of self-creation are very similar to those for self-identity, if rather more abstract and long term.

Self-creation is political in both senses. In the first sense, reflection on experience using theory points to mistakes in the account, and therefore to an understanding of how gender (and race, class, sexuality, nation) are all implicated in self-creation.

In the second sense, becoming aware of the way that self-creation is not neutral has political implications for actions. Just as with self-identity, simply becoming aware of the political influences on processes of self-creation leads to empowerment. If the construction is seen to be political, then those who have been through the process will understand the power of the collectivity in their own process of self-creation. They will gain an understanding of the blinkers which they had previously disregarded.

There are further practical implications. If selves are constructed and created in communities with others, then a politics is needed which gives space for people to find themselves with others (including in non-Western ways, like Gilroy's cultural assertions). This is a large subject. It forms the main theme of the next chapter, where I discuss autonomy both for individuals and for communities.

8 Autonomy: personal and political*

1 INTRODUCTION

In this chapter I pick up on the notion of self-creation, focusing particularly on the concepts of autonomy and independence. I use the experience of women to investigate the concept of autonomy by looking at how it enters both into gender stereotypes and into mainstream philosophy. Focusing on personal autonomy in the first half of the chapter, and on public autonomy in the second, I consider how autonomy and independence appear in the subjective experience of women and in the way they live their lives, going on to draw implications for politics.

2 GENDER STEREOTYPES, PHILOSOPHERS AND AUTONOMY

In Chapter 7, a connection was made between autonomy, in the sense of self-creation, and the emotions of dominance and cruelty, which are, I pointed out, masculine rather than feminine. These gendered connections between emotion and autonomy were found both in Rorty, and in Hegel's analysis of master and slave as the moment of finding self-consciousness and entering modernity. The philosophies that have made these misleading connections are narrowly masculine ones.

I now turn to consider more generally the questions of the relationship between gender and autonomy. I take a brief look at other philosophies besides those of Hegel and Rorty. I also consider gender stereotypes related to autonomy, just as earlier I considered the gender stereotypes related to reason and emotion. I show that the apparently gender-free notion of autonomy – or so it is usually presented – is in fact, deeply gendered. I argue that this is not true to the lives and experience of women, and that a new understanding of autonomy and its relation to dependence is needed.

I need to say something about the words I am using. 'Autonomy' is a

---

* In this chapter I draw on the following auto/biographies and poems from the annotated bibliography in Chapter 3: Yasmin Alibhai, Nayra Atiya, Joseph Brodsky, Frantz Fanon, Margaret Garner (in Gilroy, 1993), Satu Hassi, bell hooks, Erica Jong, Marialice (in Patai, 1988), Mary Seacole, Anne Seller, Liz Stanley and Patricia Williams.

word that gives some difficulty to non-philosophers, while being central to the vocabulary of philosophers. In this chapter I am taking 'autonomy' to mean much the same as 'independence'. Both terms routinely apply to the self-rule of individuals, of groups, and of states. I shall use the two words interchangeably except where I am discussing theorists who themselves use a tight definition. It is useful to have both words. 'Independence' has the advantage of familiarity. 'Autonomy' has the advantage that it is not so obviously related to 'dependence' – it takes its meaning from the even less-used term 'heteronomy', meaning 'rule by others'. It carries, therefore, the overtones of 'liberation' and 'emancipation' more obviously than 'independence' does.

Autonomy is often thought to be a problem for women. It is asserted that: they haven't got it; they are frightened of it; they are insufficiently separated from their mothers; they are too reliant on the opinion of others; they are encumbered by their families; they are absorbed by caring for their husbands; they are interested in private rather than public matters; and so on and on.[1] In other words, autonomy is often thought to present a problem for women because (1) it is a desirable quality; and (2) women don't have it.

Philosophers have contributed to this stereotyping. Rorty's and Hegel's contributions have already been noted.[2] As well as Hegel's 'master and slave', the Kantian rational autonomous being, Rousseau's *Emile*, and the citizens of the Social Contract are all fathers to the contemporary understanding of the person. This is a legacy which is deeply gendered.

Kant took the exercise of autonomy to be acting rationally in the pursuit of one's own self-chosen goals. This rational action took place in the public sphere, because in order to be the result of mature reason, reason had to be developed in the public space of universal principles. Thus Kant implicitly excluded women from full autonomy, since he apparently assumes that women rather than men deal with the personal, and that this is part of their nature.[3]

Kant is not alone in his views of women. Rousseau, too, explicitly excludes women from his vision of man. This is particularly obvious in *Emile* (1762, 1956), his influential book in which he describes an idealised education for the young boy, Emile, and for his playmate, Sophie. Emile grows up to be rational and self-sufficient, having revelled in the 'enjoyment of his natural liberty' (1956: 7) (carefully contrived as it is by his tutor) – though as an adult he is to be dependent on women, who have 'the capacity to stimulate desires greater than can be satisfied' (1956: 132). Sophie's education is to be very different from Emile's. Indeed it is essential to Emile's well-being as an autonomous adult that Sophie does not share his education; instead, she is to be 'passive and weak' rather than 'active and strong' like Emile (1956: 131). She must learn to submit to the 'hard, unceasing constraints of the proprieties ... always to be submissive" (1956: 139–40).[4]

The citizens of the Social Contract, in Rousseau's and other versions, are also males. In an engaging article on the subject, Janna Thompson begins with an alternative founding story, in which women, rather than men, set out to establish a social contract. She begins 'Each of them was a mother, grandmother, or an aunt, a sister or a daughter, most of them were several of these at once, and in connection with each identity, each had particular and sometimes conflicting responsibilities' (Thompson, 1993). They also traded, belonged to religious communities, and belonged to clubs. These women will make a contract founded on carrying out family responsibilities, which is very different from the usual social contract where individuals are assumed to be independent and self-interested. This contract may be one-sidedly feminine, but it is very useful in pointing up the inadequacies of the usual version. In particular it shows how masculine are the assumptions contained in it.[5]

3 PERSONAL AUTONOMY

3.1 Do women want personal autonomy?

It is the argument of this section that the usual meanings ascribed to personal autonomy and independence are inadequate to describe and explain the experience of women. Attention to that experience demonstrates that a different set of meanings for 'autonomy' or 'independence' is struggling to be heard. Once it is possible to hear them, it becomes possible to hear more clearly what women want – in what senses we reject, and in what senses we require autonomy. It also becomes possible to hear in what ways different groups of women (differing in their social class, nationality or race, for instance) have different perceptions of their needs and wants for autonomy.

Many women deny that they want more independence and autonomy, if that means they should be more like a particular kind of Western man: unencumbered by emotions or close personal relationships, and free of ties to the social circumstances into which they were born. They assert the value of all these things to their own lives: both the expressive life of feelings, and the social life which is rooted in ties to their family, friends, neighbourhood, culture and family history. On the other hand, women continue to want to run their own lives and do so in their own way. In other words, they want autonomy, in the sense that autonomy means deciding for oneself.

There is an apparent paradox here. Women want autonomy; they want to decide the course of their own lives – even though this may mean that they decide to continue with precisely the situations that others may define for them as ones in which they lack autonomy. I argue that there is, in fact, no paradox, but that the apparent paradox gives us a pointer to a different set of meanings of autonomy which find it hard to be heard.

Let us look at both sides of this apparent paradox. First, consider how it is that some women reject autonomy. It is not hard to see why some women deny that they want independence. Autonomy and independence are easily equated with emotional and financial self-sufficiency. It is a short step from here to seeing independence as lonely and isolating, even selfish.

Some feminists have proposed 'sisterhood' as an antidote to loneliness, but, however attractive, it is not a substitute for embeddedness in a general social life. Sisterhood is an ideal of relationships of equals based on choice, or, alternatively, a mutual sympathy based on recognition of commonalities. It is very like the relationship of fraternity, or the relationship of the Social Contract that autonomous rational man has with his fellows. Such contractual equality is rare in ordinary human life. It is not to be found in most social relationships. Of course, it must be obvious to more women than men how untypical such relationships are, since women are more likely than men to engage in a wide variety of social relationships. Consider the most usual social relationships: parent, child, colleague, neighbour, and even *real* brothers and sisters. We do not choose with whom to have these relationships. We find ourselves in them. Moreover, only a few of them are relationships of equality in respect of neediness, power, capability, strength, knowledge, time and experience. All of them are found over all the stages of human life, in which people move from relative dependency to relative self-sufficiency and back to dependency, as a result of ageing, child-bearing, sickness and changes in earning power. In Chapter 2 (section 7.4.1) I try to describe the complexity of mutual dependence and independence which characterises my own close relationships. Liz Stanley describes the changing patterns of mutual dependency in her relationship with her mother. She shows that any view that she had her own independence curtailed, when she was caring for her mother, would be hopelessly oversimplified and inaccurate.

Now consider the other side of the paradox: how is it that some women want autonomy? That women reject lonely self-sufficiency does not mean that they also reject any kind of independence. On the contrary, for centuries, and all over the world, women have demanded liberation from injustice, and the freedom to control their own lives. This struggle goes on at an individual level, and in groups of people, whether defined culturally or politically.

In my attempt to explain my own close relationships (Chapter 2, section 7.4.1) I made it clear that I do not simply *resign* myself to the need for others. On the contrary I find and create myself through them. They give me autonomy more than they restrict it. This is the tenor of Liz Stanley's article about her sick mother too. She emphasises that her changing self is grounded in material reality, including the narrations of selves and others, and, therefore, the direction she wishes to give to her life is also grounded in this material reality. The particular circumstances in which

British academics live are very different to most other women leading very different lives in the rest of the world, yet many of our responses to our entanglement with others are remarkably similar to theirs.

Other women, the world over, include their networks of relationship as part of their own wants and needs. Marialice is an example of a woman struggling to live her life in her own way as an individual. By any standards her life is a hard one, a struggle to make ends meet through long hours of paid and unpaid work. But as Patai comments:

> To see Marialice purely as a victim (is) to miss the point .... It is the self-expression of a woman who is doing what we all do: struggling to make sense of events that are beyond her control and to establish a place for herself in terms of the things that are within her control, and doing so not only through her actions but also through her representation of those actions via language.
>
> In Marialice's case, the material circumstances of her life are largely beyond her control. She cannot move into a higher income bracket which is her first and greatest need. What she has done, instead, is to humanize her surroundings, to try and forge human relations within the situations that constrain her. And she is not unsuccessful at this; it is family ties and kin networks that make life tolerable at the poverty level, where the majority of Brazil's population is situated.
>
> (Patai, 1988: 163)

Marialice does not find autonomy in the rejection of family ties in favour of self-sufficiency. Her life is different, indeed, from mine – or from Liz Stanley's – and her choices are different. However, cross-cutting the differences are similarities in the constraints we take to ourselves when deciding about the directions of our lives. Different again from Marialice and from British academics are the Egyptian women who talked to Nayra Atiya. However, like her and like me, they too place social relationships at the centre of their life narratives and the choices that they have made about the directions their lives should take.

Marialice struggles for autonomy within the constraints of her family ties. Her struggle is unwillingly against poverty, but not against her constraining cultural ties. British Asian women provide another particularly clear example of women valuing their own culture while simultaneously demanding freedom to direct their own lives. Well-meaning white British have seen the needs of Asian women as being self-sufficiency, to be achieved by escape from the extended family and its demands – as being more like white British women. Arranged marriage has been cited as an especially significant bond to burst in those Asian communities that practise it. Indeed, Asian cultural practices in general, and Muslim cultural practices in particular, are regularly described by liberals as a problem for equality, justice and freedom for girls (Harris, 1982; Hatem, 1989; Halstead, 1991). All this is denied in the writing of Asian girls and women, who rarely see their freedom in leaving their families and communities and the cultural practices which are part of themselves. Indeed there is evidence that Muslim all-girls' schools, far from being anti-feminist, help girls both in articulating their aspirations and also in their educational achievement.[6] To leave their communities would be to deny something essential in their personal identities. They continue, nevertheless, to affirm their need to be free within family and community and to criticise specific aspects of their cultures, including specific forms of arranged marriages.[7]

Are all these women – am I – wanting to square the circle? To have our various cakes and to eat them too? No, there is no contradiction here, if independence – or autonomy – is the freedom to be yourself, to speak for yourself, to determine your own life, in the knowledge that a worthwhile life includes cultural and social bonds, and in the knowledge that such bonds will last during periods of relative need for the help of others and relative responsibility to meet the needs of others.

Why does all this sound paradoxical? One reason is to be found in the power of some groups to legitimate their language as the proper one (see Chapter 4, section 3). There is an odd masculine logic underlying the use of words like 'independent'. Indeed, both 'independent' and 'dependent' are very odd words. Consider who is called a dependant. It is usually assumed that dependants are women and children economically dependent on a man: he is the breadwinner. Dependants are not usually taken to be men and children dependent on a woman for housework or for emotional support. In other words, in a traditional household, when a woman and a man are both in a state of dependence, the woman is called 'dependent' and the man is called 'independent'. Of course it is true that the woman has the more dangerous dependence. She is making herself progressively more incapable of becoming economically independent, while he remains capable of finding emotional support and domestic help in a variety of ways.

This logic of the word 'dependence' remains alive and well. In the economic climate of the late 1980s and early 1990s women increasingly became the primary 'breadwinners' for the household. Their menfolk did not usually assume the other role: there is no manly 'independence' attached to learning to do the domestic tasks of housework and emotional support. The men remained dependent on their women for these things, in order to keep up their 'independent' masculinity. Beatrix Campbell contrasts the behaviour of young men who live on run-down housing estates in England with that of their sisters. The young men turn to crime to assert their masculinity, while the young women turn to crime to try to keep the family together. Having described the striking difference between the crime committed by the two sexes she says: 'This is not to say that boys and men are bad and girls and women are good, it is simply to repeat the obvious, that men and women do something dramatically different with their troubles' (1993: 211). That is, she says: 'Crime and coercion are sustained by men. Solidarity and self-help are sustained by women. It is as stark as that' (1993: 319).

The same odd masculine logic is to be found in the language of sexual relationships. 'There ain't nothing like a dame' can be sung by a group of men without any suggestion that they are dependent or vulnerable. It is true that men have complained about the seductive power of women, but even this is a limited power. A man without a woman may be sorry for himself, but he remains a whole person. A woman wanting a man is more often supposed to be in a state of need resulting from her supposed inability to function properly without one. A woman's life is supposed to revolve round a man and his children. He gives her life meaning. Popular fantasy literature bears this out. Men's thrillers are about action in which they may get a woman as a bonus. Women's romances are about getting a man. This is all most extraordinary at the same time as being utterly commonplace.

The odd logic of independence and dependency is backed up by Western philosophy. This is not surprising, if philosophy is a community talking to itself (see Chapter 3, section 3.1).[8] Kant's view of autonomy ignores his own dependence on women. In so far as Kant notices women he thinks that they destroy their own peculiar merits by struggling after learning, but that these merits do not include the courage to use their own under-standing, as is necessary for autonomy. However his philosophy is really directed at the rational, autonomous males of the public sphere. Hegel and Rousseau spend more time discussing the place of women, but come to much the same conclusions. As has been pointed out by many commentators, both of these philosophers, in their different ways, require women to stay at home, providing a basis of moral feeling derived from the 'natural' or 'nether' worlds, while men enter the public world of citizenship with its associated fully realised state of autonomy.[9] Solomon points out:

> Some of [Hegel's] more offensive pronouncements are virtual para-phrases from Rousseau. . . . According to Hegel, women are strictly dependent and supportive, intuitive and the ethical essence of the family. Men on the other hand, are more independent and rational. Women are passive, men are active, and so on.
>
> (1983: 544)

In spite of great differences between them, all three philosophers unite in the view that women should stay at home where they are meant to be, dependent on and of service to the family, while men live a so-called independent life in the rest of the world. Women who make the mistake of trying to be like men should be sharply discouraged, since society needs their distinctive (dependent, supportive) contribution. Throughout the work of social contract theorists too, is found this view of the man in the public world: rational, just and independent with a dependent woman at home providing support. Even Rawls, writing in the 1970s, assumes male heads of households.

There are indeed competing sets of meanings for autonomy. The picture given by the philosophers is misleading. A better one (still oversimplified) is that on the one hand, there are men who are frightened of admitting their dependency. On the other, there are women who understand that social ties give their lives meaning – give them the freedom to be themselves. However, the discourse of the males is so dominating that many women's thoughts about independence are mixed up with male understandings of it. So, not surprisingly, they are frightened of the loneliness which will be theirs if they look for an independence in a male world without male privileges.

But why has the women's version not taken more root? Why have they not lived their understanding more boldly? Since women have been asserting their autonomy and taking it, as I have argued, why are so many of us still in positions where this is so hard to do? Why does Janna Thompson's fantasy of a female social contract remain so fantastic? (Why don't women just take over?) In the next section I discuss some of reasons. They are to do with the structures of violence which back up male understanding and the self-identity, and possibilities for self-creation of both men and women. There are continued efforts to make sure that women are forcibly kept in their place. In section 4, I look at how autonomy remains within women's grasp: at how we refuse to be kept in our place in public life.

3.2 Self-identity and personal autonomy

The theory of self-identity in Chapter 5, is hospitable to the pursuit of autonomy for women as well as for men. It shows that the development of self-identity is the making of a kind of web, the construction of which is partly under guidance from the self, though not in its control. That is, it is an account which takes it as central that people make themselves, though not in circumstances of their own choosing. Not only is the theory broadly hospitable to the pursuit of autonomy but also the conclusions drawn from Chapter 5 are close to the conclusions about independence and autonomy as found in women's lives. These are that autonomy is to be found in being yourself, speaking for yourself, and deciding the course of your own life, in the knowledge that a worthwhile life includes social ties which will change the self that is being, talking and deciding. In Chapter 5 it was stated that each individual creates her own identity, but that creation takes place in the various communities of which she is a member, and is, indeed, continually in a process of construction by those communities. The development of self-identity is a process reliant on the exercise of autonomy. If someone exercises less autonomy she will develop an identity, of course. The development can be more or less autonomous. Further, autonomy can be enhanced and increased at any point, and the particular self-identity, as so far developed, used as a basis for further development.

In Chapter 5 the processes of exclusion and inclusion were emphasised as productive of self-identity. During Chapters 6 and 7 it became increasingly apparent how far such processes were processes based on violence, humiliation and fear, as well as on love and affiliation. The members of dominant groups stay dominant by maintaining or colluding in structures of fear and violence, built on inflicting fear of harassment, ridicule, loneliness and physical violence. They, themselves, are kept in line, too, by the fear that such structures will be turned on them.

Those who have benefited from the structures of violence – so far as being the oppressors rather than the oppressed is a benefit – are the ones who have the greater influence in building structures. They therefore influence the possibilities for autonomy of those who do not have as much influence, as well as the possibilities that they themselves will have. Think of Marialice, of the Egyptian women who spoke to Atiya, and of British Asian women: their lives are constrained at every turn by public decisions by groups which do not include them. However, those who make the public decisions have already been influenced by the particular collusions and negotiations that each one of them has made with the structures of fear and violence. It is wrong to think of the division between personal decisions and public decisions about what to do as a chasm. Rather, each set of decisions depends on the other.

We can draw out the following implications for the concept of autonomy. The notion of autonomy as it applies to the lives of women and other people includes the following strands: freedom to be and to continue to be, in directions influenced by the agent, and freedom to make public decisions about matters which influence the possibilities of individual freedom for all people. Thus there are three interconnected strands: freedom to make oneself, freedom to live that self without fear of the consequences, and freedom to participate in public decisions that affect oneself.

3.2.1 Freedom to make oneself

The individual deciding for herself is at the centre of a notion of autonomy applicable to the lives of women. This is a freedom to make your self in recognition of the way the self is made in communities although it is not determined by them. Thus there is a need for *space* for the self to be formed both in and against various communities of others and also out of the material conditions in which it finds itself.

Making oneself both in and against the community is easier if there is a variety of communities. The variety makes it easier to see that the term 'woman' refers to overlapping networks of constructions, and that the individual can find herself within and against them. Moreover there is a requirement for recognition that being with others does not necessarily curb your autonomy, though having *no* others will do so. Of course, some kinds of interactions with others are debilitating and oppressive while other kinds are enriching. In the long term even oppressive kinds of interaction (short of death) can be used for enrichment, though doing so is hard, and sometimes only possible for exceptional people.

The process of making oneself in and against communities can be seen in various examples. For instance consider the stories that black and Asian women in Britain spin.[10] They take from the rich variety of communities that they inhabit to make something which is their own identity, forged from love, resistance and their particular material circumstances. Other examples are provided by various other feminist women who insist on their own identity even if they do not fit what some other feminists want, for instance if they like domesticity on the one hand or military life on the other. Jong's poem (pp. 48–9) describes the ambiguities of feminists liking housework. In Chapter 2, section 7.1.2, I talked about felt contradictions about being a feminist but liking particular aspects of technology.

The politics of autonomy needs to ensure enrichment rather than debilitation, and also to leave space for previously debilitating interactions to be transformed into enrichment. In particular there is a need for generous patterns of cultural and political life, and the reduction of fear. By 'generous patterns' I mean patterns which allow individuals room to take them on, move between them, and transform them.

In Chapter 7, I referred to Gilroy's argument that the self-consciousness articulated by Frederick Douglass and Margaret Garner owes a great deal to African and black cultural forms, and also to their own specific forms of masculinity and femininity. In my terms, they were both availing themselves of patterns which they were of, but which they could re-create, in order to produce something new building on the old. Garner said in court, through Mr Jollife her lawyer, that she would go singing to the gallows rather than be returned to slavery. As Gilroy argues, in saying this she was joining 'a moral and political gesture to an act of cultural creation and affirmation' (Gilroy, 1993: 68). The popularity of the Garner narrative bears this out. Garner was taking from the narratives of femininity, blackness and white legal conventions to make herself, in so far as she was able to in the circumstances. Those who are less brave and imaginative than Garner need a politics which allows for change, development and individual patterns without facing fear. Already it is clear how interwoven are the three strands of autonomy which I named.

3.2.2. Freedom to live that self without fear of the consequences

Fear keeps people in their place, as defined for them by the powerful. Margaret Garner was indeed exceptional. Throughout this book I have been emphasising the power of fear to keep exclusions and inclusions intact. The fear induced in different groups is particular to them – for instance, in young women, whether they are to be scared of being thought to be sexually active heterosexuals, lesbians, or sexless; or whether they are to be made to fear just for being black or Asian; or having particular disabilities; or some combination of these. However, the means of inducing fear are remarkably similar.

Fear is induced through verbal and physical violence, through ridicule and condescension, or through disregard mixed with high visibility. I have described a number of examples which show these different methods used for different groups. Such fear reduces the scope for ways of living and being, from dress to the expression of affection, to the enjoyment of intellectual activities, to self-confidence, to going for a walk even. This comes out in any number of autobiographies. See for instance the experiences noted by Atiya, Brodsky and Williams. I referred in earlier chapters to other examples: Alibhai, Hassi, hooks and Seacole (in Chapter 5); Fanon and Seller (in Chapter 7). I, myself, describe going for a walk, under conditions of mild harassment in Chapter 2, section 7.2.3. Even such mild harassment altered my scope for ways of living and being.

Compare this account of mine with those that valorise cruelty and fear. In particular, compare it to the stories told by Rorty and Hegel. There is little choice in these stories to be the one inflicting the pain, the road to autonomy for Rorty. However it easy to see the exercise of autonomy within them, wrenched as it is from fear. Hegel who thinks that submission is a precursor to selfhood did not consider stories like these. The fear that is induced does not promote obedience and discipline as he imagined. He says: 'Without having experienced the discipline which breaks self-will, no one becomes free, rational and capable of command' (1971: 175). This sounds more like army training than the realities of life-long exclusions. Fear is not the royal road to self-confidence and wholeness. The increase of autonomy requires a reduction rather than an increase in cruelty and domination. Again it is clear how interwoven are the strands which make up autonomy.

3.2.3 Freedom to participate in public decisions affecting oneself

The interaction of the strands which make up autonomy show the mistake in standard theories, both those which emphasise the individual making his own decisions, and those which emphasise the primacy of a social contract. Public decisions and public behaviour influence the possibilities for each individual in exercising her autonomy, as she creates herself.

Moreover the individuals who take public decisions are neither self-sufficient nor equally needy. The myth that lonely self-sufficiency is either possible or desirable has resulted in untenable social contract theories.[1]

Politics is not just about equal respect and equal rights for self-sufficient individuals. It is also about human beings making themselves and being made in social webs. Therefore politics is about responding to the changes that result in individuals working out new patterns of being, and about creating spaces for people to make themselves, and, in particular, it is about reducing fear. It is also about recognising the importance of public decisions in matters that have been deemed part of the private world of women and family. Thus it is about dealing with the periods of relative need and relative responsibility that affect us all. Again, Janna Thompson's compelling story about a women's 'social contract' is relevant (see section 2). However it cannot give the whole story, because any social contract story is only a utopian myth of origins. In fact, as Spivak says, we need a practical politics of the open end: 'Given our historical position we have to learn to negotiate with structures of violence, rather than taking the impossible elitist position of turning our backs on everything' (1990: 101).

4 PUBLIC AUTONOMY

4.1 Public autonomy and public life

In the last section the focus was on personal autonomy. I drew the conclusion that personal autonomy is inextricable from the politics of public decisions. The word 'autonomy' originally referred to public life, to the autonomous city state. This is no longer the case. 'Autonomy' is just as likely to refer to the personal life of an individual, as explored in the first part of this chapter. In order to refer to public life, as opposed to personal life, I shall refer to 'public autonomy' – meaning by this the conditions under which individuals contribute to the rule of law and of state. That is, I take it that I have personal autonomy if I can order my own personal life and I have public autonomy if I can contribute to the ordering of public life: institutions, laws, customs, culture.

4.2 Do women want to take part in political autonomy?

Just as meanings ascribed to personal autonomy and independence are inadequate to describe and explain the experience of women, so with public autonomy. There is a gender bias in the assumptions and arguments which contribute to the understanding of the power and participation of individuals and groups in the ordering of public affairs.

It would be easy to say that women do not want to take part in public life. History tells us that over the centuries they have not done so. The history that I learnt at school was the history of men's actions. To be sure, this was partly because history as I was taught it was the history of wars. But in my all-girls' school we did not spend more time than necessary on wars. We learnt about the great revolutions which shaped the modern world: the French, Russian and American revolutions, the industrial revolution in England and the enacting of the laws which frame the British welfare state. I learnt about some women in this history, but very few in comparison to the men. Women, like the Pankhursts and the Misses Buss and Beale, made brief appearances to fight for the rights of women. Otherwise, men were the enactors of laws and the movers of revolutions. Only a very few women joined them. There were some Queens (Boudicca, Elizabeth I, Victoria), some famous wives and mistresses (Eleanor of Aquitaine, Anne Boleyn, Nell Gwynne), some social reformers (Florence Nightingale, Elizabeth Fry) and a small number of others (Joan of Arc, Charlotte Corday, Marie Curie, Rosa Parkes).

It could be said, with some justice, that my school history did not tell the full story. Women have fought for a place in public affairs and they have fought for public causes. For instance, we could have learnt more about the participation of women in working-class movements in the last century. The history of the fight for women's suffrage and women's education in public institutions could have been given more prominence.

The teaching of history in England is not different from that in other countries, as far as the under-reporting of women is concerned. To take just one example, Mernissi describes how the standard histories she grew up with in her own country of Morocco led her to believe that women had never been rulers in Muslim, especially Arab, countries. Her research showed that history contains several such women taking and using power. However, so fully have they been erased from modern histories, that a colleague of hers, faced with the evidence she had collected about the existence of Arab women heads of state during the Middle Ages, asserted she must be quoting the *Arabian Nights*! She says:

> The journey into the past in search of these forgotten queens invites us to take another look at what was inculcated into us in our adolescence. [We find that] the pleasures of love can be combined with the conquest of power.
>
> (Mernissi, 1993: 117)

The fact remains that prominent women are few by comparison to men, whether we look at the origins of the trade union movement, or at Muslim rulers. However, history also shows that women have always wanted to take part in public affairs -- to combine love and power -- even though it was made so hard for them to do so. The question remains: if women have been trying to get a place in public affairs why are they so unsuccessful? In the West there is a reasonable measure of formal equality of opportunity in education and in other procedures which would allow women into public office. In the rest of the world too, there are now fewer obstacles in the way of women who would take political actions, in spite of serious recent set-backs from the various forms of backlash, including the rising tide of nationalism and religious fundamentalism (especially in Christianity, Islam and Hinduism): witness the existence of women heads of state around the world, even in old, traditional countries.

It has been suggested that one answer to the question of the scarcity of women in public life is to be found in the discourse of 'private' and 'public'. It has been particularly difficult for women to take part in public affairs when the discourse of private and public is one which assigns women to the private, and men to the public realm. According to these arguments, to be in public life is to be positioned as male.[12] Mernissi (1993) describes the powerful discourse which surrounds women, the veil and public life, in traditional Islam. Odeh (1993) describes how Arab anti-Western sentiments increase the pressure on Arab women, who share such sentiments, to express their views by wearing the veil. She goes on to show that they are then put in an ambivalent position with regard to the discourse of private and public, since they wish simultaneously to work out of the house, and also to wear the veil with its associated rhetoric encouraging them to stay at home.

There is a lot to these arguments, but they do not give the whole picture. There must be something else stopping women entering public life. If the discourse of 'public' and 'private' was so powerful, it should also have confined women to working in the home rather than taking paid employment outside. However, the dichotomising of 'public' and 'private' has not stopped women entering the labour force either in the West or, as Odeh's article shows, in Arab countries either. In both kinds of countries, women have subverted the discourse and overcome practical difficulties in order to take paid employment outside the home. Subverting the discourse and overcoming the practical difficulties should not be too difficult for women desiring to enter public life, however male-defined public life has been in the past. This is especially so, since many women (like the equivalent men) who would enter such public office would be relatively well-off, with enough resources to deal with many of the practicalities of personal life, like cleaning, cooking and some of the care of children and the aged.

If the private/public dichotomy is not enough to explain the lack of women in public life, what is an alternative explanation? I suggest that the reasons for women's absence are analogous to those for the supposed lack of personal autonomy in women. Just as the problem of personal autonomy was seen to be a problem for women – but turned out to be a problem of language and understanding, so also for public autonomy. Women do indeed want public autonomy, and have begun to take it. However it is not easy to see this, given public life as defined in the history books, and present-day 'politics as usual'.

I argue that the problem is precisely one of the discourse of 'private' and 'public', but not in the sense given above. Rather, what is needed is a re-conceptualisation of what counts as private or public. Before I start to discuss this, note that I have avoided the word 'private' in my own arguments, although it is the one favoured in the discourse which puts the individual against the public domain. I have preferred to use the word 'personal', because I think it is less question-begging. What is needed is a re-thinking of the language in which the discussion is couched. Just as the usual use of 'independence', 'dependence' and 'autonomy' make it hard to see when women are, in fact, being personally independent (*pace* masculine logic), so equally for the concepts of 'private', 'personal' and 'public'.

4.3 Political autonomy: the personal, the private and the public

It has been argued that there are areas of personal autonomy which require and/or presuppose action on a larger scale than the simply personal, i.e. on a scale beyond the face-to-face or the individual levels of action. These are public actions. They produce a number of spheres of political action. Some of these are directly related to what are traditionally termed women's issues, such as contraception, abortion, harassment, child-care, and sex discrimination in employment practices. Other issues that women have seen as vital to their own autonomy and well-being are not, at first sight, traditionally in the realms of the self, or even of 'women's issues', like the environment (eco-feminism) or war (peace women).

Women have taken effective political action in all of these areas. Changes have happened owing to a variety of actions ranging from academic writing to direct action; from patient small-scale local work to large-scale media happenings; from local campaigns in particular work places to internationally reported campaigns like Greenham and SEWA, the trade union movement of scattered, self-employed and home-based women in India.[13] There have been changes in the micropolitics of political activism. Political questions are now seen to include questions of who does the washing up; who minds grandparents or babies; and whether a sexual partner is sadistic. Political movements are now seen to include networks of friends, activists and colleagues, who bring children to their meetings if necessary, and arrange matters to take account of other dependants and social obligations. Only some of these campaigns are politics in the sense of party politics and public office, or even normal pressure group politics. Indeed some of them have depended on distance from such (Eisenstein, 1991).

Change is apparent, within education, laws, policies and cultural expectations. In England, girls are now achieving so well in their public examinations, that there is worry expressed in the newspapers and on the television about boys' underachievement. The discourse surrounding laws and rights, and some of the material factors too, have become more feminist. Margaret Hodge, who was labelled as a 'loony left feminist' when she was Labour councillor in Islington in the early 1980s, points out '10 years later, things for which we were pilloried have become orthodox. Staff nurseries, ethnic monitoring, equal opportunity recruitment policies: Opportunity 2000 [a Conservative Government document] promotes these' (quoted in an article in the *Independent*, 7.6.94).

Parmar (1990) discusses the place of cultural productions in the politics of the articulation of British black feminism and its activisms, using photographic work by black women and poetry by June Jordan. She asserts the significance of visual and written works of art in securing an authentic language for black and migrant women, which at the same time addresses the differences among them. This kind of cultural politics is a basis for more traditional political actions. In her discussion of *Elle* magazine, Stuart (1990: 33), points out that women's glossy magazines may dismay the feminist establishment, but they can give young women space to transgress traditional boundaries of sexual difference and flout anachronistic notions of femininity.

The public–political actions of women have been effective.[14] Though I should emphasise that at the same time as noting the achievements it should also be noted that there is no room for complacency. Any achievement is accompanied by resistance. Faludi (1992) convincingly traces some of the backlash in the present, also remarking on the evidence of it over the centuries. Spender has traced the erasure of women's political and intellectual work in her books. There is the fact that feminism is now unfashionable for young women. Stuart (1990) discusses some of the reasons for this in the difficult relationship of what she calls 'popular feminism' to be found in the media and what she calls 'professional feminism' found in academia or activist local politics. In some cases spoken attitudes have changed, but there has been little to no progress in other areas: women's pay is one dreadful example (Stuart, 1990). Still, even with that caveat, it is undeniable that all the areas mentioned above have been the subject of effective interventions by women and women's movements.[15]

The different examples of change on the large scale show how women take public autonomy. The examples are examples of a set of public actions, but not of public actions that can be distinguished from private actions. Earlier I referred to the more traditional views about the division between the private and the public, as found in the theories of Western philosophy. A challenge to those views is provided by the alternative conception that the examples point up. They point the way to a different view of political action.

Decisions about contraception, sexual harassment and child-care would be 'private' in the traditional sense. Against that tradition, women have shown that these issues may be personal, but they are also public. Decisions about them are decisions with public implications and the society as a whole influences the decisions that can be taken, thus requiring a public response. Equally, the deployment of nuclear weapons and the protection of the environment have been thought to be 'public' in the sense that solutions to issues should be found through public institutions. Equally, against that tradition, women have shown that these issues may be public, but they are also personal.

It is not just in the content of public actions that the division between personal and public needs to be re-thought. Women have shown that personal response taken in public modes is also effective. Men sympathetic to feminism used to complain that women were not properly organised, and would be more effective if only they became so. Such complaints are still heard, to the effect that women are still too emotional, insufficiently detached and rational. The bafflement expressed in these complaints comes, I suggest, from a conflation of the idea of 'public action' with 'action through public institutions' (as opposed to private institutions, like the family). However, women have shown the falsity of this conflation. They have not only formed committees and joined political parties. They have pinned photographs of their grandchildren to the wire at the air base at Greenham Common, and in India they have sung songs about the oppression of women, both to policemen arresting them, and in village street plays (Seller, 1985; Bhushan, 1989). Women have used argument in the traditional sense, but they have also used jokes, cartoons, demonstrations, slogans, novels, films, art, street theatre. They have also noticed the ways in which arguments themselves come to be accepted, through communities which validate them. In Chapter 2, section 7.4.2, I describe one of these ways, the establishment of a women and philosophy network, explicitly exclusive of men: this ploy uses the exclusivity of dominance against itself, as well as avoiding the games of exclusion that take place in all the other arenas of philosophy where men are found in large numbers relative to women. It should be noticed that this is a politics of rationality in the second sense of political that I distinguished in Chapter 7. Using an understanding of the ways that different judgements are validated by a new community and entered into circulation, women can begin to re-define what is taken to be rational by men.

4.4 The politics of selves

Given a better understanding of public autonomy, it is now possible to move on to practicalities. It is possible to see how a theory of what to do might be drawn up, given the reality rather than the rhetoric of changes wrought by women. This is a suggestion about a theory of practical politics, and the ways in which a variety of public spaces contribute to women's ability to take part in public life. That is, it is about a politics of selves which goes beyond both kinds of politics often associated with the phrase 'the politics of identity'.

I have deliberately used a new term like 'politics of selves' rather than the old term 'politics of identity', in order to signal that there is a possibility of going beyond old understandings. In the past, the term 'politics of identity' has been the subject of much well-deserved criticism.[16] This is directed at both the main versions: categorical, essentialist politics and cultural politics. I have shown that categorical essentialist politics must be mistaken. Nothing can be assumed from the bare fact of sex, race or sexuality, except that these facts make a difference. Individual human beings growing up in specific social circumstances make that difference in any number of ways. Cultural politics is a harking back to old cultural circumstances and, while it acknowledges the social roots of identity, it stops further development, negotiation and the forging of new alliances. As Stuart Hall says:

> It seems to me that it is possible to think about the nature of new political identities which isn't founded on the notion of some absolute, integral self and which clearly can't arise from some fully closed narrative of the self. A politics which accepts the 'no necessary or essential correspondence' of anything with anything.
>
> (quoted in Parmar, 1990: 108)

The politics of selves I am suggesting is a politics in the second of the two senses of 'politics' which I explained in Chapter 6. It focuses on how self-identity and the processes of self-creation both do affect and should affect practical actions, because practical large-scale communal action affects personal autonomy. What this politics might look like is something I take up in Chapter 10 after discussing authenticity.

Part III
Changing

9 Communication and change*

1 INTRODUCTION

An important theme has been emerging from the discussion of the first two parts of the book. This is the theme of personal change and its relationship to political change. This theme will provide the focus of Chapter 10, where it will be discussed in terms of authenticity. However, it is not possible to examine it in any depth without first addressing another underlying theme of the book: the question of language. So before I can address questions of personal and political change more directly, it is necessary to make a diversion into a discussion of the theory of language. Language is the subject of this chapter.

The main themes related to language which are to be found in the book so far are: (1) the possibility of expressing oneself; (2) the possibility of communicating the expression to others, and (3) the way that both expression and its communication are productive of change in the people who are involved and also of change in the means of expression and communication – that is, in language. In this chapter, I pick up on those themes in order to bring together an account of language, and to explain communication and self-expression, using questions originally posed in Chapters 2 and 3 about the possibilities of speaking with those who spoke other languages. I go on to look at language change – and the politics of language change.

2 A THEORY OF LANGUAGE

The theory of language I develop locates itself primarily within analytic traditions (Wittgenstein, Grice, Davidson) rather than in structuralism and post-structuralism. But I draw on both. The distinction between the two traditions can be exaggerated. As Wheeler remarks, there are relatively few people who are familiar with both Davidson's and Derrida's work. To those few, he says, the conclusion that 'some of the basic ideas

---

* In this chapter I draw on the following auto/biographies from the annotated bibliography in Chapter 3: Joseph Brodsky, bell hooks, and Patricia Williams.

and (perhaps) insights that move their respective arguments are the same for the two thinkers' will 'be scarcely news' (1986: 477). Both traditions work from the central notion that any item used as a sign or a symbol can only be understood in relation to all the other signs or symbols that make up a system of communication. What they do with this notion is what distinguishes them; the analytic tradition continue to develop truth conditions which will show the objectivity in the sciences, while structuralists and post-structuralists focus on the political implications of discourse.

In what follows, by the word 'language' I mean 'that with which we express ourselves and communicate'. Expression and communication are much more important than particular words or grammatical structures – but depend on them. Thus, I am taking the view that language is primarily a system for expression and communication rather than description, but that language also needs to be understood as a system of words and syntax (together with other symbolic items, like gestures, intonation, and facial expressions). Since communication is prior, the words and syntax are not simple referents. They are understood only as elements of whole sentences used in communication, all of which are understood against shared background assumptions. In Chapter 2, section 1, I distinguished 'language' in this sense from what I called 'tongues', which are particular human languages like French, Swahili or Arabic, marked precisely by particular words and grammatical structures, gestures and intonations, and which have grammar books and dictionaries to define their correct usage. I continue to use the word 'tongue' in this sense.

Communication is possible because human beings combine a common interest in expression and communication with a capacity to initiate and understand what communication is. That is, they are *able* to communicate, usually having learnt ways in which to do so from others who already know. Moreover, they *want* to communicate. So they want to communicate *something*. Such learning is only possible for beings who can already make an effort to communicate.[1] Babies show this clearly.

Research by a number of investigators shows how babies learn particular systems of communication, rather than actual communication itself. Young babies show a preference for faces and speechlike sounds, and generally a baby's activity towards people is more elaborate than any acts directed towards the rest of the world. Babies initiate communications with their mothers about objects, and are probably able to do this before they can respond to the parent's own attempts to initiate communication. Parents teach a baby or child how to communicate by interpreting the conversational contribution and responding to it. Children are more likely than their parents to initiate the topic of conversation, and the parents use their skills in responding to the meanings in a language that is well, adapted to the individual child's ability to understand (Trevarthen, 1978; Wells, 1981).

People retain their ability to think up new ways of expressing themselves and communicating. It is a striking feature of human life that people regularly come up with new ways of communicating either out of necessity, or just for fun. Consider the astonishing speed with which families, social groups and nation states develop their own ways of understanding each other in dialects, slang and jokes and in their artistic and cultural expressions.

The process of communication was described by Grice (1957). It is an account which focuses on acts of communication, which may or may not be spoken words, but could include gestures, facial expressions, dances, drawings, or any other suitable action. Any of these actions are acts of communication if the person who does them hopes to produce a state of mind in a second person (perhaps expressed in an action). However, simply producing the state of mind is not enough to make the action communicative. It is necessary for the second person to know that the first one was trying to communicate. The state of mind of the second one depends on her knowledge that the first person was trying to communicate with her. There are any number of ways to produce states of mind in others, which do not involve communication: spiking a drink with a drug, surreptitiously treading on a foot, putting a sweet in a crying child's mouth. Each one of these acts becomes different in its effects if it is, in fact, communicative. The process, as expressed in the academic philosophical language in which Grice himself was comfortable, is as follows: a person P does an action A so as to induce a belief, action or feeling B in person Q, intending that Q should be aware of the reason P did A. Moreover, Q's awareness is part of the reason that Q does B.

Any such action depends on a host of background assumptions, based on shared knowledge and attitudes. Some acts of communication require a great deal of such shared knowledge while others need comparatively little – as anyone knows who has tried to make themselves understood without using a common tongue. I do not speak Romanian. Yet on a recent visit to Romania, buying cheese at the market was easy. The cheeses were displayed, the act of shopping was well understood on both sides, and numbers are easy to explain with fingers or with a pencil and paper. However as soon as the transaction went wrong, our shared knowledge and assumptions were inadequate. Trouble arose over a misunderstanding about the change. Suddenly we all felt the need for a common tongue as well as a common understanding of shopping. The shared knowledge of a tongue is a part of the normal assumptions of communication for most conversations.[2] When words are spoken (with proper syntax, intonation and accompanying gestures) in the knowledge that the hearers take them to be attempts at communication, the speaker is able to communicate with the hearer. Unusual instances of usage can then be understood: new utterances and conventions regularly appear in human groups as a result of the Gricean mechanism.

The theory is able to explain the creation and discovery of experience by language. When someone has a perception of a situation – a perception which is already mediated by language, of course – she can attempt to communicate it. Such a communication is, inevitably, an expression of her perception. To the extent that the perception is communicated it is symbolised; the symbols are communicated and understood in relation to the other symbols that make up the system of communication. Thus the perception is already constrained and altered by the symbols that are already available to the partners. However it is not determined by them, owing to the communicative part of the Gricean mechanism. As Taylor says:

> Men are constantly shaping language, straining the limits of expression, minting new terms, displacing old ones, giving language a changed gamut of meanings. . . . They can only be introduced and make sense because they already have a place within the web, which must at any moment be taken as given over by far the greater part of its extent.
>
> (1985: 232)

Part of what is communicated is expressive. Communication and expression are dependent on each other, even if, in the case of a mature language user, it is possible to do one without the other, as I explain in this chapter.

Earlier in the book I described efforts to communicate which go beyond standard uses of language. For instance, in Chapter 3, I quoted Joseph Brodsky as saying that some experiences were impossible to render into English. So what does he take himself to be doing when he tries to communicate his Russian experiences in English? Similarly, what does Patricia Williams take herself to be doing in trying to talk about rights and needs to her colleague, although she says that ultimately they will not understand each other (Chapter 2, section 4)? Clearly, in both cases, something is being communicated which may not lead to entirely satisfactory understanding, but which goes beyond the limitations of the words and sentences. Both Brodsky and Williams implicitly rely on the Gricean mechanism. In Chapter 2, I described my own attempts to communicate across languages and tongues – see section 7.2.2. Clearly such attempts relied on a Gricean mechanism, as does learning the names of feelings as described in Chapter 6, section 2.2.

Communication and expression are further constrained and altered by the nature of the public space which is created between the participants in the conversation. An act of communication creates a public space: the participants need to understand that a communication of a certain kind is going on. However, that understanding itself affects what kind of communication can go on, since it will help to define what can be said and by whom. Children learn this, often painfully, at primary school, where they discover that the teacher has the power to define a public space. For instance, when a whole class of 7-year-olds sit companionably on the carpet for a discussion, it is the teacher who decides whether this is a public space of the kind where impersonal information is exchanged, rather than one where jokes are told or information relayed about family members.

One way of understanding how this public space is established is through the notion of 'conversation rules': the conventions which govern who may speak, when, about what and for how long. Conversation rules are a way of mutually defining public spaces – within well understood conventions of doing so. Conversation rules were discussed in an influential paper by Grice (1975). He argued that certain rules were necessary for a successful conversation, for instance that all participants observe a 'cooperative principle'. For him, the cooperative principle requires that all parties give as much information as is needed to be truthful, relevant and not vague or ambiguous.

Grice presents these rules as universal, failing to notice that what can be said and how it can be said varies according to social circumstances and according to gender, class, race, nationality – both in homogeneous groups and in mixed ones. In her carefully researched investigation into the views of the Sudanese and of expatriates working in the aid sector in Sudan, Leach (1991) points out that codes of conversational courtesy in Sudan mean that local people were unable to voice their dissatisfactions with the degree of effective consultation with local people by expatriate consultants, because of, rather than in spite of, the good personal relationships that they enjoyed.

The serious mistake Grice has made is in not noticing that for many groups the principles on which they cooperate are not ones in which information exchange is paramount. They may be more attuned to amusement, to caring for feelings, or to preserving status, for instance. Holdcroft (1979) criticises Grice for not noticing the different rules that apply in various educational settings such as lectures and examinations. However, the mistake is deeper than this. Conversations in which caring for feelings or preserving status are important considerations are not necessarily about information exchange at all. Nevertheless, they help define the public space in which meanings can be made.

A second facet of this mistake is in not noticing the effects of power. A public space is not only defined by the purposes of a conversation. It is also defined politically. In a group of human beings, not all kinds of persons are equal in power, both in the traditional sense of the 'power that says no' and the Foucauldian 'productivity of power'.[3] This power is part of the space that is defined and the rules that define it. For instance, to enter a conversation at all requires that one is positioned as a male or a female. (Possibly this is the reason I was discomforted by not knowing if Ray was a boy or a girl; see Chapter 2, section 7.1.3.) It also requires that one is positioned in various other ways according to social structures as particular kinds of male or female – servant, boss, black, white, co-patriot, alien – with implications for the meanings available to him/her.

These positionings should not be thought of as fixed. When women talk in a mixed sex group they are positioned as women and this has an effect on their contributions to the conversation. When women talk in a single sex group they are still positioned as women and this still has an effect on their contributions to the conversation – but the effect is different. Women in single sex groups talk with different conversation rules, both from women in mixed sex groups and from men in single sex groups.

Thus there are different conversations going on, with different rules and different meanings – a different public – political space. Women talk to each other (as do black people and working-class people, half of whom are women) and they take the opportunity to develop their own systems of meaning. These systems of meaning include meanings attached to words and sentences and also ways of understanding the public space of language. What is created is a counter-discourse to the dominant discourses, though drawing on them. British women have always known that a 'woman's work is never done' at the same time as they know their husbands would like them not to work. They know that men are 'really just little boys' at the same time as they know that women will be referred to as girls all their lives in situations where men will not be referred to as boys.

Using the rules developed in one form of discourse it is possible to flout the rules of another. The effect of this might be to change the space defined – through a process of Gricean communication. The other participants will react to the flouting, and interpret it, thus themselves helping to re-create the public–political space. In the process it is entirely possible that meanings attached to words or sentences will change. One need only think of telling jokes or of irony to understand how great a change might be achieved. Such re-creations, like the direct coining of new word and sentence meanings can only take place in the context of the public spaces and conversation rules which already exist.

So far I have been concentrating on spoken language. Written language has similar features, losing some of the social constraints, and acquiring some new ones. Like speech, writing may have the giving of information as its main goal. More often it does not. Either way the conventions which govern writing create particular public–political spaces depending on the assumed audience. Bell hooks discusses the kinds of decisions she has to make when writing her books. Coming from a working-class black community herself, she is careful about not excluding them unnecessarily. While arguing strongly for the importance of abstract theory, she takes control over the convention of including footnotes when discussing it. She points out that footnotes indicate to her community that a book is only for the college educated. So she leaves footnotes out. She describes how she was warned that 'the absence of footnotes would make the work less credible in academic circles' (1989: 81). She also discusses the way that assuming black women as her primary audience upset the white women who were used to taking it that feminist writing was addressed primarily to them (1989: 15). This topic is explored in this book in Chapter 2, where I also comment on how little it is addressed by the mainstream.

While the continued existence and maintenance of language depends on Gricean communication, a lot of communication can proceed without recourse to it. This is because human beings live in groups which already have tongues. It is characteristic of tongues that utterances and gestures have become frozen into habits and rules.[4] These are the habits and rules of grammatical, lexical, gestural and social meanings: the stuff of linguistic and discourse analysis. They are the subject matter for socio- and psycho-linguistic research into patterns of language use.[5] They are also the stuff of analyses of symbolic structures and metaphors of the kind popular in structuralist and post-structuralist research.[6]

Frozen language is utterly familiar. When British shop assistants say 'Anything else?' automatically and in a standard intonation, they are not being communicative in the Gricean sense. Nor is there any need for a communicative response. The phrase is as frozen in meaning as a traffic light turning red. Indeed, language in its totally frozen form is to be found in machines. The automatic part of the job of a canteen assistant has been replaced by the snack machine; that of a bank-teller by the cash dispenser. Another example of a different kind of frozen language is in the psychological and social assumptions which underpin it. I remark on frozen metaphors, collocations and dualisms later on in this chapter.

Frozen social language includes conversation rules, which themselves have been built up in political contexts, as explained earlier. Thus the assumptions on which Gricean intentions are built will include assumptions of power differentials. Therefore, the perceptions and meanings built up in the group will reflect that disparity. If, over time, men are more structurally powerful, then the perspectives of men will carry more weight. Thus a language is marked by its history, which includes the social history of power differentials; the frozen parts of the language include frozen social history. To return to the example of men being more powerful with regard to defining discourse: even if the status of women changes, the historical state of affairs will still be reflected in the language – which will thus lag behind social changes.

The value of this theory of language is that it explains both the power of language to determine thought and action and also the limits of its ability so to do. We use conventions and rules which are frozen history, in discussions which depend on an element of frozen language. However, since most human communication is at least partly Gricean, it is possible for the language to melt as the Gricean element is increased. Indeed language would be impossible if the rules were rigid. All of it would resemble our interchanges with snack machines and bank dispensers.

Changes in language may be slow but they are commonplace. The study of changes in language over time is a well-established branch of linguistics. Less well studied is the question of how far such changes can be directed. That is, there has been less attention paid to the question: if language can melt, how far is it also possible for its users to melt it deliberately, especially for political reasons? Certainly such attempts are made, and certainly they are resisted. Indeed, politically motivated efforts to change language are often seen to be destructive of language itself. Consider this remark by Stephen Kanfer: 'The feminist attack on social crimes may be as legitimate as it was inevitable. But the attack on words is only another social crime – one against the means and the hope of communication' (cited in Cameron, 1992: 101). Deborah Cameron comments: 'Poor, poor language, attacked in its innocence by feminists intent on destroying its virtue. Lucky for language that so many men are eager to protect it' (ibid.).

3 EXPRESSING ONESELF AND COMMUNICATION WITH OTHERS

I now turn to look directly at a particular issue of expression and communication, the question posed in Chapters 2 and 3: how far are we stuck in our own language? or, more precisely, how far can we understand those who speak another language – or be understood by them? This question was also raised in Chapter 4 in relation to the construction of an epistemology which depended on people talking overlapping languages. The discussion in this chapter draws on and supplements the earlier one.

It is necessary to look more carefully at what is shared by those who speak a language. A language is made up of its lexical items – words – together with rules for combining them. It is also made up of its rules for establishing public–political space. The words are used to refer to things (which may be supposed by the speaker to be real or imagined, literal or metaphorical) or to form the syntax. It is also made up of functions: the acts which are performed by particular uses of words. Each of these are expressions. To repeat what was said earlier, neither self-expression nor communication can be discussed in isolation from the other. Since what is communicated is dependent on the act of communication itself, the symbols used (in both their frozen and melted aspects) and the public–political space which has been created, what is communicated is properly called an 'expression'. It is not a transparent reporting of an entity independent of language.

Some of the ways of creating space, and some of the items and functions, refer to things and actions which are nearly universally shared. Examples would be a greeting or the word 'baby'. Any speaker of a particular tongue will know how to greet someone, and the term for a baby. Nevertheless, it needs to be noted that even 'Hello' and 'baby' are not exactly translatable into other tongues. There is wide variation in the conditions under which a greeting can be exchanged, and who counts as a 'baby'.

Some of the ways of creating space, and some of the items and functions refer to things and actions which are shared only by particular groups. These groups have languages which are not necessarily identical with the tongues in which they are couched. Some languages are subsets of tongues. Some languages cross tongues.

One way in which a language can be a subset of a tongue is local language, often called local dialect. Thus the ways of greeting in Nottingham ('Eh up!' as well as 'How are you?') are not exactly the same as the ways of greeting in Sydney ('G'day', as well as 'How are you?'), although people from both these places would say that they spoke English. The function of greeting is shared, but not all the lexical items are. Similarly there are numerous lexical items which are specific to a dialect.

Another way that a language can be a subset of a tongue is where tongues cross national boundaries (as they so often do as a result of the worldwide migration of peoples over the last few centuries). Lexical differences between different Anglophone nations are well known. British people are more likely than Americans to be able to identify a 'chip buttie'. The British have 'yoghurt' while Indians have 'curds'. Function may also be specific to one set of English speakers: British people are likely to know the functions (and the correct responses to) the statements 'Oh no you haven't!' or 'What do you think of it so far?' Other Anglophone nations or speakers of English as a second language are less likely to have this information.

I have discussed tongues and dialects first, because they are so familiar. Languages which are not identifiable as dialects share the same features. I shall take philosophy as an example of a language which is a subset of a tongue. In Chapter 2, I mentioned Davidson's (1986) article, 'A nice derangement of epitaphs', with its allusions to various cultural items. It seems that the lexical items that an academic philosopher needs include Mrs Malaprop and *Finnegans Wake*. Think, too, of 'straw men', 'epistemology' and 'the evening star'. Functions that need to be used include methods of argument (the adversarial method) or expressions of disagreement couched as 'this is odd'. Foreign philosophy students studying in England can learn to 'speak philosophy' quite adequately, while still finding it hard to follow conversations on buses or understand what is going on in a children's TV show.

Overlap occurs for both lexical items and for functions. From the point of view of any one language there is a series of concentric circles. At the centre of the circles are those who speak it very well indeed and communicate quickly and easily. Working outwards from the centre there are those who share some of the items and functions but do not recognise them all. Where the circles are drawn will be arbitrary. The place where one turns into the other is fuzzy. Think of the progress of dialects. Nottingham is eight miles from Derby. Just where does a Nottinghamshire way of speaking turn into a Derbyshire way of speaking? Just when can someone say they are now able to speak like a philosopher – or like an academic feminist?

Some aspects of such languages would cross boundaries of tongues: 'talking like a women' may be one such a language. Being of the 'Black Atlantic' may be another, as Paul Gilroy persuasively argues. Other possibilities include areas where the skill is in many ways not context-bound: being a mother, or doing mathematics would be examples. Of course the languages of those mothers or mathematicians who speak the same tongue will be closer than those who do not.

Languages overlap. As I said earlier, from its own perspective each one of them may be pictured as a series of concentric circles, with the real thing, the pure language itself, at the centre, becoming more diluted or muddied at the outer wheels, where dialects or improper versions are found. The picture which included all the languages would be much harder to describe. For instance, the language of academic philosophy has a clear overlap with that of the language of highly schooled Western males. (This is why Davidson can assume a recognition of Mrs Malaprop and *Finnegans Wake*.)

The existence of overlap means that some kind of translation is possible – the existence of non-overlap makes translation difficult. Each of us has an idiolect made up of a particular pattern of pieces of language. We can choose to use what we share, to explain what we do not. Or we can choose only to speak to those with whom we share nearly everything. When there is less than total overlap, Gricean communication comes into its own, to fill in the gaps.

It is important to remember that the overlap includes an overlap of assumptions and rules about public–political space. Many of the examples I have given could have been taken as examples of this. Take the 'Eh up!' greeting in Nottingham. It both defines and assumes a particular space which is not only public but also political – in terms of social class and, to a lesser extent, racial politics and the politics of North and South in England. The possibility exists to change this space, by playing with the parameters and expectations. However, any such change would have to take into account the already well-understood assumptions which govern its use and the space it creates and draws on.

The question of this section was: how far are we stuck in our own language, and under what conditions can we understand those who speak another language – or be understood by them? My response so far is as follows.

First, it is important to be more careful about the term 'language'. The problem in the question is a false one in that 'another language' is not usually a true description – there is a false problem raised by assuming that there are sharp, clear boundaries between one language and another.

On the contrary, the existence of overlap means that it is possible to understand across tongues and across shared activities, values and experiences. On the other hand, where there is little overlap there is little chance of communication. Second and supplementary to this answer, is the conclusion that in so far as I want to make others understand me, I have to share a set of perspectives, or set of activities with them. We have to negotiate these within the public–political spaces we create in any conversation.

This is not a comfortable response, because it gives no clear-cut answer. It demonstrates the reasons for tensions, which can only be acted on, not dissolved. Depth and breadth of understanding of others have to be weighed against each other. Similarly, the importance of making the difficult effort to listen to those who are most oppressed needs to be weighed against the importance of listening to those who can be understood. In coming to terms with these tensions I generated a set of principles, a working document, which appears in Chapter 3. They also provide a springboard for a politics of language, and, in particular, a politics of selves, which I explore further in the next chapter.

4 COMMUNICATION IN THE ACADEMY

The conclusions I have reached are different from those of most contemporary English-speaking philosophers of language. In order to show this, I focus on the symposium by Davidson, Hacking and Dummett (LePore, 1986) and on Rorty's reply to Lyotard (Rorty, 1991). These philosophers have serious differences with each other, but there are surprising similarities in the perspectives they take in their enquiries. My own enquiry is rooted in understanding the self and its politics, which led me to an interest in speaking and listening to others, in conditions of social injustice. My own political position as both marginal (for example as a woman) and as privileged (for example as white and middle-class) gives me a particular set of perspectives. There is no doubt that both Dummett and Rorty demonstrate an interest in justice. None the less, their perspectives will inevitably have been limited by their positions.[7]

There are three main areas in which I want to criticise the narrowness of perspective in the academy for the way that it distorts the account of language that has been presented. The first is that the theory appears to be modelled on a view of conversation as a lecture or seminar, supplemented with reading the newspaper, or as the occasional conversation with taxi drivers or with neighbours over the garden fence. The second criticism is that it is assumed that translation between languages is achieved by observation rather than by joining in. Third, I draw attention to the place of politics, which is largely ignored in the academy.[8]

The first criticism is that language interactions are seen as telling and learning. Both Hacking and Dummett rightly criticise Davidson for focusing on monologue. However, their preferred model seems to be one of hearer and speaker taking turns as they exchange views and information about compassion and babysitting (LePore, 1986: 457). They both have an idea that the hearer interprets (or simply understands) the speaker. I am reminded of the progress of University lectures, tutorials and seminars – and of how different they are from so many other conversations and interactions. Quite ordinary interactions include episodes in which the participants struggle to understand the point of an interchange, or to assert status, or to negotiate social or political attitudes. Each of these can be described as Speaker, Hearer, and turn-taking, but to do this distorts the description into one where there is merely an exchange of information or argument.

For the participants in the LePore symposium, oddities of understanding are things like malapropisms, or (following Putnam's earlier series of investigations) questions of identification, such as the identification of a boat as a 'ketch' or a 'yawl' by non-specialists talking to each other. Why is malapropism or this kind of exact identification so salient for these philosophers? My view is that their discussion is heavily influenced by the model of a turn-taking information exchange. But malapropism and dealing with identification is relatively easy. Moreover they are much less immediately relevant than the problems of communication that beset so many of us others, every day, often with the significant material result of being unable to communicate or express ourselves well enough to participate as we should like in a number of spheres.

Rorty is nearly as narrow, and equally bound by privilege. He too is influenced by the lecture–tutorial–seminar model, but he also takes aesthetic self-expression as one of the most significant functions of language. This is just as much of a distortion. Just like running seminars and giving lectures or tutorials, aesthetic self-expression is much easier for the powerful from institutional strongholds of privilege. The cultural politics I discussed at the end of Chapter 8 is predicated precisely on the difficulties that less privileged people have in making a cultural impact.

Even Charles Taylor, whose work I have drawn on extensively, fails to see the political implications of some of his work, because the examples he uses are so apolitical. He is concerned, as I am, to criticise the model of Speaker and Hearer exchanging information. His examples are of people creating public space with others like them: conversations with strangers in trains about the heat, or between acquaintances at cocktail parties, who share an ironic stance to the social world in which they find themselves. He entirely misses the kind of conversations he might have as a man who finds himself among feminists, and suddenly finds himself tongue-tied, or as the white man who is in a gathering of black people, and waits before entering the discussion.

The second criticism is related to the model of translation between languages as achieved by observation rather than by interaction and joining in. In this model little notice is taken of the fact that social groups do things together, trying to achieve common processes and ends, rather than, like the people talking about ketches or yawls mentioned above, simply making 'laconic comments on the passing show' (Quine, 1960: 5). Social groups notice their environment, including the human environment, in terms of what they are trying to do together. Quine makes a great deal of the difficulty for a linguist in discovering whether 'gavagai' means 'rabbit' or 'rabbit part', or even 'animal', or 'white'. This is because he imagines his linguist observing and asking questions. If the linguist had a common interest with the natives in eating, photography, religion or fur-trapping she would quickly find out these things. Unfortunately Quine's view of language learning as derived from observation rather than social interaction is taken up by later philosophers in the tradition. Charles Taylor remarks that Quine's and Davidson's theories of radical translation are 'framed as theories elaborated by an observer about an object observed but not participated in' (Taylor, 1985: 255).

Rorty, in reply to Taylor's charge, argues that such a procedure is appropriate, comparing learning a language to a biologist learning about squids by prodding them (1991: 108). More usually the debate is set up as a story of traditional anthropology, in which an anthropologist learns a language and a culture by observation. This story is part of the problem. It assumes an 'us' and a 'them' who are clearly distinguishable. But, as I have been arguing, this is to ignore the overlap between languages, and the possibilities of multiple patterns of overlap. The assumption is damaging to the theory because it is so oversimplified. More realistic questions about translation are by-passed, together with their interesting theoretical implications: translation within us, among us, with those who are much like us, with those who are a bit like us. In fact it is very hard to think of anyone who could be said to be an unequivocal 'them' to our 'us'.[9] Another metaphor, similar to the one of biologists and squids, or anthropologists and natives, is found in the debate between Rorty and Lyotard who talk in terms of islets of language and the causeways between them. In distinction to this, my view is one in which language is fractured, overlapping, fragmented, and ever-changing as a result.

Since the issues of translation are so oversimplified, there are serious omissions in the mainstream discussions. There is no account of the double vision so often spoken about by marginals.[10] Spivak (1992: 186) talks of the importance of surrender to the text, and of the different import that ideas have in context (see Chapter 3, section 4.1). In my terms, she uses the idea of surrender as a way of discussing the difficulties of creating public space and establishing the degree of overlap that exists in it:

In translation... we feel the selvedges of the language-textile give way, fray into *frayages* or facilitations. Although every act of reading or communication is a bit of this risky fraying which scrambles together somehow, our stake in agency keeps the fraying down to a minimum.

(Spivak, 1992: 178)

There is no discussion of these matters, even as ideas to puzzle over in order to help work out a theory of meaning in translation. Therefore no attention is given to issues related to hybrids, fragments, double consciousness. The discussion is seriously weakened by these omissions.

The third and last criticism is the omission of the existence of power differences in social groups. Politics sometimes appears, but not at a fundamental level where it would affect the formation of the theory. Dummett discusses the political significance attached to minority languages by their speakers, but he does so only to further the argument that there is such a thing as a language. Rorty, of course, simply argues away the language of the less powerful (see Chapter 7, section 2.1). He talks of persuasion, seemingly seeing it as a rational enterprise untainted by power and passion. In a discussion of ethnocentricism, he ignores the possibility that his liberal views may be forced on less powerful peoples through the force of arms and capital – and in doing so ignores the testimony of history.[11]

A chilling example of the spread of liberalism is to be found in Taussig's careful historical analysis of the imposition of Western trading relationships understood in terms of barter and contract on to peoples who lived in a society of gift exchange and what Roger Casement called at the time 'affection as root principle of contact with their fellow men' (Taussig, 1987: 19). The invaders took pains to describe what they were doing, even to themselves, as no more than a combination of persuasion together with the keeping of the rule of law but, as Taussig shows, the move to liberal capitalism was achieved through terror.

In less extreme cases the existence of power differences affects discourse. This is all ignored in the mainstream accounts. There is no acknowledgement of the feeling that anyone would have to wait and listen, humbly, before joining in and understanding. There is no sense of trying to be heard and simply being irrelevant to the conversation, even when the words are heard and understood – or of always being in the spotlight as one of a visible minority. Patricia Williams describes all this vividly. As a result there is no discussion of those at the margins, nor of power as constitutive of communication.

5 CHANGING LANGUAGE: POLITICAL CHANGE AND LANGUAGE

In this section I pick up on the point made at the end of section 2, about language change. Language changes all the time. Many of these changes have political dimensions – and are vigorously resisted for political reasons. The question is whether language can, in fact, be made to change for political reasons – and so whether it is worth fighting the resistance to such changes and making the effort to try and make changes.

The task of changing language can address itself to surface level changes or to deeper structures of language. I shall discuss both. However, it seems evident that the difference between surface level and deep structure is not always where a quick glance would take them to be. Some apparently simple changes are hard to make and this is, no doubt, because they are tugging at some deep-seated reason not to change. As Deborah Cameron comments:

> The more we hear anti-feminists bleating that language is 'trivial' or a diversion from 'the real issues', the more we may suspect they are protesting too much: perhaps the issue of language has an extra-ordinary subterranean importance for those critics who deride feminist concern with it.
>
> (1992: 2)

Most straightforwardly, it is possible to unpack and display oppressive, (male, racist, heterosexist, etc.) assumptions underlying the logic and rationality of ordinary communication in words. Part of my argument in this book has relied on this procedure, in displaying, for instance, the odd logic underlying descriptions of emotion and independence.

There are other ways of reclaiming the language. Words may have to be invented. Ways of speaking may have simply eliminated certain concepts. In her illuminating discussion of learning the language used by defence strategists, Carol Cohn shows that 'technostrategic' language has eliminated the word 'peace':

> No matter how well-informed or complex my questions were, if I spoke English rather than expert jargon, the men responded to me as if I were ignorant, simpleminded or both. ... I adapted my everyday speech to the vocabulary of strategic analysis. ... The word 'peace' is not a part of this discourse. As close as one can come is 'strategic stability', a term that refers to balance of numbers and types of weapons systems – not the political, social, economic and psychological conditions implied by the work 'peace'. Not only is there no word signifying peace in this discourse, the word 'peace' itself cannot be used. To speak it is immediately to brand oneself as a soft-headed activist instead of an expert, a professional to be taken seriously.
>
> (1987: 708)

Cohn is describing how words can get excluded from a language. In recent times there have been a number of words coined that now seem to describe significant parts of experience: gender, sexism, assertiveness, sexual harass-ment. Coining a new word is more like driving a wedge into a crack in a wall than putting a torch on to a previously unilluminated part of the stonework. The wall may prove to be obdurate. Or the stone may shift to make room for the wedge – and indeed may break up all together, leaving room for new wedges. Thus ordinary, everyday language has now changed to accommodate some of the new words, changing their meaning in the processes. Other new words are in the processes of being excluded again.

Cameron points out what has happened to the word 'person' – an example of masculine logic reasserting itself:

> Consider the short, sad career of the sex-neutral suffix 'person', as in *chairperson, spokesperson.* . . . *Person* has become a kind of euphemism for *woman*. It is hard to recall any instance – in speech anyway – of its applying to a man.
>
> (1992: 121–2)

Something similar has happened to 'assertion', which was meant to be contrasted with 'aggression', but has now come to mean much the same, at least as applied to women. The named thing has disappeared from view again.

It is not just nouns that need changing. It is also important to pay attention to pronouns, insults and even collocations, and also to the conversation rules that make up the public–political space for discourse. Dealing with these can be described as changing what Spivak calls the rhetoric, which 'must work in the silence between and around words in order to see what works and how much' (1992: 179). The use of pronouns ('we' as well as 'he' and 'she') is now routinely put under scrutiny, as I have done in this book. Insults and who can make them are changing. There is now an understanding of the political implications of using the feminine as an insult. Indeed there is a reappropriation of some insults for feminist purposes: Virago, the publishing house, is a famous example. In describing the conversation rules of lecturing, public speaking, and publishing, Patricia Williams simultaneously subverts them. In describing what the audience and editors take to be objectivity and straightforwardness, she casts doubt on their judgements, while continuing to transgress the rules of objectivity and straightforwardness in her own book. Similarly, the decision that bell hooks made not to use footnotes in her theoretical writing has helped to subvert and change the conventions available for everyone else.

Just as there has been effective resistance to changes of nouns, there has been resistance to changes of rhetoric. The sorry story of the campaign to lampoon 'politically correct' language, and to brand it as the misuse of power by bigots is another example of an effective campaign to stop the political change of words, pronouns, insults, and conversation rules. The relative lack of power of those demanding changes in language contrasts strangely with the extraordinary virulence of the campaign, and the speed with which it got going. I will suggest some reasons for this odd state of affairs in the rest of this section.

Frozen language is more than individual words and phrases, and it is more than rhetoric and conversation rules. At a deeper level it can be examined for its metaphoric structure. Here we get closer to the reasons for the resistance and recalcitrance of the dominant forms. The metaphors that structure our thinking may also need to be changed. One familiar to philosophers is the 'argument is war' metaphor (Lakoff and Johnson, 1980). Ayim describes what she teaches in her philosophy classes:

> We value our sharper students whom we might openly praise for their penetrating insights ... [because] we require an able opponent with whom we can parry in the classroom, so as to exhibit to the others what the thrust of philosophical argument is all about. This behaviour is somewhat risky however, as we must take care always to have the upper hand, to win thumbs down. . . . If we find ourselves pressed for time at the end of the lecture, with our back to the wall, or as it is occasionally even more colourfully expressed, between a rock and a hard place, we may have to resort to strong-arm tactics, to barbed comments, to go for the jugular, to cut their argument to pieces, to bring out our big guns or the heavy artillery.
>
> (1987: 23)

It is hard even to imagine argument as being friendly, collaborative, or conversational, although there are some attempts being made to do so. Compare Jane Martin:

> A good conversation is neither a fight nor a contest. Circular in form, cooperative in manner, and constructive in intent, it is an interchange of ideas by those who see themselves not as adversaries but as human beings come together to talk and listen and learn from one another.
>
> (1985: 9)

It is easy to see that increasing the range of metaphors for argument would open the way to a variety of processes of argument.

The example 'argument is war' is a useful one for me to use in this book which uses philosophical argument, because it is an easy example for the philosophically minded to understand. It is also easy for us argumentative philosophers to appreciate the real consequences of using it. It is particularly useful for feminist philosophers who typically find cut and thrust argument less fun than do the mainstream. Lakoff and Johnson (1980) describe many more such metaphors. Their argument that metaphors systematically structure the language can be used for feminist purposes.

A metaphor of sexuality systematically pervades the language. It is necessary to note that this is a metaphor which draws on the peculiarities of sexuality as it is assumed by the dominant discourse: in the first place there are two and only two sexes (homosexuality is assimilated to the Other.) At the same time sexuality is marked by the many differences of class, race, age, and not least, sexual orientation. Thus a metaphor relying on sex draws, on the one hand, on duality (heterosexual men and others), and on the other hand, on multiple difference which is all the 'residue' against which the male can define itself and with which sexual relationships of one kind or another exist. These are the many 'others' against whom the dominant WASP man defines himself – and who he finds sexually inferior and often desirable. As well as females there are blacks, lower classes, orientals, slaves, children and animals, the 'bits of skirt', the 'rough trade', the 'dusky maidens' and the 'poofs'.

The existence of this metaphor has been the subject of analysis by feminist critics working in a number of traditions. Evelyn Fox Keller (1985) traces the use of sexual imagery in the history of modern science, using a psychoanalytic framework of object relations. Luce Irigaray, writing from a Lacanian perspective (while remaining critical of it), argues that the duality arises from the sexual structuring of the language, though she does not speak of metaphor, but rather of the imaginary (Irigaray, 1985; Whitford, 1991). Both argue that the existence of dualism in thinking is associated with sexuality.[12]

In dualist thinking, a concept that describes the world can be unitary. It picks out a single class of cases, leaving everything else as chaotic residue (to use a term used by Irigaray). Alternatively, it can be binary. It picks out two classes, which are defined as different from each other and mutually incompatible.

That dualism arises from a sexual imaginary or metaphor is significant because it ensures that, where it exists, the two concepts can never be equally valued. Even where the female is accorded value, it is always less than that accorded to the male. Indeed, to question the value of a concept which is structured as masculine, such as rationality, independence or autonomy, is to question the value of masculinity and the male sex organ. The strong feelings attached to sexuality attach themselves to these concepts and the dominant (masculine) culture will affirm them out of fear of the feminine. Questioning of this stance would be radically subversive: in danger of attacking all that is held dear. The result is that thought is short-circuited and that the concepts are ill-understood.

From this section it is possible to see that there are possibilities of change and also some reasons for the resistance to it. The account points to the strong influence that language exercises on the way we think, but also shows how language might evolve and change as a result of thinking and political action. It also shows why language is in a state of flux, and gives further reasons why understanding is partial and vision is double.

There is neither optimism nor pessimism about the possibility of intentional language change in the long term. All the examples have been of short-term change, and there are powerful forces acting against reform. However, at least it is certain that the changes that I have been discussing are significant for individuals. Individual women change profoundly as a result of a new understanding of language. They change both their use of language and their understanding and assessment of language of others. Thus their authentic self-expression and their political communications are affected. This is the topic of the next chapter.

10 Changing selves: personal and collective change*

1 INTRODUCTION

It is time to return to the questions posed at the beginning of the book: 'How did I come to be myself? And is what I take to be myself my real self?' These questions have been unpacked further as the book has progressed. It is now possible to understand the questions in more detail: 'Is this my real self that experiences, acts, is, feels, thinks, decides to do things for herself?' 'Is it still really me after changes to my feelings and ways of understanding and reacting to them?' 'As I change, am I being true to myself?' Alternatively, these questions can be phrased in terms of selves or fragments rather than in terms of a single self: 'There are different bits of myself, which appear and act in all the different circumstances of my life: which of these bits are really me?' 'Am I being hypocritical as I change according to the company I keep? Or, rather: when am I being my real complex self, and when am I being hypocritical?' 'When I change one bit of myself, must I work on all the other bits, if I am to be true to my new self?'

These kinds of questions must be fundamental for any politics of liberation. Liberation invites a re-assessment of oneself, and an encounter with change. It is convenient to discuss these questions in terms of the idea of authenticity: am I acting authentically? Is this an authentic feeling? How is it that some changes in myself feel as though they enhance my authenticity, while others leave me uneasily feeling that I am behaving falsely?

Since what is at issue is a politics of liberation, I also look briefly at what such a politics might look like for us, both individually and collectively. Authenticity is addressed in section 2, and politics in the creation of change is the subject of section 3.

---

* In this chapter I draw on the following auto/biographies and poems from the annotated bibliography in Chapter 3: W. E. B. Du Bois and Richard Wright (in Gilroy, 1993) and Grace Nichols.

2 AUTHENTICITY

Questions of authenticity underpin the book as a whole, but have mostly been left inexplicit. They have surfaced particularly clearly at various stages in the book. In Chapter 5, section 1.2, I discussed the importance to feminist thinking of the concepts of shrouds and fragmented selves and of a feeling described as the 'loss of a real self'. This idea was extended and developed in section 2.4.1, where it was argued that those people whose acceptance into groups is conditional upon them meeting norms imposed on them, may feel they are not being authentic. The examples given were: being 'good' children, or acting like a real boy. Questions of authenticity also appeared in Chapter 6 and Chapter 7 where the issue of trusting one's own feelings, and of changing them, were central to the argument.

In Chapter 8 the theme of authenticity was implicit in the discussion of the apparent tension between creating oneself through others, while being oneself. It was also implicit in the discussion of collective expressions of autonomy. I drew on work by Parmar who discusses the creation of authentic works of art by black and migrant women which asserts both their unity and their differences. In Chapter 9, I discussed the relation between communication and expression, pointing out that communication depended on there being something to communicate – but that the 'something' was itself formed (in part) by the means of communication. Authenticity of expression and communication needs to be understood in this framework.

Several issues need to be explored. They are: spontaneity, change over time, fragmentation and political change. First I say more about what is at issue, and then I go on to consider them in more detail in sections 2.1, 2.2 and 2.3.

First there is the question of the possibility of recognising authenticity. This is important because it is the starting point of the interest in the idea, as the questions at the beginning of the chapter indicate. The issue is one of recognising authentic actions and feelings when they occur (or fail to do so). In Chapter 2, section 7.2.2, I said how expressing love of children through valentine cards embarrassed me, even though I recognised the feeling being expressed as one I shared. The expression, however, felt unnatural to me: false, inauthentic. In section 7.4.1, I described how living with, rather than in spite of, others gave me the freedom to be myself. Evidently, spontaneity is taken to indicate an authentic feeling or action. There is a strong element of an 'individual in the here and now' in the feeling of being authentic. Authentic feelings and emotions come unbidden, are unforced. They are not the result of some cleverness by those skilled at playing on our response to music or to pictures, or on a crowd's reactions, nor are they the result of old habits now emptied of meaning. Authentic emotions are typically contrasted with sentimentality, with shallowness, or with mob hysteria.

If something is considered or planned, if it merely follows the crowd, if it 'feels unnatural' or 'forced' then it is less likely to be judged 'really me', or 'true to myself'. These are not considered, reflective judgements about self based on evidence and data. Rather, they are a considered, reflective reporting of spontaneous feelings (both remembered and current).

The strong element of individual spontaneity in the feeling of being authentic also applies to those claiming to be authentic members of groups – or worrying about their lack of authenticity. In Chapter 2, section 7.1.2, I discuss various aspects of this. The narratives of Chapter 3 are full of examples of how people are caught between knowledge of their spontaneous reactions and knowledge of reactions proper to the group with which they identify. Gilroy describes how this affected the black intellectuals Du Bois and Wright, and how they attempted to resolve the situation.

Spontaneity is of the present, it is 'now'. However, it masks a second issue which needs clarification: the importance of time and change in the recognition of an authentic feeling or action. I have argued that the self is constructed through time. Thus spontaneity, rooted in the present, gives only a snapshot of an authentic self. There can be no unchanging authenticity to be found in this way, since the self is in a process of construction. However, the feelings of 'really me', 'true to myself' and 'being myself' (expressed in the questions of the opening paragraph) seem to be indications of something more lasting than a snapshot. More-over, the recurrence of questions of authenticity in Chapters 5–9 show that such questions keep imposing themselves. This is something which needs exploring and explaining.

A further complication is introduced by the view that the self is frag-mented. This is another issue which needs clarification. If 'the self' in question is actually more like 'the selves' the answer to finding something more lasting is not to be found in seeking a coherent, transparent, unity to the self, of the kind Descartes and Hume were looking for. If frag-mented selves want to be true to themselves, then they do not mean they want to be true to some particular one clearly understood and unified self.

Finally there is the issue of the importance of authenticity in a politics of liberation. Without some grasp on authenticity, there is a mystery surrounding the identity of the liberated selves who are acting, feeling, being, changing. Therefore, an understanding of authenticity is essential. It is the key to understanding what is being called for in a liberation movement. In Chapter 8 I argued that liberation is, at least partly, about allowing people to act as they feel they want to, without fear of reprisal from those who oppress them. Equally it is, at least partly, about allowing people to speak for themselves, and to be themselves rather than having to pretend, to pass, to deny some part of themselves.

2.1 Time and the self

The first two of the issues identified above are spontaneity and change over time They need to be considered together, since each one so easily masks the other. To repeat, phrases like 'really me' typically get their purchase in situations where the experience of spontaneity is important. The experience of immediacy and individuality cannot possibly be giving the whole story. It leaves out any reference to how the self was constructed. So it is unable to take account of the importance of time to the construction of self.[1] Moreover, it stresses the personal against the social; no notice is taken of the way the social is integral to the personal. As I have argued throughout the book, every 'I' is a fragment of a 'we' – indeed of several 'we's.

Arguments in earlier chapters, beginning with Chapter 5, showed that social interactions are crucial to constructing the self. Social interactions are not snapshots. They persist over considerable lengths of time, sometimes over a life-time. In Chapter 6, I showed how emotions change over time. The theme was taken up with regard to autonomy in Chapter 8. In sum, the self may be experienced as feeling, acting and being, authentically, in the here and now. But there is no such 'here and now' for a self that is not a result of what has happened in the past – and what is expected in the future. It may be that we may act authentically in the present, but, if so, that authentic, spontaneous, immediacy is in fact firmly rooted in time, especially in past social interactions. The tensions generated by this argument have been central to discussion of authenticity in philosophy.

The tensions fuel Heidegger's idea that there is a possibility of release from 'thrownness' into authenticity. This idea has been heavily influential on later accounts of authenticity. 'Thrownness' is a term coined by Heidegger which expresses that Dasein has Being-in-the-World as its way of Being. The world is not external to, and added on to, Dasein (1962: 174). He argues that: 'Thrown into its "there", every Dasein has been factically submitted to a definite "world" – its "world"' (Heidegger, 1962: 344). For Heidegger, the conscience attests that authenticity is possible. It also indicates that authenticity is 'uncanny' – a state of mind of anxiety (or 'anxiety of conscience'). 'Being-guilty' (1962: 342) indicates that one's own Dasein (being) has been disclosed in the uncanniness of its individualisation. He says:

> Resoluteness, as *authentic Being-one's-Self*, does not detach Dasein from its world, nor does it isolate it so that it becomes a free-floating

'I'. And how should it, when resoluteness as authentic disclosedness, is *authentically* nothing else than *Being-in-the-world*?

(1962: 344)

For Charles Taylor too, there is a tension between authenticity as an idea of self-determination and acknowledging that the construction of self depends on circumstances. He argues that the ideal of authenticity in modern times is an ideal of individuality transcending social roles: 'the ideal of authenticity. As this emerges, for instance with Herder, it calls on me to discover my own original way of being. By definition, this cannot be socially derived but must be inwardly generated' (Taylor, 1991: 47).

And yet, he says, identity 'crucially depends on my dialogical relations with others' (1991: 48). The result is a continuing tension, which is too easily polarised:

> The fact that there is tension and struggle means that it can go either way. On one side are all the factors, social and internal, that drag the culture of authenticity down to its most self-centred forms; on the other are the inherent thrust and requirements of this ideal.
>
> (Taylor, 1991: 77)

This will be bad news for anyone who hoped for a definitive solution.

Frazer and Lacey express an allied dilemma for feminist politics in terms of a debate between liberals and communitarians. They say that these two dominant ways of understanding selves and others polarise three binary oppositions: agency and structure, self and other, and individual and community.[2] Thus liberals are unable to explain the importance of society and social relations to the creation of a self, and communitarians leave no room for any criticism to arise within a culture:

> On this communitarian view of personhood, the woman who lives in a sexist and patriarchal culture is peculiarly powerless. For she cannot find any jumping-off point for a critique of the dominant conception of value. . . . Within a communitarian framework, who is to say that a community with gender segregation and hierarchy in its labour market is not preferable to one without such a hierarchy, and how are they going to get to the stage of saying it?
>
> (Frazer and Lacey, 1993: 151)

The dilemma appears particularly sharply in terms of the linguistic turn in philosophy too, in so far as a 'we' expresses itself through language. For if, with the analytic philosophers, we speak language which is objective in so far as it meets truth conditions, then we are cast as observers and authenticity does not arise as an issue. If, on the other hand, with the structuralists and post-structuralists, we are created by language, then it is difficult to see how we can be authentic. For if we have been created by our language (if language speaks us, rather than we speak language),

where is there room for human agency or creativity? Subjectivity and
agency are a continuing difficulty for this set of theorists. Rorty argues,
that there is room for agency and creativity, that it is possible for us to
create ourselves through language (and not just be spoken by it, as most
people are), but that such freedom is only to be found in those few creative
artists who are untrammelled by relationships with others (see Chapter 7).

In contrast to these views of language is the view explained in Chapter
9. There I showed how language shapes, as well as is shaped by,
expression. To put that abstract argument more colloquially, the relation
is captured quite well by the everyday phrases, 'saying what I mean,
meaning what I say'. A particular form of expression can fail to communicate a perception – but on the other hand particular forms of expression
can reshape what is being communicated, so that they give precise meaning to a half-formed feeling, thought or attitude. Authentic expression
takes time to establish; it is a long-term project which depends on saying
and re-saying, over a period of time. The form of expression and the act
of communication can continue to shape and re-shape each other until a
satisfactory result is achieved.

The tensions within the issues of spontaneity and long-term construction
can be resolved in terms of the ideas of *becoming* and of *agency* – and of
the way each affects the other. These ideas underpin the arguments about
changing selves and the creation of a web of identity. The metaphor of a
web is useful in understanding both 'becoming' and 'agency' (with 'web'
understood here as tapestry, weaving, crochet and lace, rather than as a
spider's web). At first sight, needlewomen seem free to create whatever
web they fancy. A longer look shows that this impression is misleading.
Webs are always made in a temporal and social context, and they get their
meanings from that context. There are only some patterns available. Still,
a needlewoman does have room for manoeuvre. The design of the finished
article is not fixed prior to its making. New webs are invented using the
old ones as motifs. Consider the Bayeaux tapestry again, first mentioned
in Chapter 1, and compare it to the tapestries made in medieval times or
the late twentieth century, in Europe or elsewhere. It would not have
been possible for the makers of the Bayeaux tapestry to create medieval
tapestries – and vice versa. The context of the assumptions about tapestries
from which they drew was only partly visible to them. We of the twentieth
century cannot create a Norman tapestry either, because our context is
also different. A modern copy of a Norman tapestry is just that: a copy.
Divergence from conventions would be a mistake for the modern copy; for
the Normans it would have been creativity.

Just as webs are made in context, an ever-changing context to which
the new web contributes, so selves are always in a process of becoming.
Just as webs are creations of particular makers, so selves are constructed;
a self has agency. Just as making a web that expresses the wishes of the
maker is a creation, even though she is working in previously fixed

patterns, so 'being me' means creating a self as well as living within the patterns of a particular time and place. Agency occurs within context – and no self could explain the context within which she had agency, any more than a needlewoman could explain the full context in which any given article was made.

Agency and becoming, therefore, cast further light on two of the arguments of this book. First, the construction and maintenance of 'I' or 'self' is both with and through others (you, they, we). The processes of construction and maintenance take place between individuals in small-scale, face-to-face groups. As emphasised throughout the book, it also takes place in communities of others who may be chosen or, through processes of exclusion and inclusion, they may be imposed on the self. Second, these processes of construction and maintenance are not necessarily conscious at the time; nor are they always remembered. They take place throughout a person's life and leave their traces on future selves. Some of them – such as the effects of sexism and racism – are precipitated by views that others have of features of an individual, regardless of her previous perception of the salience of these features.

This is an argument that agency is possible but only within a pre-existing, but changing, context which cannot be fully known. Thus, agency does not necessary imply a self who always knows just what she is doing. The idea of becoming shows why not. The processes described in the theory are ones in which a person comes to understand some of her earlier choices and reactions (and their constraining circumstances) and uses this knowledge to re-direct the shape of the web. That there can be a self which is not fully conscious of its agency is a startling notion for much standard philosophy. The debates about 'the death of the subject' have, until recently, tended to assume a fully conscious Cartesian subject. It is also a debate which is alive and well in the analytical tradition, where it appears as a discussion about how far the 'I' is conscious, and how far the self is different from a person, a human being or a consciousness.[3]

So, finally, what is 'authenticity'? It is to be understood in relation to agency and becoming. To be authentic requires acting at one's own behest both at a feeling level and also at an intellectual, reflective one. The feelings are the spontaneous enactment of the agency. The context of that agency in terms of the wider context needs to be taken into account. This is the intellectual reflection on the action, which may well change what future feelings arise spontaneously. So the present time remains important, but authenticity has to be achieved and re-achieved. Each action changes the context and requires understanding if authenticity is to be retained. Simply acting on what you feel will not answer. Nor will acting on what you think. Both are required, and it is difficult to know which to emphasise at any stage. The re-introduction of the term 'autonomy' into the explanation may help clarify the idea: autonomy comes from agency which takes place within a context of becoming. The more both agency and context are acknowledged, the more autonomous is an action and the more authentic is the self.

Take the example of Marion Milner's three books which were first mentioned in Chapter 4, section 4.2. They report a project in which she tries to understand herself better, in order to improve her control over her own life. To do that she needs to discover her preoccupations. She does not assume that she already has the raw material, but makes efforts to find out the 'facts' in various ways – and is surprised by them. She finds out some things she did not know about herself, like her feelings about religion and her tendency to masochism. She also finds she changes with time – for instance her religious preoccupations change radically. This is an account of a person endeavouring to discover her authentic self: it is not an effort to discover some essential self which she was born with. Her account of thinking which leads her to discover this authentic self is one which requires a receptivity to herself, and to her world. Thus she is indeed acting at her own behest both at a feeling level and also an intellectual, reflective one.

Grace Nichols expresses the significance of both context and agency in her poem 'Holding my beads' (see p. 52). In this section, I continue to use her poems as expressive of much of my own view of self.

2.2 'The self' and 'selves'

It may reasonably be objected that throughout this chapter, and indeed the book, I have persistently used the terminology of 'self' or 'the self', and of 'I'; and that these are formulations which do not catch much of what I have to say about the fragmentations of identity. This is, in part, a good example of the difficulties of expression and communication. If I were to use a phrase like 'selves' it would sound as if I were referring to more than one embodied person. 'Self', like 'I', is used in standard English to mark a difference from 'we', 'you', 'he', 'she', 'they', and the selves which come with them. It might, perhaps, have been easier to express multiplicity if the English tongue had collapsed 'I' into 'we' as it has collapsed 'thou' into 'you'. As it is, talk of 'we' or of 'selves' is misleading within the context and assumptions which mark expressions in English. As I explained in Chapter 9, any expression is constrained by language although it can use it as a springboard for new meaning.

My hope is that the terms 'self' and 'I' lose some of the assumptions that presently surround them in theoretical discourse, so that they can be used without implying a unified, transparent subject, but still maintain the distinction, based on embodiment, between 'I' and 'you'; 'I' and 'we'. I think that this should be possible because 'I' in ordinary English is hospitable to notions of fragmentation, much more so than much of the Western traditions of philosophy, particularly those rooted in Kantian liberalism or in the unified subject of various Cartesian traditions. In ordinary language it is commonplace to talk of sides or streaks in a person: 'She has an unexpectedly sentimental side to her character' or 'She is kindly, but she has a real streak of malice' or 'I didn't know I would do that – but I did.'

The self for which I argue is compatible with the self found in the statements of ordinary language; it is very far from being the transparent unified subject of so much Western philosophy. Rather it is characterised by incoherence in its beliefs and actions, is not easily understood by itself, is only partly avowed: it can, however, be distinguished from you, even while acknowledging that it has been both created and maintained by us, together.

I now add to the two statements in section 2.1 summarising my central arguments about the self. A third argument is that the self is made up of a number of different, sometimes incompatible, 'selves', all of which, taken together, make up the self as a whole. A self can participate in different, partially incompatible communities. It is not unusual for a self to be surprised by itself, as different 'selves' take precedence. A fourth argument is that it speaks and is constrained by a number of different, overlapping, languages and discourses. This is all expressed particularly well in Grace Nichols' poem 'In spite of me' (see pp. 51–2).

I argue that authenticity is more likely to be reached by an acceptance of the fragmentary nature of the self, than by clinging hopelessly to a dream of unity. In order to see this argument, it is necessary to look again at the fragmentation of self. Some of the fragmentation comes about from political structures of oppression: fragments of self can be described in terms of gender, race, class, sexuality and so forth. So I look first at fragmentation using the categories of the oppressor and the oppressed. Almost every individual falls on *both* sides of these divides, depending on what kind of oppression is at issue. Those who are absolutely 'one of us' – always in the position of privilege – are few and far between. Just as rare are those who have no position of privilege. Thus it is normal for any one individual to build up habits which reflect that they are oppressed, in some contexts, while they have other habits which reflect that they are oppressor in others. In each case there will be obscure views of some things and clear visions of others, since the different perspectives provide different vantage points.

Only some of the fragmentation of self comes about from political structures of oppression. There are other reasons for fragmentation. Selves can be fragmented because of material conditions and experiences and interests that do not fit readily into categories of oppressor and oppressed. For instance, fragments of self can be described in terms of regional differences, particular experiences like migration or parenthood, or affiliations of interests, such as a passion for hill walking. In England, for example, Asian British living in Lancashire view themselves as different from Asian British living in London. Migrants, of whom I am one, overlap with a variety of other migrants, some of whom find migration deeply mixed with race (e.g. from the Caribbean), or ethnicity (e.g. from Poland) while some others do not (such as myself migrating from an African colonial childhood).

All these fragments are marked by material conditions and by languages, discourses. Women typically have different experiences from men, yet they may overlap in some respects, such as class, or interests in walking. Young South Asian women in Lancashire have different experiences from young South Asian women in London, yet share common experiences of racism, or of sexism (Mirza, 1995). Migrants share some experiences of dealing with strangeness, yet have serious differences in other respects, depending on their race or on their political reasons for migrating.

The acceptance of fragmentation is the relinquishing of an inappropriate dream of purity, as well as a relinquishing of the wish for the unity of the subject. It implies a celebration of 'hybridity, impurity, intermingling, the transformation that comes from new and unexpected combinations of human beings' (Richardson, 1991: 8). Indeed, the problem of fragmentation takes on an entirely new look when it is recognised that most people will not identify 100 percent with any group in which they find themselves.[4] We are all hybrids. A group need not strive after purity. To do so is to force its members into making a more than 100 per cent identification, a condition in which much of their experience and interests are stifled.

Once hybridity is recognised in general, it can be further seen that, in particular, multilingual abilities are widespread and normal. Communication takes place through a network of languages, which arise from material conditions of the users, which is why there are so many of them. As argued in Chapter 9, a member of a group can use the language of that group, more or less well. Moreover, only by struggling with the language she is using, is it likely that she expresses herself well (see section 2.1). She can also use the language of other groups to which she belongs – and translate from one to the other, or use the language of another group to disrupt the language of the first (see Chapter 9, section 2 and some of the examples at the end of that Chapter).

In the past feminists have had a dream of sisterhood and a common language. Recognition of hybridity and multilingualism shows that, so far from this being desirable, differences between women and their different languages, combined with the points of overlap between them, actually improve the possibilities of political change. Differences provide a space for alternative perspectives to grow, and for alliances to form, making space for collective change.

It is always easier to see those inequalities and injustices which adversely affect us, than those we (unintentionally) inflict on others. But having had to deal with those inequalities and injustices which adversely affect us, it is easier to be brought to see how we are dealing out similar inequalities and injustices to others. Having seen institutional sexism in operation, even by well-meaning men, it is easier for me to be brought to see the operations of institutional racism practised by myself and others, without thinking that makes me ill-intentioned. As I judge how far sexism in men is pernicious by their willingness to change when institutional sexism is brought to their attention, so too can I equally judge racism in myself. Moreover, because I can describe myself as both oppressed and oppressor, it is easier for me to overlap in experiences with others who are also both oppressed and oppressor, even if their areas of oppression are different. Thus we can forge a language in which to discuss the matter, and the contexts in which we express agency become clearer.

Fragmentation is an ordinary condition of human selves. The question then arises what response the self should make to its own fragmentation. It may feel as though the different fragments of the being are at war with themselves. Or it may be that some coalition of the fragments is possible. I have chosen a word like 'coalition' rather than 'consensus' because 'coalitions' imply a mixture of tolerance, including one fragment ignoring another, with negotiation. The self that acts and speaks in one role need not always enquire too closely into the self that acts and speaks in another. However, the differences may cause pain and discomfort, and require resolution of some kind. I describe some of this in Chapter 2. In section 7.1.2 I described more or less successful coalitions I achieved over my own 'belonging' to various groups. In the same section, I also described my observations of children working out coalitions of their own in their own fragmented selves. Grace Nichols' poems express an acceptance of difference within herself, together with a tension about it that is a source for the creation of the poems.

In the previous section (section 2.1), I said that authenticity requires acting at one's own behest both at a feeling level and also at an intellectual, reflective one, and that authenticity has to be achieved and re-achieved. Fragmentation helps this process of achieving authenticity. Not only does it show us difference, but also it impels re-assessment and change as we both act in the present, as we are now, and at the same time reflect on our own incoherence. This dual process of action and reflection is a source of insight and further change. The acknowledgement of the complexity of ourselves is a pre-condition for self-transformation, in so far as transformation is needed.

The process is difficult, slow and painstaking. There is a thin line between bad faith (self-deception) and authenticity. Sartre's discussion of bad faith shows one reason for this. He discusses the case of a 'paederast' who refuses to admit that he is one (1958: 63):

While recognising his homosexual inclinations, while avowing each and every particular misdeed which he has committed, [he] refuses with all his strength to consider himself '*a paederast*'. . . . Here is assuredly a man in bad faith who borders on the comic since, acknowledging all the facts which are imputed to him, he refuses to draw from them the conclusion which they impose.

However, Sartre says, in some ways, the man is right (1958: 64):

He plays on the word *being*. He would be right actually if he understood the phrase 'I am not a paederast' in the sense of 'I am not what I am'. That is, if he declared to himself, 'To the extent that a pattern of conduct is defined as the conduct of a paederast and to the extent that I have adopted this conduct, I am a paederast. But to the extent that human reality can not be finally defined by patterns of conduct, I am not one.'

In so far as the man is trying to change himself, rather than simply lying about what he does, he is using contradictions within himself to reflect on what he does, in terms of other parts of himself, in order to transform himself. In so far as he is doing this, he is trying to achieve authenticity.[5]

The analysis of this section shows that Sartre is only presenting part of the case. The man could also reflect on his dislike of being labelled a 'paederast'. He can use the self which is homosexual to reflect on the self which hates the idea. Each fragment can reflect on the other, thus allowing for a wider range of resolutions. It is obvious, too, that this reflection is helped by participation in a number of different communities. If there had been Gay Pride marches in Paris in the 1940s, he could have given more space to his gay self and encouraged it to ask questions of the homophobic self. Good faith is rooted in the context. Sartre was wrong to place it entirely in isolated consciousness.

In effect a person can 'try on' one self, and hold to it, and then, another time, 'try' on another, meanwhile reflecting on both. To some extent, then, achieving authenticity may mean behaving with irony, at least some of the time. It certainly means uncertainty. Since, as I have said, we have a limited ability to understand the context in which we live, and since we are ourselves fragmented, it is easy to make mistakes. Many of our actions, attitudes and perceptions have become habitual, or have their roots in forgotten situations, but which yet express important sides of ourselves. Overriding these habitual actions and attitudes is a necessary part of transformation, but to do so may be to abandon some other part of ourselves which we had not properly noticed.

Consistency may not be the best resolution to divisions within the self. There are different coalitions possible. Consider the situation when a person has been diagnosed as having a fatal disease. Denial or acceptance are not the only possible options either for her or for those who love her. Nor will the same resolution be appropriate for different fragments of herself, for instance, as parent, as colleague or as member of various communities.

Maintaining any such resolution of different sides to the self is difficult, and requires constant reflection and reappraisal. Authenticity is best seen as a continuing process, one which requires constant effort. As I noted earlier, both Heidegger and Taylor also describe the achievement of authenticity as a continuing, difficult struggle, marked by tensions and temptations to be inauthentic (Heidegger) or by the ignoring of one or other side of the pull towards individual and social (Taylor). Authenticity is an exercise of a politics of the self, in which transformation of some or all of the self is possible, but which acknowledges that such transformation starts with what is there already. This is freedom but not a total freedom to create oneself.[6] A self is always rooted in its past. Grace Nichols' poem, 'Epilogue' (see p. 52), expresses the view powerfully and succinctly.

2.3 Authenticity and change

I am now in a position to return to the questions with which I began the chapter. Knowing what feels like 'me' is important but may change, indeed will change. The agent has some control over how it will change and will contribute towards creating the new 'me'. However it must be recognised that it is only a contribution. All the other selves also exercise some control over such a creation. Decisions and choices are made against a shifting background. Being alert to who you are requires discovering yourself in a number of ways as well as through simple introspection. It is an important part of finding or creating 'me'.

Worries over what is a real self, over which bits of oneself are the real self, are shown to be a useful invitation to listen to oneself and find out. The worry turns into a problem of authenticity and autonomy: having acknowledged discomforts, what is the best way to resolve them? Decisions can be made about which parts of the self need transforming and how far it is possible to do that. It is essential to acknowledge that there exists no unity of the self, no unchanging core of a being. Such a belief is a fancy, and will mislead the self into seeking to establish it. Being true to oneself does not mean seeking after such a core. It means undertaking the difficult business of assessment and transformation within a changing context of self. Authenticity requires re-assessing the changing self, not preserving a sameness.

3 CREATING CHANGE

I now focus on the possibilities of making change happen. This question has arisen in earlier chapters, particularly in Chapter 8 in relation to public autonomy and in Chapter 9 in relation to changes in language. In this section I take up these themes as they have arisen out of attention to authenticity: to changes in selves during which they remain true to themselves. Thus I turn to the issue of creating a politics of personal and public change which preserves and creates authenticity; personal and collective change as it starts from a concern with self and selves.

Inevitably this will be a somewhat sketchy discussion. I am not hoping to solve major problems of political theory and organisation in a few pages. However, I think it is important to show how such problems might be tackled in the light of my account of how self-identity is constructed both collectively in a variety of overlapping communities, and also at an individual level.

3.1 Personal change: learning from others and from our own divided selves

Change is inevitable: it comes from the interaction of selves with each other and with material circumstances. Change is also self-directed. How should it be directed? How is it possible to make change happen?

Learning is derived not just from observing and experimenting, but also from trying to enter into a genuine discussion. In Chapter 3, section 5, I discussed this in terms of listening, openness to persons and engagement. The discussion of language in Chapter 9 gives a basis for a deeper understanding of the issues as they were presented earlier. In particular, the analysis of the establishment of public spaces in which communication and expression can occur shows what is involved in listening, openness and engagement. It points up the importance of 'surrender'[7] as well as of 'participation'. In Chapter 3, I quoted Anne Seller (1994) reflecting on her stay in an Indian University, explaining some of the difficulties of maintaining a dialogue in terms of its content. She also discusses some of the difficulties in establishing public space. She had tried, without success, to set up a seminar which would be a forum for discussion, a place of dialogue, in which people would feel they could speak freely:

> I was surprised to discover within myself a commitment to liberal principles so deep that I was at a loss when they were not used to define my working space. . . . At the same time . . . my attempts to put them into practice could be a piece of cultural hegemony.
>
> (Seller, 1994: 237)

As time went on, she resolved this in terms of response and ways of being with others, terms reminiscent of openness and surrender as well as of participation. In this case there is a happy ending. But as Seller shows, Strickland is right in her view that openness and engagement is an uncomfortable process, productive of conflict, tension, anger, hurt and defensiveness, as well as of resolution and of the pleasures of new inclusions and loves (1994).

Change also arises from our own, individual, fragmentations of self. The more we are members of different communities and the more we are each multilingual, the more opportunities we have for change. It takes courage to instigate self-reflection which calls oneself into question. Openness to ourselves is not always a comfortable process, any more than is the process of openness to others. There may be tension, anger, shame and defensiveness in discussions with oneself too. In Chapter 2, section 7.1.2, I reveal some of this discomfort, both in reflections on my identity and in reflections on my reactions to others.

Thus the self changes over time, partly through having the attitudes required for engagement with and openness to persons, partly as a result of having the courage and patience to listen to our own fragmented selves. This is self-direction up to a point, but is not enough by itself. It is also necessary to understand the power operating in the context in which we live. I am referring here more to a Foucauldian 'productivity of power' than to 'the power that says no' (see Chapter 9, n. 3). In Chapter 3, I explained why simple listening is not enough. The few with loud, powerful voices drown out the softer, less powerful voices of others. In Chapter 9, I pointed out the difficulties of making changes in language, given the capacity of others to reverse them.

In Chapter 3, I suggested some principles which guide an individual actively seeking out less powerful voices. A longer-term solution is the development of a politics based on a collective wish to learn from each other. This is a collective as well as a personal endeavour. It is to this I turn in section 3.2.

3.2 Collective change: working with others

In this section I argue that there are a number of requirements for collective change, such that it allows for the exercise of autonomy and the maintenance of authenticity. I argue that the Women's Movement as a whole – and indeed any other liberation movement – needs its members to take part in the following: cultural politics, organization round issues and academic reflection, all of which need to be framed by the attitudes of vigilance, subversion and the willingness to dream impossible dreams. A continuing theme of this argument is the mutual dependence of the personal and the collective. The personal ability to instigate change depends on a collective endeavour. Likewise the collective endeavour is meaningless without the personal.[8]

It is impossible for any one individual to immerse herself in cultural politics, at the same time as taking an active part in collective organising around issues, at the same time as undertaking academic reflection. The important point is that, collectively, we need to be working towards all of them at once. Individually we can focus on one or two or even, over a life-time, all three. Here, again, the metaphor of a web is useful.

Together we can make a web, but we need not each work on all of it, all of the time. Networking and overlap mean that it can be a collective effort, which draws on all aspects of collective change, rather than just on one.

Before collective change is possible, people need to speak for themselves, and define themselves: to put it another way, they need to work out their own authentic resolutions. This can come about through cultural politics. Cultural politics requires time and space in which to generate cultural creations and to respond to the creations of others. So it may be necessary first to organise around the issue of getting such time and space, whether this is a room of one's own, or the provision of child-care.

In order to organise you need to know who you are – even though 'who you are' is in a state of change.[9] In so far as people can speak for themselves and define themselves, which is itself a collective, political act, then they can bring that to collective organising around issues. So some kind of cultural politics may be needed just to start organising round issues. Thus, neither cultural nor organisational politics is prior to the other.

Neither cultural nor issue-based politics can advance without sustained collective reflection. This is academic work. Feminist theory puts ideas together, picks over the ideas of others and asks awkward questions of ourselves. Theory is not distinct from practice. On the contrary, there is a multiplicity of ways in which academic work – collective reflection – furthers practical outcomes, be they cultural creations or changes in material conditions.

Collective actions take place through a combination of action and words. Just as for personal change, collective change can be an extremely uncomfortable process. Sometimes, happily, it is a source of new ways of being together but, equally, since collectivities are marked by disagreement and tensions, there are also incommensurable arguments and violent actions. They arise in all of these modes of action: cultural politics, organising round issues and academic reflection.

The process of dealing with collective change depends on meeting together collectively. Meeting together means having an agreed meeting place – a public space – where different people come together, to love and to fight. This space need not be a physical place. Although meetings can be in person, they also occur through publications, or through media reporting of events. The process of dealing with collective change also depends on working out ways of dealing with the differences that are at the root of the fights. Thus, there are two issues which need to be taken up, even if very briefly: (1) public spaces; (2) pluralism and difference. I can only make some comments about this: a thorough discussion would be a subject for another book.

3.2.1 Public spaces

In Chapter 8, and again in Chapter 9, I introduced the issue of what counts as a public space, a space in which we can meet, negotiate, fight, and learn how to love each other, or how to live with our differences one way or another. Benhabib, in her useful chapter called 'Models of public space', concludes that the Habermasian model of public space is one which best 'captures the role of democratic debate' (1992: 107). She defends this view even though Habermas himself has tried to 'establish overly rigid boundaries' between public and private, the good and the right. Her claim is that the discourse model can, in fact, accommodate feminist challenges to the public/private distinction. I agree with her that the discourse model is an advance on the liberal model, but I think it does not go far enough. It retains an untenable distinction between public and personal, framed by a misleading narrowness of scope in what counts as 'political'.

Benhabib states that she is restricting the scope:

> The model of public space is the one implicit in Jurgen Habermas's work. . . . By situating the concept of 'public space' in this context, the discussion is restricted from the outset to normative political theory. The larger sense of *Offentlichkeit*, which would include a literary, artistic and scientific public will not be of concern here.
>
> (1992: 89)

She goes on: 'The public sphere comes into existence whenever and wherever all affected by general social and political norms of action engage in a practical discourse, evaluating their validity' (1992: 105).

But I have argued to the contrary. Public space is any place where political, collective action can take place, be it cultural politics (including the literary and artistic), or the politics of practical discourse related to organisation around issues, or academic reflection intended to reflect on either or both of the first two. In her inspiring article, Madhu Bhushan (1989) describes how women in Vimochana, India are undertaking a dual process of political practice and cultural innovation with respect to women's issues. In her article, she herself, of course, is contributing to academic reflection on their collective actions. The politics of language is another example of ways in which cultural, activist and academic politics interweave and benefit from each other.

3.2.2 Pluralism and difference

Attempts to deal with difference in collective, public affairs have so far been met with little success. Anne Phillips discusses the issue by distinguishing what she calls 'conventional pluralism', in which groups are organised around interests, and 'radical pluralism' which focuses on 'identity politics', in which groups 'are defined by a common experience of exclusion or oppression' (1993: 17). She shows how conventional pluralism has failed to represent various excluded groups, including minorities and women. She also points out difficulties that have arisen in various practical attempts in England, in the Netherlands and in the USA, in trying to represent and empower such groups using identity politics as a starting point.

While Phillips discusses multiple identities, she has not accepted all its consequences for a future politics of interest or identity.[10] She characterises identity politics as though there is not an overlap between groups, and distinguishes it sharply from the politics of interest groups which she characterises as 'groups that overlap in their membership and are organised around issues that may only be moderately felt' (1993: 17). She contrasts them to identity groups, where 'the intensity of identity politics is less amenable to a politics of accommodation or compromise, and is far more likely to encourage fragmentation or mutual hostility' (ibid.).

I have argued to the contrary. Identity groups overlap and may well have gained their identity precisely by organising around issues. People can participate collectively, publicly, in a number of modes, including cultural, issue-led and academic ones. Indeed since there is a collective need to have all these ways, it is important that all the different modes co-exist. Thus it is necessary to have a combination of forms of organisation at the level of national or local government. This implies a politics of some representative government together with a large number of pressure groups. Some groups, of course, would need resources just to organise themselves. The provision of this should be a priority in a democratic system.

There is an obvious problem with the fragmentation and fluidity of this model. The very fact that it is so fragmented and fluid means that it is all too easy for it to dissolve into no politics at all, allowing the status quo to reassert itself. Of course this has been the continual complaint of outsiders about the Women's Movement as a whole, and of any number of aspects of it, such as the Greenham protests: 'If only you women got properly organised you might achieve something.' On the other hand, it is important to keep the politics alive and responsive. This is more likely to happen if all the modes of politics are framed by the attitudes which I mentioned at the start of the section: vigilance, subversion, and the willingness to dream impossible dreams.

Vigilance is needed to ensure both that the status quo is not returning, and also that the fluidity of politics is not stiffening into rigidity. There needs to be continual alertness to who is being excluded and how. There are any number of ways to express concerns about these. Vigilance is exasperating to those who are relatively powerful, since it is inevitably critical of even the best of efforts. A democratic politics should encourage it, none the less.

By subversion I mean the use of ambiguity and compromise. This has been described by Spivak as 'the practical politics of the open end' (see Chapter 8, section 3.2.3). Subversion will be needed in any society which falls short of perfection. Like vigilance, subversion is exasperating to those who are relatively powerful. However, the relatively powerless need to practise it and to teach each other how to do so. It is an important way in which an individual can express her own particular identity in relation to the context in which she finds herself.

Finally there is the importance of the willingness to dream impossible dreams. To change oneself personally and collectively, requires a leap of the imagination, from the current assumptions and patterns into new forms of identity. Such leaps of the imagination can be expressed as dreams. The prevalence and influence of Utopian thinking in feminist literature is not an accident. It is an essential part of the creation of new self-identities, personally and collectively.[11]

4 PATCHWORK

I started the book with a metaphor of webs. I end with an extension of that initial metaphor, a metaphor of patchwork. My argument about the construction of self shows that, like patchwork, making a self is relatively easy, though it always takes time and attention. However, again like patchwork, making a good one is very hard indeed. Understanding which pieces of old cloth will fit into the whole is a difficult and painstaking matter. Like patchwork, the construction of an authentic, autonomous self depends on the context of each fragment, and where it fits within the overall design. Like patchwork, it is hard to say how many makers there are and where all the pieces came from.

Trying to reduce all our complexities of self-identity to relatively simple designs and simple stories, of the kind that mainstream philosophy tells, has resulted in inappropriate stories about ways in which to deal with our personal and collective dilemma. It is a simplicity which has contributed to sameness and oppression. Infinitely preferable is the variety, confusion, colour, hotchpotch, kaleidoscope, medley, motley, and harlequin of patchwork selves.

Notes

1 QUESTIONS OF THE SELF: QUESTIONS OF SELVES

1 The Bayeaux tapestry, an eleventh-century creation, is not just an historical curiosity immured in a museum in Normandy. Although the Norman conquest of England it depicts is no longer news, 800 years after its creation it is still a source of conflicting political explanations. For instance, the French and English schoolchildren who visit it hear different accounts of it and have different aspects of it highlighted.

2 John Donne, *Devotions*.

3 I take this phrase from Sneja Gunew's article (Gunew, 1990). See also Chapter 4, section 3.

4 Ray Monk provides a particularly accessible discussion of this project as it manifests itself in British academic philosophy (Monk, 1992).

5 For instance the issue merits a chapter in Friedan's pathbreaking book of the early 1960s. Also see Rowbotham (1973) and *Feminist Review* (1989).

6 See for instance the work of Carol Gilligan (1982) and many of the contributors to Harding and Hintikka (1983) and to Garry and Pearsall (1989).

7 The book is derived from my writing of ten years and more. It draws on a series of papers that I have written for a variety of audiences, and with a variety of purposes. They have been completely re-written for the sake of drawing them together into a coherent story. So the book grew as an organic whole. It has now been produced as a linear entity from Chapter 1 to Chapter 10, but the writing of it was anything but linear.

Short sections of the following will be found in the body of the text often spread over more than one chapter. 'Auto/biography and epistemology', *Educational Review* 47 (1), 1995; 'Making a difference: feminism, postmodernism and the methodology of educational research', *British Educational Research Journal*, 1995; 'Self-identity and self-esteem: achieving equality in education', *Oxford Review of Education* 19 (3), 1993, pp. 301–317; 'The politics of identity, the politics of the self' (with Anne Seller), *Women: A Cultural Review* (special edition on gendering philosophy) 3 (2), 1992, pp. 133–144; 'Autonomy and the fear of dependence', *Women's Studies International Forum* 15 (3), 1992, pp. 351–362; 'Standing alone: dependence, independence and interdependence' (with Richard Smith), *Journal of Philosophy of Education* 23 (2), 1989, pp. 283–294; 'Feminism, feelings and philosophy', in M. Griffiths and M. Whitford (eds), *Feminist Perspectives in Philosophy*, London: Macmillan and Indiana University Press, 1988.

2 USING AUTOBIOGRAPHICAL ACCOUNTS

1 There are a number of theoretical versions of the view that our perception of the world is determined by our language. A traditional version was the linguistic theory known as the 'Sapir–Whorf hypothesis', which drew on empirical evidence about the number of words for snow among Arctic-dwelling people and the grammatical structures in the North American Hopi language. Lacan provides a recent version of linguistic determinism. For Lacanians, language is a system of signs which speaks the speakers, rather than the other way about.

2 I have to say that when I have mentioned this problem to other feminist philosophers, they have not always understood my problem. They have said that I should see the process as writing for myself, to work out my own point of view. However, I fail to see how this is possible. The notes I write literally for myself would be incomprehensible to anyone else. They use a shorthand that could only be comprehensible to me, since 'I' and 'me' share both memories and interpretations.

3 From my position as adult I find such delight at 6 a.m. heroic.

4 Peter Bowbrick comments that she might have been responding to the *porkishness* of the word 'hog'. I agree. Part of the interest of the story is just that negotiation is not and could not be entirely explicit, especially for a 6-year-old. However at age 6 she was well on the way to establishing deep roots of identity based on religion and nationality, as well, no doubt, on gender and class. She may also have been developing a more complex appreciation of hogs, porkishness and Judaism.

3 OTHER LIVES: LEARNING FROM THEIR EXPERIENCES

1 This phrase owes its genesis to the discussion of 'tourism of the soul' in Donna Haraway (1991), *Simians, Cyborgs and Women*. I discuss it further in section 4.4 below.

2 Examples are Piaget in children's cognitive development, Kohlberg in theories of moral development and Goldthorpe *et al.* (1980) on political behaviour and demographic change in Britain.

3 This is discussed by Dale Spender in her *Man-made Language* (1980) and by Deborah Cameron in her *Feminism and Linguistic Theory* (1985, 1992).

4 I do not think this is a mistake on the part of Elvin; see Sharon Shih-jiuan Hou (1986). I am grateful to Yung Ming Shu for providing this reference.

5 In Egypt, Ahmed and el Sa'adawi are eminent. (Ahmed, 1988; el Sa'adawi, 1980). The Moroccan Fatima Mernissi is world famous for her carefully researched, challenging scholarship (1987, 1993). Algerians like Marnia Lazreg (1994), Maire-Aimee Helie-Lucas (1994), Cherifa Bouatta and Doria Cherifati-Merabtine (1994) are all writing critiques both of and from within their own societies.

6 Consider, for instance, a notion like 'freedom' or 'equality' as discussed for Islam by the Moroccan, Fatima Mernissi. Or the ideas of personal identity contained in *Two Lives: my spirit and I*, by the Kenyan, Jane Tapsubei Creider. There certainly exist Islamic scholars in the West – but the overlap between them and the mainstream intellectual life of the West is regrettably small. Kenyan scholars have even less impact.

7 See Sidonie Smith (1993).

8 See, for instance, Carrithers *et al.* (1985) and Jung Chang's best-selling novel, *Wild Swans*.

9 See, for instance, Stephen Butterfield (1974), David Vincent (1981), Doris Sommer (1988), Regina Gagnier (1991) and Sidonie Smith (1993).
10 This move has sometimes been rejected at a later stage: see, for instance, Radha Kumar (1993) on the movements for women's rights and feminism in India.
11 I quoted the rest of this passage earlier in Chapter 2.
12 I am thinking of interpreters that I have already mentioned, like Spivak and el Sa'adawi who have a knowledge of the West. Another is Meena Dhanda, who is mentioned later in this chapter.
13 This is true in a single society or between societies, internationally. Within education, the exotic is brought into school, as anti-racists have explained, through the syndrome referred to as 'saris, samosas and steel bands'. Teachers tell about 'other cultures' through particular instances of cultural difference, and risk merely reinforcing stereotypes while inoculating their students against any real engagement with the details of a changing cultural and political scene in their own country.
14 The film is the latest in a long line of European renderings of the Arabian Nights as tourism as a taste of the exotic. The book has acted as a lens by which Westerners can see the 'Orient' – and fail to see real places and people (Said, 1978; Kabbani, 1986).
15 I understand that Aladdin's face is made up of elements of current popular non-Arab film stars: thus he has the forehead of one, the smile of another and the chin of a third.
16 Meena Dhanda is someone who lives and works in two cultures and is able to interpret one to the other. Also see note 12.
17 I acknowledge the influence that 'Memo to oppressors' in Richardson (1990) has had on my thinking about this.
18 I tend, for instance, to bring an awareness of international perspectives to meetings of British women, since I come from a family of migrants. I learn from colleagues who bring a sharper awareness of British social class or of French or Italian views.

4 THEORY AND EXPERIENCE: EPISTEMOLOGY, METHODOLOGY AND AUTOBIOGRAPHY

1 There is little consensus about the meaning of 'postmodernism'. The key ideas include the insistence on the situatedness of human thought and on the impossibility of discovering a neutral transcendental reason or an autonomous self-legislating self. Knowledge, so far from being the 'mirror of nature', is particular to the discourse(s) in which it is produced. The self, so far from being an empirical, knowable or perceivable object, is a subjectivity produced by the discourse in which it finds and positions itself. This subjectivity is in a state of change, as it positions and re-positions itself in terms of (at least) gender, race and class and is changed and reacts to the changing discourse.
  In my view, 'post-structuralism' is best understood as a variant of 'postmodernism' partly because postmodernism is such a wide, ambiguous term. Foucault and Derrida are representative – and influential – examples of poststructuralist thinkers. They insist that events and situations have to be analysed and understood in the interplay of discourse and subjectivity at particular times and places. Both of them also insist on the importance of language as constitutive of reality and subjectivity, even while its parts shift their meanings according to circumstances.
2 This was a mistake that was made early in the development of feminist epistemologies, and is an idea which still lingers, if only in the minds of some

newcomers to thinking about these issues. This is why it is important to note that feminist epistemology is not necessarily opposed to anything that males have supposed about knowledge! Equally, of course, there is no such thing as the postmodern or the post-structuralist perspective. The terms are used to refer to a range of positions which share some common ground.

3 Garry and Pearsall (1989), Nicholson (1990), Stanley (1990), Braidotti (1991), Grant (1993), Rose (1994) and Lennon and Whitford (1994).

4 In particular it is taken up in Chapter 6, and then provides the basis for further arguments about autonomy and authenticity in the rest of Part II. In Part III, I discuss changing ourselves, including our language.

5 For one critique of such a position see Midgley 1988, and, again, but more generally, as an argument about innate characteristics, Midgley, 1994. Also see Fuss (1989) for an interesting discussion of essentialism and post-structuralism.

6 See, for instance, Chodorow (1978), Benjamin (1990), Brennan (1989) for a variety of perspectives on this issue.

7 I say more about this in Chapter 9.

8 I am sure there are other suitable methods which would fall within the methodological principles. It is not my concern to discover them here.

9 Brodzski and Schenck (1988), Schenck (1988), Jackson (1990), Smith (1993); but see Elbaz (1988).

10 See, for instance, the discussions in Personal Narratives Group (1989). Also Stanley (1992).

5 WANTING AND NOT WANTING TO BELONG: ACCEPTANCE AND REJECTION

1 Later in the chapter I draw attention to similarities with other structures of race, class and colonialism.

2 Including the way language differentially enters into the experience and subjectivity of an individual depending on sex, as explained in Chapter 4.

3 I am grateful to Debbie Epstein for this form of words, which resonates, of course, with Marx's famous statement about men making history.

4 'For my part I must plead the privilege of a sceptic, and confess that this difficulty is too hard for my understanding' (Hume, 1962: 331).

5 B. Williams (1973) was an early, influential example of these studies.

6 For a sustained discussion see Parfit (1984).

7 The split was usually there as a result of an operation which was supposed to help epilepsy. See Gazzaniga and LeDoux (1978). Also see Nagel (1979).

8 Note how Grimshaw, Benhabib and Flax turned to other traditions, and Almond stuck to moral theory rather than personal identity as a source of help.

9 Feminist (or anti-racist) versions of critical theory and communitarianism are more likely to include the personal and political, respectively. Examples include Patricia Williams for critical theory, and Elizabeth Frazer and Nicola Lacey for communitarianism.

10 I made some comments about this in the last chapter. See sections 2.1 and 2.2, especially notes 1, 2 and 3.

11 I have quoted Benhabib on this in Chapter 7, p. 132. Also see Lovibond (1989) and Hartsock (1990) for well-known formulations of this warning.

12 She comments bitterly: 'Neither these claims [about the dangers of postmodernism] nor the evident emotional investments were illuminated in this particular encounter' (Flax, 1993: 132).

13 In what follows in this section and the next I make no exhaustive analysis of the body, nor of the recent explosion of literature about the body. I only go

into enough detail about material conditions (especially, and including, the body) to show how, so far from there being givens, or brute constraints, the ways in which material conditions constrain us are mediated by the social, particularly by language.

14 It may be noted how influenced this argument has been by philosophical arguments about intentionality. Also see Chapter 6, note 6.

15 See Twumasi (1986) for this view which comes from within, rather than from outside a society more usually studied by outsiders from the West.

16 This thesis is coherent with mind/brain identity but so are various philosophical positions opposed to it.

17 My use of the term 'resistance' is independent of the various definitions attached to it in social theory. In particular, it should not be confused with Foucault's use of the term. As becomes apparent in the rest of the chapter, I focus not only on resistance by an agent towards categories imposed on her by others, but also on other forms of resistance by the agent in relation both to single others, and to groups of others.

18 This taxonomy of groups is more complex than those found in Haraway (1991) and Young (1990), which depend on affinity.

19 Research seems to show that children do not realise just how important genitals are for gender – though they see them as important for their own sake. They are unsure, for instance, whether they might gain or lose a penis, and who else has genitals like their own. According to this research, clothes are an important marker of gender, as are toys.

20 There appears to be anecdotal evidence that in the early 1990s boys feel that they have to choose between being 'real boys' and 'good at school', in a way that they did not in earlier periods when girls lagged behind boys in their educational achievements.

21 'Coconut' is a term of abuse applied by black people to those black people who they consider to be acting white: black on the outside, white on the inside.

22 See Connell (1989), and Jackson (1990).

6 FEELINGS, EMOTIONS, RATIONALITY, POLITICS

1 See Chapter 7, section 1.2.2 for more explanation of these terms and their use.

2 The role of emotion in these general cognitive processes is a subject of dispute among social psychologists. The summary in Nisbett and Ross (1980) is still useful.

3 Compare Whitford (1988); Bock and James (1992). Older, but still influential, arguments can be found in Elshtain (1981), Susan Griffin (1982), Lloyd (1993b, first edition 1984) and Haste (1986). I say more about this in Griffiths (1988, 1992).

4 Compare the interesting discussion by Philip Cohen in Cohen and Bains (1988).

5 See Oakley (1992) for a useful overview.

6 Intentional objects are the objects of psychological acts like believing, thinking, wanting. They have been much discussed in philosophy: one reason for this is that they have been used to distinguish a particular set of states of mind.

7 It is fair to say that Kenny uses a wider range of examples than the other two, because he recognises that occurrent feelings have some significance in individuating an emotion. However, he still falls into the trap of defining emotions in such a way that the place of such feelings among defining criteria for emotions is ambiguous.

8 That is, when discussing love he talks of the lover and his beloved (who is a she). He does give one mention to a mother's over-possessive love for her grown-up daughter.

9 Oakley (1992: 19).

10 Peters (1975) goes so far as to talk of the irrational bonds of family, thus emphasising the lack of rational cognition in the emotion of love.

11 See Kenny (1963: 92).

12 In what follows I shall make no attempt to distinguish feeling and emotion, simply using them as ordinary English speakers do.

13 Compare the discussion of the broken tricycle in Williams (1973: 211).

14 This judgement is based on evidence which is necessarily difficult to collect, given problems of translation. See, for instance, Ekman (1973; 1979).

15 According to Chris Akwesi, University of Cape Coast, Ghana, personal communication.

16 It is, of course, always going to be difficult to describe what cannot logically be put into words, because it is pre-linguistic by definition.

17 See Spelman (1989).

18 Bernard Williams (1993) discusses shame, and when it is appropriate in Britain or the USA.

19 Compare the comment by Frazer and Lacey (1993) quoted in Chapter 10, p. 177.

20 See e.g. Charles Taylor (1982), Margaret Whitford (1988, 1991), J. Evans (1993).

21 This distinction is similar but not identical to the one in Evans (1993) between 'rationality$_1$ – purposive, adaptive behaviour' and 'rationality$_2$, the rationality of process' to be found at the centre of decision theory and studies of logicality in reasoning.

22 A fuller account would include correctness and consistency. Correctness is about knowing if the end was achieved – whether you got it right. The argument about consistency would bring in a discussion about 'grue', as first discussed by Goodman (1973).

23 My definition of rationality contrasts with others which implicitly or explicitly assume that the means and ends have to be specified before the action begins.

24 One consequence is that preferences are not necessarily transitive. This has been a problem for psychology and economics based on such a unified model. For instance see the discussion in Over and Manktelow (1993).

7 EMOTIONS OF THE SELF: SELF-ESTEEM AND SELF-CREATION

1 My argument is with the Rawls of *A Theory of Justice*. He has now modified his views on self-respect and self-esteem.

2 This is a generalisation, of course. See Verma and Mallick (1988), Coultas (1989), Griffiths (1993).

3 In the late 1980s and early 1990s Madonna was helpful to them in this ploy.

4 This is a feminist issue. The situation is similar in the USA, according to Patricia Williams who comments that, while she likes being single, 'Sometimes when I walk down the street and see some poor black man lying over a heating vent, I feel I'm looking into the face of my companion social statistic, my lost mate – so passionate, original, creative, fine-boned, greedy, and glorious – lying in the gutter' (1993: 195).

5 It is likely that self-esteem will rise more slowly than reason would indicate, because emotions are inscribed in our perceptions, reactions, friendships, habits and reactions. These take time to change.

6 hooks (1993) is an extended discussion of some strategies of self-recovery. I did not come across this book until my own was written.
7 It is unfortunate that equal opportunities policies often address racist and sexist abuse separately. As Cohen (in Cohen and Bains, 1988) shows, when real people are involved the two are not separable, any more than are the categories 'race' and 'gender'. There are insults specific to particular forms of racism for each sex.
8 Rorty includes oppressive domination as a form of cruelty.
9 There have been various arguments discussing Hegel's analysis in relation to feminist arguments. For instance, see Harding (1986), Assiter (1988), Vogel (1987), Benjamin (1990) and Lloyd (1993b).
10 See note 9

8 AUTONOMY: PERSONAL AND POLITICAL

1 It may necessary to reiterate the cautions I gave about stereotypes in Chapter 6, section 1.2, in relation to who believes them, and about whom.
2 For some feminist responses to Hegel, see Hodge (1987) and Benhabib (1992), as well as those I mentioned previously, in Chapter 7.
3 See Grimshaw (1986), Hill (1987) and Lloyd (1993b) for some more details.
4 See Martin (1985) for a more thorough discussion.
5 Also see the thorough analysis of social contracts from a feminist perspective in Pateman (1988).
6 Kaye Haw (1995).
7 See Amos and Parmar (1987); Brah and Minhas (1985); and Westwood and Bhachu (1988). More fictionalised accounts are to be found in the Asian Women Writers' Workshop (1988) and Chatterjee and Islam (1990). See Bhushan (1989) on similar criticisms from within a South Asian culture.
8 I am talking about a locally specific difficulty: English has problems in this area. So does Western philosophy. Not all languages and theoretical systems have such difficulties. For instance, the juxtaposition of autonomy and dependence, natural to English (and other European languages), is difficult to translate in the Philippines (Andres and Ilada-Andres, 1987). Filial piety (and the dependence it represents) is central to Confucianism.
9 I am oversimplifying drastically. See, for instance, Lloyd (1993b) for a little more detail, and Solomon (1983) for more.
10 See note 7. Also Emecheta (1986) and Zhana (1988).
11 See note 5.
12 These arguments are to be found in both Benhabib (1992) and Young (1990).
13 See, for instance, Seller (1985); Mitter (1986).
14 Of course, changes always have a number of causes. I am drawing attention to *some* of them.
15 See Afshar (1991), Yuval-Davis and Anthias (1989), Toubia (1988), for a description of many of these set-backs together with both the advances which are being set-back and also the resistance which women are putting up to the set-backs.
16 For instance, see *Feminist Review* (1989), Griffiths and Seller (1992).

9 COMMUNICATION AND CHANGE

1 Taylor (1985) points out that Herder was the first to formulate an expressive theory of language, which developed from the earlier expressive theory of the cosmos. He also argues that although expressive theories are less congenial to

the analytic tradition than purely communicative ones, the two are always interlinked.

2 Davidson is rightly criticised by Dummett (1986: 475) for assuming that all taxi drivers speak English. That another human being shares our tongue (or does not) is an assumption which has to be acknowledged in an analysis of encounters in language.

3 See Fitzsimmons (1994) for a discussion of this distinction.

4 I am drawing on and extending an early account given by Bennett (1973). Bennett calls this kind of communication which does not rely on Gricean mechanisms, 'Plain Talk', and argues that: 'Plain Talk is not a vehicle of merely marginal and dependent kinds of meaning. On the contrary, it is behaviourally indistinguishable from much of what occurs at the very centre of ordinary human language' (1973: 170)

5 For instance, see Coates and Cameron (1988).

6 For instance, this is what Lévi-Strauss and Barthes are doing. Braidotti (1991) gives some examples of feminist analyses.

7 Their perspectives are likely to have been *limited*, but they will not have been *determined*, as I have been arguing throughout the book. There is, of course, no particular masculine perspective that I am criticising here.

8 Obviously, this last criticism would not apply to most French theory, but I am not concerned to criticise that theory here. Criticisms levelled at French theory would likewise not necessarily apply to the English-language philosophy which is my concern here.

9 See Said (1993) for a sustained discussion of cultural connections in the small world of the late twentieth century.

10 For instance, see Lugones (1989), hooks (1991), Gilroy (1993).

11 Rorty (1991): in an essay called 'On ethnocentricism: A reply to Clifford Geertz'.

12 Also see the arguments about dualism and binarism in relation to feminist thinking in Frazer and Lacey (1993). They argue that Derridean deconstruction offers resources for a feminist re-appraisal of binary oppositions in mainstream political theory – if used cautiously.

10 CHANGING SELVES: PERSONAL AND COLLECTIVE CHANGE

1 See Lloyd (1993a) for a sustained discussion of time, self and narrative.

2 See Chapter 9, note 12. Frazer and Lacey themselves are not polarising and dichotomising, which is precisely what they complain of in others. They are remarking on the dichotomies that others use – and showing how they are often false polarities. Neither liberalism nor communitarianism fits into a unitary compartment easily defined against the other, and the various individuals who are characterised as one or the other do not take up similar positions with respect to the polarities of agency, structure, etc., either.

3 Owen Flanagan (1991) argues that a narrative identity must be a conscious one. Christman (1991) argues that a transparent self is required if autonomy is not to be absent, or, at best, incomplete.

4 An idea and a form of words I take from Stuart Hall, in a talk he gave at the conference called 'Changing identities: socialism and the politics of difference', University of London Union, May 1989.

5 Also see the interesting discussion of several real and hypothetical situations in Haight (1980).

6 It is unlike Sartre's, rootless, decontexualised, existential, decisions.

7 This is Spivak's term. See Chapter 3, section 4.1, and Chapter 9, section 4.

8 I have distinguished cultural politics and organisation around issues. Iris Young

(1990) draws a similar distinction between autonomy and empowerment. But my analysis would disagree radically with hers just on the possibility of separating autonomy and empowerment in the way she does.

9 Political philosophy-as-usual tends to assume no problems with authenticity in the senses developed above: people know who they are and what they want. This is a mistake as I have shown.

10 Also see Young (1990) for a discussion of the difficulties of representational politics and difference. In my view she reifies the political divisions she so usefully analyses, thus preventing her analysis from dealing with changing identities.

11 Though see Sue Mendus (1995) for some cautionary tales.

Bibliography

Afshar, Haleh (1991) *Women: development and survival in the Third World*, London: Longman.

Ahmed, Leila (1988) 'Between two worlds: the formation of a turn of the century Egyptian feminist', in B. Brodzki and C. Schenck (ed) *Life/lines: theorizing women's autobiography*, Ithaca and London: Cornell University Press.

Alibhai, Yasmin (1989) 'A member no more', *Marxism Today*, December.

Allsebrook, Annie and Swift, Anthony (1989) *Broken Promise: the world of endangered children*, Sevenoaks: Hodder and Stoughton.

Almond, Brenda (1988) 'Women's right: reflections on ethics and gender', in M. Griffiths and M. Whitford (eds) *Feminist Perspectives in Philosophy*, London: Macmillan.

Amos, Valerie and Parmar, Pratibha (1987) 'Resistances and responses: the experiences of Black girls in Britain' in M. Arnot and G. Weiner (eds) *Gender and the politics of schooling*, Milton Keynes: Open University Press.

Andres, Thomas D. and Ilada-Andres, Pilar, B. (1987) *Understanding the Filipino*, Quezon City, Philippines: New Day.

Angelou, Maya (1984) *I Know Why The Caged Bird Sings*, London: Virago.

Asian Women Writers' Workshop (1988) *Right of Way*, London: The Women's Press.

Assiter, Alison (1988) 'Autonomy and pornography', in M. Griffiths and M. Whitford (eds) *Feminist Perspectives in Philosophy*, London: Macmillan.

Atiya, Nayra (ed.) (1988) *Khul Khaal: five Egyptian women tell their stories*, London: Virago.

Averill, J. R. (1979) 'Anger', in H. E. Howe, and R. Dienstbier (eds) *Nebraska Symposium on Motivation*, London: University of Nebraska Press.

Ayim, Maryann (1987) 'Warning: philosophical discussion, violence at work', *Women and Philosophy*, special issue of *Resources for Feminist Research* 16(3): Ontario Institute for Studies in Education.

Bedford, Errol (1957) 'Emotions', *Proceedings of the Aristotelian Society* 60.

Benhabib, Seyla (1992) *Situating the Self: gender, community and postmodernism in contemporary ethics*, Cambridge: Polity Press

Benjamin, Jessica (1990) *The Bonds of Love*, London: Virago.

Bennett, Jonathon (1973) *Linguistic Behaviour*, Cambridge: Cambridge University Press.

Bernauer, James and Rasmussen, David (1991) *The Final Foucault*, Cambridge, Mass.: MIT.

Bhushan Madhu (1989) 'Vimochana: women's struggles, non-violent militancy and direct action in the Indian context', *Women's Studies International Forum* 12(1).

Blackburn, Simon (1984) *Spreading the Word: groundings in the philosophy of language*, Oxford: Oxford University Press.

Bock, Gisela and James, Susan (eds) (1992) *Beyond Equality and Difference: citizenship, feminist politics, female subjectivity*, London: Routledge.

Bouatta, Cherifa and Cherifati-Merabtine, Doria (1994) 'The social representation of women in Algeria's Islamist movement', in V. M. Moghadam (ed.) *Identity Politics and Women*, Oxford: Westview Press.

Brah, Avtar and Minhas, Rehana (1985) 'Structural racism or cultural difference: schooling for Asian girls', in Gaby Weiner (ed.) *Just a Bunch of Girls*, Milton Keynes: Open University Press.

Braidotti, Rosi (1991) *Patterns of Dissonance*, Cambridge: Polity Press.

Brennan, T. (ed.) (1989) *Between Feminism and Psychoanalysis*, London: Routledge.

Brodsky, Joseph (1986) 'Less than one', in *Less than One: selected essays*, Harmondsworth: Viking.

Brodzki, Bella and Schenck, Celeste (eds) (1988) *Life/lines: theorizing women's autobiography* Ithaca and London: Cornell University Press.

Butterfield, Stephen (1974) *Black Autobiography in America*, Amherst: University of Massachusetts.

Cameron, Deborah (1985, 1992) *Feminism and Linguistic Theory* (second edition), London: Macmillan.

Campbell, Beatrix (1993) *Goliath: Britain's dangerous places*, London: Methuen.

Carrithers, Michael, Collins, Steven and Lukes, Steven (eds) (1985) *The Category of the Person: anthropology, philosophy, history*, Cambridge: Cambridge University Press.

Casdagli, Penny, Gobey, Francis and Griffin, Caroline, with the Neti Neti Theatre Company (1990) *Only Playing Miss!*, Stoke-on-Trent: Trentham Books.

Chadwick, Henry (1991) 'Introduction' *Confessions* (trans. Henry Chadwick) Oxford: Oxford University Press.

Chang, Jung (1993) *Wild Swans: three daughters of China*, London: Flamingo.

Chapkis, Wendy (ed.) (1981) *Loaded Questions: women in the military*, Amsterdam: Transnational Institute.

Chatterjee, Debjani and Islam, Rashida (eds) (1990) *Barbed Lines*, Sheffield: Bengali Women's Support Group and Yorkshire Art Circus.

Chodorow, Nancy (1978) *The Reproduction of Mothering: psychoanalysis and the sociology of gender*, Berkeley, University of California.

Christman, John (1991) 'Autonomy and personal history', *Canadian Journal of Philosophy* 21 (1) (March).

Coates, Jennifer and Cameron, Deborah (1988) *Women in their Speech Communities: new perspectives on language and sex*, London: Longman.

Cockburn, Cynthia (1991) *In the Way of Women*, London: Macmillan.

Cockburn, David (1991) *Human Beings*, Cambridge: Cambridge University Press.

Code, Lorraine (1984) 'Toward a "responsibilist" epistemology', *Philosophy and Phenomenological Research* XLV (1).

—— (1988) 'Experience, knowledge and responsibility', in Morwenna Griffiths, and Margaret Whitford (eds) *Feminist Perspectives in Philosophy*, London: Macmillan and Indiana University Press.

Cohen, Philip and Bains, Harwant (1988) *Multi-racist Britain*, London: Macmillan.

Cohn, Carol (1987) 'Sex and death in the rational world of defense intellectuals', *Signs: Journal of Women in Culture and Society*, 12(4).

Cole, Robert Wellesley (1960) *Kossoh Town Boy*, Cambridge: Cambridge University Press.

Connell, R. W. (1989) 'Cool guys, swots and wimps: the inter-play of masculinity and education', *Oxford Review of Education*, 15(3).

Coultas, Valerie (1989) 'Black girls and self-esteem', *Gender and Education* 1(3).

Creider, Jane Tapsubei (1986) *Two Lives: my spirit and I*, London: The Women's Press.

Daly, Mary (1979) *Gyn/Ecology: the metaethics of radical feminism*, London: The Women's Press.

—— (1984) *Pure Lust: elemental feminist philosophy*, London: The Women's Press.

Davidson, Donald (1986) 'A nice derangement of epitaphs', in Ernest LePore (ed.) *Truth and Interpretation: perspectives on the philosophy of Donald Davidson*, Oxford: Basil Blackwell.

Dennett, Daniel (1978) *Brainstorms*, Hassocks: Harvester.

—— (1991) *Consciousness Explained*, Harmondsworth: Penguin.

Dhanda, Meena (1994) 'Openness, identity and acknowledgement of persons', in K. Lennon and M. Whitford (eds) *Knowing the Difference: feminist perspectives on epistemology*, London: Routledge.

Diamond, Irene and Quinby, Lee (1988) *Feminism and Foucault*, Boston, Mass.: Northeastern University Press.

Dummett, Michael (1986) ' "A nice derangement of epitaphs": some comments on Davidson and Hacking' in Ernest LePore (ed.) *Truth and Interpretation: perspectives on the philosophy of Donald Davidson*, Oxford: Blackwell.

Easlea, Brian (1986) 'The masculine image of science: how much does gender really matter?' in Jan Harding (ed.) *Perspectives on Gender and Science*, Brighton: The Falmer Press.

Eisenstein, Hester (1984) *Contemporary Feminist Thought*, London and Sydney: Counterpoint.

—— (1991) *Gender Shock*, London: Allen and Unwin.

Ekman, P. (1973) 'Cross-cultural studies of facial expression', in P. Ekman (ed.) *Darwin and Facial Expression*, London: Academic Press.

—— (1979) 'Facial expressions of emotion', *Annual Review of Psychology* 30.

el Sa'adawi. Nawal (1980) *The Hidden Face of Eve: women in the Arab world*, London: Zed Books.

—— (1986) *Memoirs from the Womens' Prison* (trans. Marilyn Booth), London: The Women's Press.

—— (1989) *The Circling Song*, London: Zed Books.

Elbaz, R. (1988) *The Changing Nature of the Self: a critical study of the autobiographic discourse*, London: Croom Helm.

Elshtain, Jean Bethke (1981) *Public Man Private Woman: women in social and political thought*, Oxford: Martin Robertson.

Elvin, Mark (1985) 'Between the earth and heaven: conceptions of the self in China', in Michael Carrithers, Steven Collins, and Steven Lukes (eds) *The Category of the Person: anthropology, philosophy, history*, Cambridge: Cambridge University Press.

Emecheta, Buchi (1986) *Head Above Water*, Glasgow: Fontana.

Evans, J. (1993) 'Bias and rationality', in K. I. Manktelow and D. E. Over (eds) *Rationality: psychological and philosophical perspectives*, London: Routledge.

Faludi, Susan (1992) *Backlash*, London: Chatto and Windus.

Fanon, Frantz (1952, 1986) *Black Skin, White Masks*, London: Pluto Press.

Feminist Review (1989) 'The Past Before Us: twenty years of feminism' (special issue) 31, Spring.

Fitzsimmons, Annette (1994) 'Women, power and technology', in Kathleen Lennon and Margaret Whitford (eds) *Knowing the Difference: feminist perspectives in epistemology*, London: Routledge.

Flanagan, Owen (1991) 'Identity, gender and strong evaluation', *Nous*, XXV, April.

Flax, Jane (1983) 'Political philosophy and the patriarchal unconscious: a psycho-analytic perspective on epistemology', in Sandra Harding and Merrill Hintikka, (eds) *Discovering Reality: feminist perspectives on epistemology, metaphysics, methodology and philosophy of science*, Dordrecht: Reidel.

—— (1987) 'Postmodernism and gender relations in feminist theory', *Signs: Journal of Women in Culture and Society* 12(4).

—— (1993) *Disputed Subjects: essays on psychoanalysis, politics and philosophy*, London: Routledge.

Foucault, Michel (1979) *The History of Sexuality: an introduction* (trans. Robert Hurley), London: Penguin.

—— (1986) *The Use of Pleasure* (trans. Robert Hurley), London: Penguin.

—— (1988) *The Care of the Self* (trans. Robert Hurley), London: Penguin.

Frazer, Elizabeth (1989) 'Feminist talk and talking about feminism', *Oxford Review of Education* 15(3).

—— and Lacey, Nicola (1993) *The Politics of Community: a feminist critique of the liberal–communitarian debate*, Hemel Hempstead: Harvester Wheatsheaf.

Fricker, Miranda (1991) 'Reason and emotion', *Radical Philosophy*, 57.

Fuss, Diana (1989) *Essentially Speaking: feminism, nature and difference*, London: Routledge.

Gagnier, Regenia (1991) 'Feminist autobiography in the 1980s' (review essay) *Feminist Studies* 17(1).

Garry, Ann and Pearsal, Marilyn (1989) *Women, Knowledge and Reality: explorations in feminist philosophy*, Boston: Unwin Hyman.

Gazzaniga, M. and LeDoux, J. E. (1978) *The Integrated Mind*, London: The Plenum Press.

Gilborn, David (1990) *'Race', Ethnicity and Education*, London: Unwin Hyman.

Gilligan, Carol (1982) *In a Different Voice*, Cambridge, Mass.: Harvard University Press.

Gilroy, Paul (1993) *The Black Atlantic: modernity and double consciousness*, London: Verso.

Goldthorpe, J. H. (with Llewellyn, C. and Payne, C.) (1980) *Social Mobility and Class Structure*, Oxford: Oxford University Press.

Goodman, Nelson (1973) *Fact, Fiction and Forecast*, Indianapolis: Bobbs Merrill.

Grant, Judith (1993) *Fundamental Feminisms: contesting the core concepts of feminist theory*, London: Routledge.

Grice H. P. (1957) 'Meaning', *Philosophical Review* 66.

—— (1975) 'Logic in conversation', in P. Cole and J. L. Morgan (eds) *Syntax and Semantics*, vol. III, San Diego: Academic Press.

Griffin, Susan (1982) *Made from this Earth*, London: The Women's Press.

Griffiths, M (1988) 'Feminism, feelings and philosophy', in M. Griffiths and M. Whitford (eds) *Feminist Perspectives in Philosophy*, London: Macmillan.

—— (1989) 'Why philosophy needs feminism', *Cogito*, 3(3).

—— (1992) 'Autonomy and the fear of dependence', *Women's Studies International Forum* 15(3).

—— (1993) 'Self-identity and self-esteem: achieving equality in education', *Oxford Review of Education* 19(3).

—— and Seller, Anne (1992) 'The politics of identity, the politics of the self', *Women: A Cultural Review* (special edition on gendering philosophy), 3(2).

—— and Whitford, Margaret (1988) (eds) *Feminist Perspectives in Philosophy*, London: Macmillan and Indiana University Press.

Grimshaw, Jean (1986) *Feminist Philosophers*, Brighton: Harvester.

Grimshaw, Jean (1988) 'Anatomy and identity in feminist thinking', in M. Griffiths and M. Whitford (eds) *Feminist Perspectives in Philosophy*, London: Macmillan and Indiana University Press.

Gunew, Sneja (1990) 'Feminist knowledge: critique and construct', in S. Gunew (ed.) *Feminist Knowledge: Critique and Construct*, London: Routledge.

Haight, Mary (1980) *A Study of Self-Deception*, Hassocks: Harvester.

Halsey, A. H. (1985) *Change in British Society* (4th edn), Oxford: Oxford University Press.

Halstead, Mark (1991) 'Radical feminism, Islam and the single-sex school debate', *Gender and Education* 3(3).

Haraway, Donna (1991) *Simians, Cyborgs and Women: the reinvention of nature*, London: Free Association Books.

Harding, Sandra (1986) *The Science Question in Feminism*, Milton Keynes: Open University Press.

—— (1991) *Whose Science? Whose Knowledge?*, Milton Keynes: Open University Press.

—— and Hintikka, Merrill (eds) (1983) *Discovering Reality*, Dordrecht: Reidel.

Harris, John (1982) 'A paradox of multicultural societies', in *Journal of Philosophy of Education* 16(2).

Hartsock, Nancy (1990) 'Foucault on power: a theory for women?' in Linda Nicholson (ed) *Feminism/Postmodernism*, London: Routledge.

Hassi, Satu (1986) 'About loneliness', in Mona Dahms and Janni Nielsen (eds) *Women Challenge Technology: European conference on women, natural sciences and technology*, University of Aalborg.

Haste, Helen (1986) 'Brother sun, sister moon: does rationality overcome a dualistic world view?' in Jan Harding (ed.) *Perspectives on Gender and Science*, London: Falmer Press.

—— and Baddeley, Jane (1991) 'Moral theory and culture: The case of gender', in William Kurtines and Jacob Gewirtz (eds) *Handbook of Moral Behaviour and Development*, Hillsdale, NJ: Erlbaum.

Hatem, Mervat (1989) 'Egyptian, Levantine-Egyptian, and European women 1862–1920', in *Women's Studies International Forum* 12(3).

Haw, Kaye (1995) 'Why are Muslim girls more feminist in Muslim schools?' in M. Griffiths and B. Troyna (eds) *Anti-racism, Culture and Social Justice*, Stoke on Trent: Trentham.

Hegel, G. F. W. (1931) *The Phenomenology of Mind* (1841 edition, trans. J. B. Baillie) (second edition), London: George Allen and Unwin.

—— (1971) *Hegel's Philosophy of Mind* (Part III of the *Encyclopaedia of the Philosophical Sciences* 1830) (trans. William Wallace) together with the Zusatze in Boumann's text (1845) (trans. A.v. Miller), Oxford: Clarendon Press.

Heidegger, Martin (1962) *Being and Time* (trans. John Macquarrie and Edward Robinson), Oxford: Basil Blackwell.

—— (1966) *Discourse on Thinking* (trans. John M. Anderson and E. Hans Freund), New York and London: Harper Torchbooks.

—— (1971) *Poetry, Language, Thought* (trans. Albert Hofstadter), New York and London: Harper and Row.

Helie-Lucas, Marie-Aimee (1994) 'The preferential symbol for Islamic identity: women in Muslim personal laws', in V. M. Moghadam (ed.) *Identity Politics and Women*, Oxford: Westview Press.

Heller, Agnes (1984) *Radical Philosophy*, Oxford: Blackwell.

Heron, Liz (1985) (ed.) *Truth, Dare, Kiss or Promise: girls growing up in the fifties*, London: Virago.

Hill, Thomas, E. (1987) 'The importance of autonomy', in E. Kittay and D. Meyers (eds) *Women and Moral Theory*, Rowman and Littlefield.

Hodge, Joanna (1987) 'Women in the Hegelian state', in Ellen Kennedy and Susan Mendus (eds) *Women in Western Political Philosophy*, Brighton: Wheatsheaf.

206 *Bibliography*

Holdcroft, David (1979) 'Speech acts and conversation', *Philosophical Quarterly* 29(115).

hooks, bell (1989) *Talking Back: thinking feminist, thinking black*, London: Sheba.

—— (1991) *Yearning: race, gender and cultural politics*, London: Turnaround.

hooks, bell (1993) *Sisters of the Yam: Black women and self-recovery*, Boston: Southend Press.

Hou, Sharon Shih-jiuan (1986) 'Women's literature', in William Nienhouser (ed.) *The Indiana Companion to Traditional Chinese Literature*, Bloomington: Indiana University Press.

Hume, David (1739, 1962) *A Treatise of Human Nature, Book I* (D. G. C. McNabb, ed.), Glasgow: Fontana Collins.

Irigaray, Luce (1985) *This Sex which is not One* (trans. Catherine Porter), New York: Cornell University Press.

Jackson, David (1990) *Unmasking Masculinity*, London: Unwin Hyman.

Jaggar, Alison (1983) *Feminist Politics and Human Nature*, Brighton: Harvester.

—— (1989) 'Love and knowledge: emotion in feminist epistemology', in Ann Garry and Marilyn Pearsall (eds) *Women, Knowledge and Reality*, Boston: Unwin Hyman.

Johnson-Odim, Cheryl and Strobel, Margaret (eds) (1992) *Expanding the Boundaries of Women's History: essays on women in the Third World*, Bloomington: Indiana University Press.

Kabbani, Rana (1986) *Europe's Myths of the Orient*, London: Macmillan.

Kant, Immanuel (1948) *Groundwork of the Metaphysic of Morals* (trans. H. J. Paton), London: Hutchinson.

—— (1956) *Critique of Pure Reason* (trans. Norman Kemp Smith), London: Macmillan.

Keller, Evelyn Fox (1985) *Reflections on Gender and Science*, New Haven: Yale University Press.

—— (1986) 'How gender matters or why it's so hard to count past two' in Jan Harding (ed.), *Perspectives on Gender and Science*, Brighton: The Falmer Press.

Kelly, Elinor (1991) 'Bullying and racial and sexual harassment in schools', *Multicultural Teaching* 10.

—— and Cohn, Tessa (1988) *Racism in Schools – New Research Evidence*, Stoke-on-Trent: Trentham Books.

Kenny, Anthony (1963) *Action, Emotion and Will*, London: Routledge and Kegan Paul.

Kincaid, Jamaica (1981) *At the Bottom of the River*, London: Picador.

—— (1983) *Annie John*, London: Picador.

Kumar, Radha (1993) *The History of Doing: an illustrated account of movements for women's rights and feminism in India 1800–1990*, London: Verso.

Lakoff, George and Johnson, Mark (1980) *Metaphors we Live By*, Chicago: University of Chicago Press.

Lazreg, Marnia (1994) 'Women's experience and feminist epistemology: a critical neo-rationalist approach', in K. Lennon and M. Whitford (eds) *Knowing the Difference: feminist perspectives on epistemology*, London: Routledge.

Leach, Fiona (1991) 'Perception gaps in technical assistance projects: the Sudanese case', in Keith Lewin and Janet Stuart (eds) *Educational Innovation in Developing Countries*, London: Macmillan.

Le Doeuff, Michele (1991) *Hipparchia's Choice: an essay concerning women, philosophy, etc.* (trans. Trista Selous), Oxford: Blackwell.

Lees, Sue (1993) *Sugar and Spice: sexuality and adolescent girls*, Harmondsworth: Penguin.

Lennon, K. and Whitford, M. (eds) (1994) *Knowing the Difference: feminist perspectives in epistemology*, London: Routledge.

LePore, Ernest (ed.) (1986) *Truth and Interpretation: perspectives on the philosophy of Donald Davidson*, Oxford: Basil Blackwell.

Lifton, Robert Jay and Markusen, Erik (1991) *Genocidal Mentality*, London: Macmillan.

Lloyd, Genevieve (1986) 'Selfhood, war and masculinity', in C. Pateman and E. Gross (eds) *Feminist Challenges: social and political theory* (second edition), London: Allen and Unwin.

—— (1993a) *Being in Time: selves and narrators in philosophy and literature*, London: Routledge.

—— (1993b) *The Man of Reason: 'male' and 'female' in western philosophy* (second edition) London: Routledge.

Lorde, Audre (1984) *Sister Outsider*, California: The Crossing Press.

Lovibond, Sabina (1989) 'Feminism and postmodernism', *New Left Review* 178.

Lugones, Maria (1989) 'Playfulness, "world"-travelling and loving perception', in Ann Garry and Marilyn Pearsall (eds) *Women, Knowledge and Reality*, Boston: Unwin Hyman.

—— and Spelman, Elizabeth (1983) 'Have we got a theory for you! Feminist theory, cultural imperialism and the demand for a woman's voice', *Women's Studies International Forum*, 6.

MacIntyre, Alasdair (1981) *After Virtue*, London: Duckworth.

Mahfouz, Naguib (1990) *Palace Walk* (trans. William Hutchins and Olive Kenny) New York and London: Doubleday.

Makeba, Miriam, with James Hall (1988) *Makeba: my story*, London: Bloomsbury.

Malan, Rian (1991) *My Traitor's Heart*, London: Vintage.

Marcil-Lacoste, Louise (1983) 'The trivialisation of equality', in Sandra Harding and Merrill Hintikka (eds) *Discovering Reality*, Reidel.

Martin, Jane Roland (1985) *Reclaiming a Conversation*, New Haven: Yale University Press.

Mbilinyi, M., Shostak, M. and Prell, R.-E. (1989) 'Narrator and interpreter', introduction to Part 4 of Personal Narratives Group, *Interpreting Women's Lives: feminist theory and personal narratives*, Bloomington: Indiana University Press.

Meehan, Elizabeth and Sevenhuijsen, Selma (eds) (1991) *Equality, Politics and Gender*, London: Sage.

Mehta, Ved (1985) *Vedi*, London: Pan.

Melzack, Robert (1973) *The Puzzle of Pain*, Harmondsworth: Penguin.

Mendus, Sue (1995) 'Strangers in paradise: the unhappy marriage of feminism and conservatism', *Women's Philosophy Review*, 13 (Queen Mary and Westfield College, London and Nottingham University).

Mernissi, Fatima (1987) *Beyond the Veil: male–female dynamics in modern Muslim society*, Bloomington: Indiana University Press.

—— (1993) *The Forgotten Queens of Islam* (trans. Mary Jo Lakeland), Oxford: Polity Press.

Midgley, Mary (1988) 'On not being afraid of natural sex differences', in M. Griffiths and M. Whitford (eds) *Feminist Perspectives in Philosophy*, London: Macmillan.

—— (1994) *The Ethical Primate: humans, freedom and morality*, London: Routledge.

Milan Women's Bookstore Collective (1990) *Sexual Difference*, Bloomington: Indiana University Press.

Miller, Nancy (1991) *Getting Personal: feminist occasions and other autobiographical acts*, London: Routledge.

Milner, Marion (1986) *An Experiment in Leisure*, London: Virago.

—— (1934, 1986) *A Life of One's Own*, London: Virago.

—— (1987) *Eternity's Sunrise: a way of keeping a diary*, London: Virago.

Mirza, Susan and Strobel, Margaret (eds and trans) (1989) *Three Swahili Women*, Bloomington: Indiana University Press.

Mitter, Swasti (1986) *Common Fate, Common Bond: women in the global economy*, London: Pluto Press.

Moghadam, Valentine M. (ed.) (1994) *Identity Politics and Women: cultural reassertions and feminisms in international perspective*, Boulder and Oxford: Westview Press.

Monk, Ray (1992) 'An interview with Ray Monk', *Cogito* 6(2).

Morgan, Sally (1987) *My Place*, Fremantle: Arts Centre Press.

Moulton, Janice (1983) 'A paradigm of philosophy: the adversary method', in Sandra Harding and Merrill Hintikka (eds) *Discovering Reality*, Dordrect: Reidel.

Nagel, Thomas (1979) *Mortal Questions*, Cambridge: Cambridge University Press.

—— (1986) *The View from Nowhere*, Oxford: Oxford University Press.

Nichols, Grace (1984) *The Fat Black Woman's Poems*, London: Virago.

—— (1989) *Lazy Thoughts of a Lazy Woman*, London: Virago.

Nicholson, Linda (ed.) (1990) *Feminism/Postmodernism*, London: Routledge.

Nicolson, N. (1993) 'We are doing very well thank you', *The Spectator*, 13 March.

Nisbett, R. and Ross, L. (1980) *Human Interference: strategies and shortcomings of social judgement*, Englewood Cliffs: Prentice Hall.

Nozick, R. (1974) *Anarchy, State and Utopia*, Oxford: Blackwell.

Nussbaum, Martha (1986) *The Fragility of Goodness*, Cambridge: Cambridge University Press.

Oakley, Justin (1992) *Morality and the Emotions*, London: Routledge.

Odeh, Lama Abu (1993) 'Post-colonial feminism and the veil: thinking the difference', *Feminist Review* 43 (Spring).

Over, D. E. and Manktelow, K. (1993) 'Rationality, utility and deontic reasoning' in K. Manktelow and D. E. Over (eds) *Rationality: psychological and philosophical perspectives*, London: Routledge.

Quine, Willard van Orman (1960) *Word and Object*, Cambridge Mass.: MIT Press.

Parfit, Derek (1984) *Reasons and Persons*, Oxford: Oxford University Press.

Parmar, Pratibha (1990) 'Black feminism: the politics of articulation', in Jonathan Rutherford (ed.) *Identity: Community, Culture, Difference*, London: Lawrence and Wishart.

Patai, Daphne (1988) 'Constructing a life story', *Feminist Studies* 14(1), pp. 143–66.

Pateman, Carole (1988) *The Sexual Contract*, Cambridge: Polity Press.

—— and Gross, E. (eds) (1986) *Feminist Challenges: social and political theory*, London: Allen and Unwin.

Personal Narratives Group (1989) *Interpreting Women's Lives: feminist theory and personal narratives*, Bloomington: Indiana University Press.

Peters, R. S. (1975) 'The education of the emotions' in R. F. Dearden, P. H. Hirst and R. S. Peters (eds) *Education and Reason*, London: Routledge and Keegan Paul.

Phillips, Anne (1993) *Democracy and Difference*, Cambridge: Polity.

Piercy, Marge (1979) *Woman on the Edge of Time*, London: The Women's Press.

Puissi, Anna Maria (1990) 'Towards a pedagogy of sexual difference: education and female genealogy', in *Gender and Education* 2(1).

Rajchman, John and West, Cornel (eds) (1985) *Post-analytic Philosophy*, New York: Columbia University Press.

The Raving Beauties (1983) *In the Pink*, London: The Women's Press.

Rawls, J. (1971) *A Theory of Justice*, Oxford: Oxford University Press.

Richardson, Robin (1990) *Daring to be a Teacher*, Stoke on Trent: Trentham.

Roberts, Michele (1987) *The Book of Mrs Noah*, London: Methuen.

Rogers, Carl (1983) *Freedom to Learn for the 80's*, New York: Merrill.

Rorty, Amelie (1988) 'Explaining emotions', in A. Rorty (ed.) *Explaining Emotions*, Berkeley and London: University of California Press.

Rorty, Richard (1979) *Philosophy and the Mirror of Nature*, Princeton: Princeton University Press.

—— (1989) *Contingency, Irony, Solidarity*, Cambridge: Cambridge University Press.

—— (1991) *Objectivity, Relativism and Truth: philosophical papers vol. I*, Cambridge: Cambridge University Press.

Rose, Hilary (1994) *Love, Power and Knowledge*, Cambridge: Polity Press.

Rousseau, Jean-Jacques (1755, 1984) *A Discourse on Inequality* (trans. Maurice Cranston), Harmondsworth: Penguin.

—— (1762, 1956) *Emile* (trans. William Boyd), London: Heinemann.

—— (1762, 1968) *The Social Contract* (trans. Maurice Cranston), Harmondsworth: Penguin.

—— (1781, 1953) *The Confessions* (trans. J. M. Cohen), Harmondsworth: Penguin.

Rowbotham, Sheila (1973) *Woman's Consciousness, Man's World*, Harmondsworth: Pelican.

Rowe, Dorothy (1988) *Choosing not Losing: the experience of depression*, London: Fontana.

Rushdie, Salman (1991) *Imaginary Homelands: essays and criticism 1981–1991*, London: Granta.

Rutherford, Jonathan (1990) 'A place called home: identity and the cultural politics of difference', in Jonathan Rutherford (ed.) *Identity: community, culture, difference*, London: Lawrence and Wishart.

Said, Edward (1978) *Orientalism: western conceptions of the Orient*, London: Penguin.

—— (1993) *Culture and Imperialism*, London: Chatto and Windus.

Saint Augustine (1991) *Confessions* (trans. Henry Chadwick), Oxford: Oxford University Press.

Sartre, J. P. (1958) *Being and Nothingness* (trans. H. Barnes), London: Methuen.

Schenck, Celeste (1988) 'All of a piece: women's poetry and autobiography', in Bella, Brodzki and Celeste, Schenck (eds) (1988) *Life/lines: theorizing women's autobiography*, London: Cornell University Press.

Seacole, Mary (1857, 1984) (edited by Siggi Alexander and Audrey Dewjee) *Wonderful Adventures of Mrs Seacole in Many Lands*, Bristol: Falling Wall Press.

Seller, Anne (1985) 'Greenham: a concrete reality', *Journal of Applied Philosophy* 2 (1).

—— (1988) 'Realism versus relativism; towards a politically adequate epistemology', in M. Griffiths and M. Whitford (eds) *Feminist Perspectives in Philosophy*, London: Macmillan.

—— (1994) 'Should the feminist philosopher stay at home?' in Kathleen Lennon and Margaret Whitford (eds) *Knowing the Difference: feminist perspectives in epistemology*, London: Routledge.

Sha'arawi, Huda (1986) *Harem Years: the memoirs of an Egyptian feminist* (trans. Margot Badran), London: Virago.

Shostak, Marjorie (1989) ' "What the wind won't take away": the genesis of Nisa – the life and words of a !Kung woman', in Personal Narratives Group *Interpreting Women's Lives: feminist theory and personal narratives*, Bloomington: Indiana University Press.

Smith, Sidonie (1993) 'Who's talking/who's talking back? The subject of personal narrative', *Signs* (winter).

Solomon, Robert (1977) *The Passions*, Garden City, NY: Doubleday.
—— (1978) 'Emotions and anthropology: the logic of emotional world views', *Inquiry* 21.
—— (1983) *In the Spirit of Hegel*, Oxford: Blackwell.
Sommer, Doris (1988) 'Not just a personal story: women's *testimonios* and the plural self', in B. Brodzki and C. Schenck (eds) *Life/lines: theorizing women's autobiography*, London: Cornell University Press.
Spelman, Elizabeth (1989) 'Anger and insubordination', in Ann Garry and Marilyn Pearsall (eds) *Women, Knowledge and Reality*, Boston: Unwin Hyman.
Spender, Dale (1980) *Man-made Language*, London: Routledge and Kegan Paul.
Spivak, Gayatri (1988) 'Can the subaltern speak?', in Cary Nelson and Laurence Grossberg (eds) *Marxisn and the Interpretation of Culture*, Chicago: University of Illinois Press.
—— (1990) *The Post Colonial Critic: Interviews, Strategies, Dialogues*, (ed. Sarah Harasyn) London: Routledge.
—— (1992) 'The politics of translation', in Michele Barratt and Anne Phillips (eds) *Destabilizing Theory: contemporary feminist debates*, Cambridge: Polity Press.
Stanley, Liz (ed.) (1990) *Feminist Praxis*, London: Routledge.
—— (1992) *The Auto/biographical I: theory and practice of feminist auto/biography*, Manchester, Manchester University Press.
—— (1994) 'The knowing because experiencing subject: narratives, lives and autobiography', in Kathleen Lennon and Margaret Whitford (eds) *Knowing the Difference: feminist perspectives in epistemology*, London: Routledge.
—— and Wise, Sue (1990) 'Method, methodology and epistemology in feminist research processes', in L. Stanley (ed.) *Feminist Praxis: research, theory and epistemology in feminist sociology*, London: Routledge.
Steedman, Carolyn (1986) *Landscape for a Good Woman: a story of two lives*, London: Virago.
Strickland, Susan (1994) 'Feminism, postmodernism and difference', in Kathleen Lennon and Margaret Whitford (eds) *Knowing the Difference: feminist perspectives in epistemology*, London: Routledge.
Stuart, Andrea (1990) 'Feminism: dead or alive?' in Jonathan Rutherford (ed.) *Identity: community, culture, difference*, London: Lawrence and Wishart.
Taussig, Michael (1987) *Shamanism, Colonialism and the Wild Man: a study in terror and healing*, Chicago and London: University of Chicago Press.
Taylor, Charles (1982) 'Rationality', in Martin Hollis and Steven Lukes (eds) *Rationality and Relativism*, Oxford: Blackwell.
—— (1985) *Human Agency and Language*, Cambridge: Cambridge University Press.
—— (1989) *Sources of the Self*, Cambridge: Cambridge University Press.
—— (1991) *The Ethics of Authenticity*, London: Harvard University Press.
Thompson, Janna (1993) 'Can social contract theory work for women?' paper given to a meeting of the Society for Women and Philosophy, Queen Mary and Westfield College, London, November.
—— (1994) 'Moral difference and moral epistemology', in Kathleen Lennon and Margaret Whitford (eds) *Knowing the Difference: feminist perspectives in epistemology*, London: Routledge.
Thornton, Mark (1991) 'Same human being, same person?', *Philosophy* 66(255), January.
Toubia, Nahid (ed.) (1988) *Women of the Arab World*, London: Zed Books.
Trevarthen, C. and Hubley, P. (1978) 'Secondary inter-subjectivity: confidence, confiding and acts of meaning in the first year', in A. Lock (ed.) *Action, Gesture and Symbol*, London: Academic Press.

Twumasi, P. A. (1986) *Social Research in Rural Communities*, Accra: Ghana Universities Press.

Verma, Gajendra and Mallick, Kanka (1988) 'Self-esteem and educational achievement in British young South Asians', in G. Verma and P. Pumfrey (eds) *Educational Attainments*, Brighton: Falmer.

Vincent, David (1981) *Bread, Knowledge and Freedom: a study of nineteenth-century working class autobiography*, London: Methuen.

Vogel, Ursula (1987) 'Women and the Hegelian state', in Ellen Kennedy and Susan Mendus (eds) *Women in Western Political Philosophy*, Brighton: Wheatsheaf.

Walker, Alice (1984) *In Search of our Mothers' Gardens*, London: The Women's Press.

Walkerdine, Valerie (1990) *Schoolgirl Fictions*, London: Verso.

Ward, Keith (1972) *The Development of Kant's View of Ethics*, Oxford: Blackwell.

Wells, C. G. (1981) *Learning Through Interaction: the study of language and language development*, Cambridge: Cambridge University Press.

Westwood, Sallie and Bhachu, Parminder (1988) *Enterprising Women: ethnicity, economy and gender relations*, London: Routledge.

Wheeler, Samuel C. III (1986) 'Indeterminacy of French interpretation: Derrida and Davidson', in Ernest LePore (ed.) *Truth and Interpretation: perspectives on the philosophy of Donald Davidson*, Oxford: Basil Blackwell.

Whitford, Margaret (1988) 'Luce Irigaray's critique of rationality', in M. Griffiths and M. Whitford (eds) *Feminist Perspectives in Philosophy*, London: Macmillan and Indiana University Press.

—— (1991) *Irigaray: philosophy in the feminine*, London: Routledge.

Williams, Bernard (1973) *Problems of the Self*, Cambridge: Cambridge University Press.

—— (1993) *Shame and Necessity*, London: University of California Press.

Williams, Patricia (1993) *The Alchemy of Race and Rights*, London: Virago.

Woolf, Virginia (1938, 1977) *Three Guineas*, Harmondsworth: Penguin.

Young, Iris (1990) *Justice and the Politics of Difference*, Princeton: Princeton University Press.

Young-Bruehl, Elisabeth (1982) *Hannah Arendt: for love of the world*, London: Yale University Press.

Yuval-Davis, Nira and Anthias, Floya (1989) *Women – Nation – State*, London: Macmillan.

Zameenzad, Adam (1988) *My Friend Matt and Hena the Whore*, London: Flamingo.

Zhana (1988) *Sojourn*, London: Methuen.

Index